SHOOTING

≋ TO ≋

WIN

A
COACH'S GUIDE
TO
PLAYING BETTER
OFFENSIVE HOCKEY

Jean Perron

Normand Chouinard

McGraw-Hill Ryerson
Toronto   Montreal

SHOOTING TO WIN: A Coach's Guide to Playing
Better Offensive Hockey

Available in French under the title "Le hockey d'un
but à l'autre" from Gaëtan Morin Editeur Ltée
(1991) by Jean Perron and Normand Chouinard.
Copyright © Gaëtan Morin Editeur Ltée (1991).

First published in 1991 by
McGraw-Hill Ryerson Limited
300 Water Street
Whitby, Ontario
L1N 9B6

Canadian Cataloguing in Publication Data

Perron, Jean
  Shooting to win

Includes bibliographical references.
ISBN: 0-07-551281-5

1. Hockey – Offense. I. Chouinard, Normand.
II. Title.

GV848.7.P47 1991   796.96'2   C91-094009-6

2 3 4 5 6 7 8 9 0 MP 0 9 8 7 6

Cover design: Stuart Knox
Cover photograph: Bruce Bennett
Author photograph of Jean Perron: Bob Fisher

Printed and bound in Canada

To our wives,
Rita Perron and Carol Thibault,
and our lovely children
Herman, Thierry, Josée
and Lesley

TABLE OF CONTENTS _____

PART THREE
TEAM PLAY

LIST OF FIGURES _____

LIST OF SYMBOLS

Offensive player	O
goaltender	**G**
right defense	②
left defense	③
right wing	④
center	⑤
left wing	⑥

Defensive player	△
goaltender	**G**
right defense	⚠②ᐃ
left defense	⚠③ᐃ
right wing	⚠④ᐃ
center	⚠⑤ᐃ
left wing	⚠⑥ᐃ

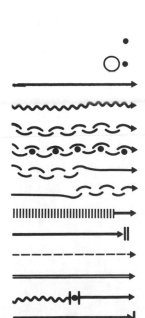

Puck

Puck carrier

Forward skating without puck

Forward skating with puck

Backward skating without puck

Backward skating with puck

Pivot, backward to forward

Pivot, forward to backward

Lateral skating

Stop

Pass

Shoot

Drop pass

Screen or pick

Moving screen

Body fake

Passing fake

Shooting fake

Checking

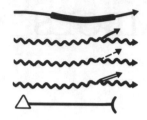

PREFACE

The historic Canada-Soviet hockey game on September 2, 1972 shocked many observers. Although the final outcome of the series placed Canada slightly ahead in terms of the win-loss column, the message was very clear: the Soviets are also masters of the game, especially in team play. Since then, many coaches, professors and technical directors have paid more attention to the nature of Soviet and European hockey.

Of course, many books on hockey have been written over the past thirty years or so. More recent texts describe the main elements characterizing the Russian-European style of play. *SHOOTING TO WIN: A Coach's Guide to Playing Better Offensive Hockey* will discuss a new way of looking at the game of hockey, of describing and explaining the fundamental principles and concepts essential to playing the game rationally. In a sense, this book is about change — a change from the way we as coaches have been trained to study, teach and coach the game to a new way of thinking about the fascinating sport of ice hockey. We have reached the point in the advancement of hockey where coaches and athletes need to understand and integrate principles of play or guidelines for action, the foundation upon which a total system of play is developed.

This book will help present and future coaches, whether amateur or professional, to develop a better understanding of the game and a stronger knowledge base for more effective coaching. Hockey players will also benefit from reading this book because it will help them acquire a fuller understanding of the reasons for their actions on-ice.

Hockey is a game of chance to some degree, but more important to us as coaches, it is a game of strategy. As in the game of chess, players must master all the different phases of the game to be successful. Our objective is to transmit the latest *theoretical* notions, through various principles and related concepts, and to make practical *application* of these in various game situations. Knowledge of both theoretical and practical perspectives is essential for successful coaching of the game.

We urge our readers to stick with us through this journey as we expose some new and innovative ideas, and expand on some of the more familiar offensive principles and concepts that relate to the tactical dimension of the game.

Lastly, we should answer a legitimate question from our readers: *for what level of coaching is this book intended?* First and foremost, we believe that all coaches, regardless of the level of hockey, can benefit from reading this book. We also firmly believe that all coaches need to know and understand the major principles and related concepts to be effective teachers. Although the main thrust of this text is on offensive tactics and team play, technical skills required to play the game will also be discussed. As we will soon discover, technical skills and tactical actions are closely interwoven. Consequently, we maintain that this book will help every coach improve his coaching methods, whether at the beginner's, intermediate or advanced level of hockey.

A Special Note

Hockey is played, coached and enjoyed by both men and women of all ages. We recognize, appreciate and fully support this fact. In writing, authors must often choose between personal pronouns such as "she" and "he," "her" and "his" to express their ideas. For the sake of convenience, we have used the masculine gender to represent both male and female. Thank you for your understanding.

Normand Chouinard
Jean Perron

ACKNOWLEDGEMENTS

There are a number of individuals who have inspired and assisted us in our venture of writing this book.

First, we are grateful to the many coaches who encouraged us to go forward with our idea of writing a hockey book on team tactics during our initial period of research. Their expressed need reassured us of the benefits and value of our undertaking.

To the players, thank you for challenging and demanding the best from us as coaches. The real test of the decisions we make as coaches is confirmed by your performance on ice.

We also convey our sincere appreciation to Wayne Gretzky for patently endorsing our book. Wayne's endorsement will help us meet our main objective of reaching out to those coaches searching to improve the game of hockey.

Finally, a very special word of appreciation is extended to our wives for their unrelenting source of motivation and encouragement throughout the project of writing this book.

I

ANALYZING
THE GAME

To analyze the game of hockey is to examine its very nature, purpose and methods, objectively and rationally. This is no easy task, since there are so many factors that can affect the outcome of a game and the performance of each athlete. However, given the literature available and the studies that have been undertaken over the past two decades, both in North America and in Europe, there is now sufficient evidence to support the need to approach the teaching and coaching of our sport in a dramatically new way — a conceptual and integrated approach. Let us begin our analysis.

1

Introduction

1.1 Prerequisites for Ice Hockey

The game of ice hockey requires four categories of preparation:

1. Physical preparation
2. Psychological preparation
3. Technical preparation
4. Tactical preparation

[handwritten annotations: physical; mental/passion think hockey; individual skills; strategy *]*

All of these categories or dimensions of the game are critically important for providing total preparation or training of the athletes (Bukac, 1977; Kostka, 1979). Depending on a number of factors, such as age, maturity, progress and the time in the season, one area of training should be emphasized more than another while maintaining a perspective on all categories. Of course, it is unrealistic to expect a coach to be an expert in all areas; nevertheless, every coach should be familiar with the general concepts under each category.

Today, especially at the top competitive levels, the head coach seeks assistant or associate coaches who can supplement and complement his own knowledge and training. Assistance is needed in a number of functions : the recruitment and selection of players, on the ice during practices, behind the bench, as an observer, and as a "video" person preparing and editing the films for the coaches.

Many head coaches, for example, have sought help in the area of goaltending, where past goaltenders seem to be the only individuals who can offer this special assistance. But assistant coaches can be generalists or specialists in a number of areas, such as the whole dimension of physical fitness, working with the defensemen, or even being responsible for special areas such as power plays, penalty killing or face-offs. The latest vogue seems to be in the psychological domain, where more and more sports psychologists, again at the higher levels of competition, are obtaining recognition and results. As a coach, at whatever level, choosing the right assistants will benefit both you and your athletes. Obtaining the necessary assistance in various areas of expertise indicates a sense of openness and willingness to learn more about the game. Few coaches, if any, can know every facet of the game in depth.

It is also important to note that all four categories of training are interrelated − one affects another. Interpreting this relationship in a positive way means that, if an athlete develops a high level of physical fitness, it will enhance or facilitate the learning of technical and/or tactical skills. Similarly, an athlete who is properly motivated and psychologically prepared will execute much more effectively in practices and games. Unfortunately, a number of corollaries are also true. For example, if an athlete has not mastered the necessary technical skills in individual puck control, stick-handling around an opponent will be extremely difficult or impossible. Likewise, if your level of physical fitness is inadequate or incomplete (let us say in the area of muscular strength), it will affect your ability to win individual battles, even though your technical and tactical skills may be sharply developed.

In summary, the main points to retain from this discussion are first, that all categories are important in terms of total preparation of your athletes and second, that these areas are interrelated. At the end of this text, under the heading of "Suggested Reading," we have put together a list of books that deal with physical, psychological and technical training for those who may wish to further their knowledge. Tactical preparation is the heart of this book.

1.2 Tactical Preparation

The world of hockey has been greatly influenced by the international scene. Through observation of many European teams in competition and practice, coaching seminars, manuals and books, and more North American coaches learning European methods of training, we now know much more about the game of hockey. International competitions such as the Canada Cup, World Championships, Olympic Games and other tournaments have also provided meaningful learning opportunities for everyone involved. Tactical preparation or training is certainly not exempt from this bilateral influence (Kostka, 1976; Boulonne, 1986).

Tactics or tactical play are the individual and/or collective actions of the players on a team that are appropriate in various situations in order to gain advantage over one or more opponents (adapted from Gagnon, 1982). Tactical preparation involves a series of activities, since obviously, before attempting to deke an opponent or use the "give-and-go," for example, the player must first master the fundamental skills of skating, stickhandling and passing-receiving.

Before turning our attention to the various types of actions/ skills used in the game of hockey, let us explore a term that is frequently misused as a synonym for tactics.

1.3 Strategy — What Is It?

"Strategy," "system" and "tactics" are popular hockey terms which are frequently used interchangeably by coaches to define a team's role or approach in a given on-ice situation. Expressions such as "our strategy for the power play," "our power play system" and "our tactical approach to forechecking" are ambiguous, unclear and confusing, not only to hockey experts, but also to the players themselves. Even the general public becomes perplexed when sports reporters use these words indiscriminately. Can all of these words really have the same meaning? Our answer, in light of progressive reform, is "NO!"

Historically, the word "strategy" has been widely used by the military. As a matter of fact, most dictionaries define the word in the context of military activity, as stated in Funk and Wagnalls' *Standard College Dictionary* (1963): "The science and art of conducting a military campaign on a broad scale: distinguished from tactics." In the *Family Word Finder* by Reader's Digest (1977), a clear distinction is made between strategy and tactics: "There's a nice difference between strategy and tactics. Strategy is an overall plan or campaign... Tactics are the techniques or ploys used to carry out the plan."

In light of these definitions of strategy which refer to an overall plan, grand design or scheme to wear the enemy down, we propose the following definition of strategy in terms of the game of hockey.

Strategy is an overall plan or approach to a game in relation to the opposition and the strengths of your team. This plan rests upon the physical, tactical and psychological dimensions of the game. In practice, this plan is reflected through a particular system of play deployed against the opposition in an attempt to exploit their weaknesses and neutralize their strengths. Yuri Morozov (1975), Soviet Junior National Team coach, captured this sense of the word "strategy":

> The Soviets have different patterns for different teams. For example, their forwards will come back much further into their own zone against Canada and Sweden but not as deep against the Czechs and Finns. A game plan [strategy] is drawn up to play the opposition according to the strengths and weaknesses [of the team] (p. 1).

In this next section, we will discuss the use of the word "tactics." In Chapter 3, the word "system" will be defined and explained in detail. We hope that this will clear up any misconceptions regarding the use of the terms tactics, strategy and systems. Now it's time to explore the types of actions or skills used by hockey players.

1.4 Types of Actions or Skills

From the most fundamental to the most advanced movements performed by one or more players, there are essentially five types of actions or skills (see Figure 1.1):

1. Technical skills
2. Combined technical skills
3. Individual tactical skills
4. Group tactical skills
5. Team tactical skills or team play

FIGURE 1.1   Types of actions or skills

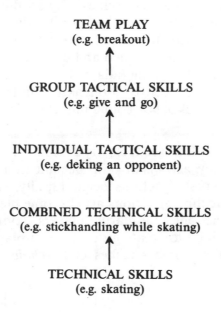

TEAM PLAY
(e.g. breakout)

↑

GROUP TACTICAL SKILLS
(e.g. give and go)

↑

INDIVIDUAL TACTICAL SKILLS
(e.g. deking an opponent)

↑

COMBINED TECHNICAL SKILLS
(e.g. stickhandling while skating)

↑

TECHNICAL SKILLS
(e.g. skating)

Technical skills   These are the basic skills or techniques required to play the game, such as skating, stickhandling, passing, receiving, shooting and checking.

Combined technical skills   These skills involve the execution of two or more technical skills, simultaneously or at least in quick succession, for example, skating and shooting, tight-turn and passing, and stickhandling while skating backwards.

Individual tactical skills   The individual actions used consciously by one player to gain advantage over one or more opponents, whether offensively or defensively (adapted from Théodoresco, 1965). Examples would include deking, faking a shot to go around an opponent, blocking a shot or screening the vision of the goaltender.

Group tactical skills   The collective actions used consciously by two or more players to gain advantage over one or more opponents, whether offensively or defensively. A few examples: give-and-go, drop pass, crisscross, screening to allow your teammate to recover the puck, covering your wing so that your backs can challenge the puck carrier at the blue line.

Team tactical skills or team play   (1) The totality of individual
and collective actions used consciously by all the players to gain
advantage over the other team, whether offensively or defensively.
(2) The totality of individual and collective actions by all the players
on a team, organized, coordinated and unified rationally with the
objective of winning the game (adapted from Théodoresco, 1965).
We often refer to these collective actions as the "unit of five." Examples
would include breakouts, counterattacks, forechecking and
backchecking.

On paper, these skills seem clearly distinct and identifiable, but
in a game of hockey, actions or skills become more difficult to tell
apart, since all types of actions occur rapidly, successively and
simultaneously. Technical actions also become blended with individual tactical actions. Similarly, players' individual tactical
actions are combined to create group tactical plays. Let's explore
this process, which some coaches call *technico-tactical*, a little
further.

1.5 Techniques and Tactics

In a game situation, most individual actions are technico-tactical in
nature. Whether you stickhandle around an opponent or simply
pass the puck, there are certain technical and tactical skills required
to successfully accomplish the play. This type of relationship
between the technical and tactical elements of any single action
can also be extended to group tactical actions. In other words, in
group tactical actions we can recognize some very technical elements as well as some more sophisticated individual tactical skills.
This relationship led us to develop the concept of the *technico-
tactical triangle*, as shown in Figure 1.2.

Essentially, this model suggests that every action taken by a
player in a game situation has technical and tactical components
which are invariably difficult to discern. As soon as you place a
player in the context of an opposing team, all of that player's individual actions automatically or instinctively become tactical by the
very nature of the situation. The technical skills of the player
translate into tactical actions used against the opponent. This is
referred to as *individual tactical actions or skills*. Since hockey is also
a team sport, individual tactical actions must be channelled

FIGURE 1.2 The technico-tactical triangle

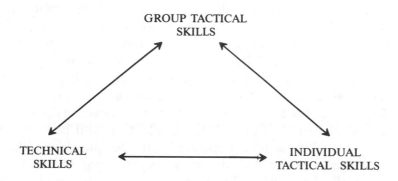

towards a group or collective effort. This concept implies that individual players must combine their actions to produce *group tactical actions or skills*.

1.6 General Guidelines for Teaching Skills

In light of this concept, the technico-tactical triangle and other factors such as age, athletic ability, playing experience and maturity, the teaching of hockey skills requires some special attention. As a teacher/coach, the element of progression and repetition in the teaching of these various actions or skills is critical when developing your seasonal plan and specific day-to-day practices which may include some off-ice (gymnasium) skills development training. We often hear it said that a certain coach is focusing too much on the technical or too little on the tactical, or vice versa. This is certainly not an easy issue to resolve, since it involves all the many factors we have mentioned. The following guidelines can provide some assistance as you develop your seasonal plan and daily practices.

1.6.1 Skating and stickhandling

Individual and combined technical skills are the building blocks for tactical actions. Of these, the most important are skating and stickhandling. Even the most elite hockey players need to work at discovering new ways of improving their skating ability. By varying the angle of attack, speed, body movements and hand maneuvers while maintaining a vision ahead, a player can greatly improve his stickhandling skills. Regardless of your level of ability, never neglect working on the fundamental technical skills, especially skating and stickhandling. As in basketball, where a player must first master dribbling skills to play an effective role in ball control, in hockey players must develop excellent skating and stick-handling abilities to maintain puck control, the main offensive principle in ice hockey. Tarasov was a firm believer in these funda-mental skills. In the Soviet Union, selection and promotion to Tarasov's hockey school depended on the player's ability to demonstrate superior techniques in skating, passing and stick-handling (Brokhin, 1978). Puck control, as we shall see later, also has a collective dimension, passing and receiving.

The Canadian Amateur Hockey Association and authors Patterson and Miller (1986) deserve credit and recognition for having addressed this concern within the hockey community by developing the *Initiation Program*. We firmly believe that every youngster or beginner in hockey should be exposed to this program by qualified instructors, that hockey associations should devote the necessary funds to deliver the program effectively, and that hockey schedules for on-ice training should be adapted to incorporate the program. A youngster's first experiences, whether in hockey, music or other socio-cultural activities, are usually the most important. A quote from the *Instructor's Manual* (Initiation Program) puts it perfectly:

> How a player gets that first taste of hockey is critical.
>
> If a beginner has fun, developing some basic skills and building confidence, there is a good chance that the player will go on to enjoy hockey for many years.
>
> But if a beginner has an unhappy, unrewarding experience, the chances are that he, or she, will quit at an early age and never discover the real joy of Canada's great game (p. 3).

1.6.2 Technical to tactical

While keeping in mind the factor of age and/or ability, the pro-gression should follow the general order described earlier. In other words, a coach should move from technical skills to combined technical skills and so on, right through to team tactical skills. Coupled with this progressive approach to teaching the various skills is the element of overlap (see Figure 1.3). Although your main objective for a particular age level may be to develop group tactical skills, there should still be some emphasis on technical skills. It goes without saying that as you practice tactical skills, you are simultaneously working on technical skills; however, the important point is to further improve technical skills you have already acquired through specific drills. It may not be the main objective of your practice, but a certain amount of time should be dedicated to this purpose. Figure 1.3 is a chart relating various hockey skills to age and ability. This chart can be used as a general guideline for teaching the various skills in a progressive manner.

FIGURE 1.3   Teaching progression of hockey skills: the relationship between age/ ability and types of skills

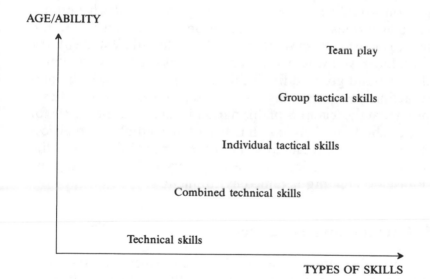

AGE/ABILITY

Team play

Group tactical skills

Individual tactical skills

Combined technical skills

Technical skills

TYPES OF SKILLS

1.6.3 Seasonal perspective

As the season advances, and again depending on the ability of the players, the coach should be progressing from technical skills to more tactical skills. Once more, it is a question of emphasis. It's crucial not to overlook the development and refinement of technical skills, but equally important if the team is to experience success, the coach must introduce the vital tactical elements of the game as the season progresses. What becomes more important to judge is the rate at which you introduce new principles and concepts within a particular season. This decision and other related issues depend on the players' ages and abilities, as well as on practical factors such as the amount of ice time, facilities and equipment, and human resources at your disposal.

1.6.4 Simple to complex to game-like

This guideline applies to whatever type of action/skill you are trying to teach. The objective here is to gradually build into the drills more and more elements that challenge the players, forcing them to execute under conditions very similar to an actual game. If, for instance, you are working on a group tactical skill such as a give-and-go, you would begin by asking your players to *slowly* perform the action at various probable locations on the ice. Next, you would get them to *increase the speed* of execution, followed by some *passive resistance*. Later, you would ask certain players to *actively* attempt to stop the give-and-go. And finally, they would try to apply the particular action in a *scrimmage*, simulating game-like conditions. Accepting that the teaching of this particular skill is appropriate for their age or ability level, the coach may require a number of practices before arriving at the final phase. For other types of skills, an entire month of regular practice may be necessary before reaching the final phase − creating a game environment.

1.6.5 Practice makes perfect

There is no substitute for hard work. This is especially true when trying to master various individual and collective skills in hockey. This implies not only repeating and perfecting the variety of skills acquired, but also maintaining the necessary *intensity, concentration* and *speed*. As coaches, we too often expect our athletes to perform during the course of a practice at a tempo way below the optimal level for effective learning. The repetition of a skill or collective actions must be accompanied by the proper physical and mental dedication. Only then do you derive maximum benefit from the learning environment and further the development of your athletes. To complete our discussion, let us now describe the main principles and components of an effective practice.

1.7 Principles and Components of a Practice

Try to picture the perfect practice. What would be happening on the ice? What elements or characteristics would be present during this wonderful practice? And as coach, what would you do to create this ideal learning environment?

First, let's look at the underlying *principles* of an effective practice for any team sport. Some of the ideas that follow were taken from Kerr (1982), Schmidt (1982) and the National Coaching Certification Program (1989).

The principles of a practice are:

A. Pre-planning and organization

(1) Set practice objectives.
(2) Divide specific responsibilities among coaches.
(3) Choose on-ice drills and practice activities.
(4) Determine time allotments for the various components within the practice.

B. Pre-practice instructions

(1) Review practice objectives and drills with players in the dressing room, using audio-visual aids.
(2) Stress the importance of individual and collective work.
(3) Reinforce total commitment to practice, physical and mental.

C. Give clear on-ice instructions

(1) Explain and demonstrate the drill.
(2) State the purpose of the drill, highlighting specific points or concepts.
(3) Use teaching cues to reinforce concepts during actual practice.

D. Create a positive learning environment

(1) Motivate players to learn.
(2) Select meaningful tasks.
(3) Stress the importance of the different tasks.
(4) Ask players/learners to set individual goals.
(5) Build in a progression from simple to complex.

E. Give positive and meaningful feedback

(1) Provide both individual and team feedback.
(2) If necessary, select an appropriate time and place for not-so-positive feedback, ending on an encouraging and constructive note.
(3) Encourage open communication among players.

F. Maximize the activity and involvement of all the players

(1) Players should be active, physically and mentally.
(2) Encourage players to visualize certain actions.
(3) Maximize the use of the entire ice surface.
(4) Provide rest periods to re-energize and prepare for the next task.

G. Make drills/exercises interesting and challenging

(1) Select drills that will develop "reading and reacting" skills.
(2) Choose drills that simulate game situations, especially transition drills.
(3) Select challenging drills to develop "hockey sense."
(4) Provide variety.
(5) Be creative, e.g., have players make up a drill.
(6) Be flexible to allow for individual needs and situational factors.

H. Evaluate the practice

(1) After the practice, coaches should share general and specific comments and reactions.
(2) Occasionally seek feedback from players.
(3) Answer the question: were the practice objectives achieved?

I. Don't forget to have fun

(1) You can have fun and meet your practice objectives.
(2) Coaches and players are entitled to have fun.
(3) Satisfaction comes from dedication and hard work.

J. Always strive to do your best

These principles are intended as general guidelines for coaches to follow in planning and organizing a practice. As we've seen, these principles can apply to virtually all team sports.

We would now like to examine the various ingredients or *components* that produce an effective practice − the design of a practice. Again, these components are generally applicable to most team sports; however, we have described them in terms of a typical hockey practice. Although the order and emphasis of these components may vary somewhat depending on certain factors such as individual and team needs, the time in the season, the amount of ice-time available and whether the ice session falls before, on or after the day of a game, they still represent the main elements of a sound practice.

The components of a practice are:

A. General warm-up

— In dressing room, mainly stretching exercises but could also include some endurance work, cardiovascular and muscular. Working in pairs is a good way to keep motivation high, and is required when following certain stretching programs.

— On-ice stretching, aerobic and anaerobic work, and agility skating with and without the puck. Create variety by having players lead the warm-up and work in small groups or by setting up stations where players move from one exercise to another. After a certain time, goaltenders should perform their specific exercises.

— Gradually build up intensity to produce warm-up effect.

B. Goaltender warm-up

— Shooting pucks by one player to work on blocker, trapper, stick and skate saves.

— Gradually increase the speed of the puck.

— Shoot pucks in quick succession to force the goalie to move rapidly from one position to another.

— Devise drills that challenge goalies from various angles and distances.

— Have players shoot using all the different shots (slap, snap, wrist, sweep and flip) from both their forehand and backhand.

C. Flow and combination drills

— Flow refers to movement; combination refers to combining skating, stickhandling, passing and receiving in the same drill.

— Try to introduce one new drill every practice; at least vary a drill you have already used.

— Have players strive for quality of execution first, then gradually increase the tempo.

D. Instrumental component

— Introduce new concepts by adding to the known content. Brief review is often necessary before proceeding to new material.

— Introduce and demonstrate the drills that will support the new concepts, first with the visual aid, then on the ice, preferably with one or more players who have already been briefed.

E. Practice component

— First, allow players to feel their way through the new drill; they usually require time to adjust their own moves. This is what motor learning experts refer to as intrinsic feedback, that is, knowledge of performance from their own senses.

— If necessary, point out any mistakes (changes that need to be made) and, if the players are mature enough, see if they can adjust accordingly. With novice players, explain precisely what you mean and demonstrate once again.

— Select drills that simulate game-like conditions.

F. Scrimmage

— Allow players to try and implement what they have learned by scrimmaging.

— Scrimmages can be half-ice, even a third, or full-ice.

— Scrimmages can be 3 on 3, 4 on 4, 5 on 5 or any combination to produce man-advantage or man-short situations.

— Scrimmages must have a purpose; they must work some aspect of the game, e.g., forechecking, defensive alignment.

G. Fitness component

— Work primarily on anaerobic endurance, especially the lactic component. This requires work lasting approximately 45 seconds. Of course, you must build up to that gradually and have the right work-rest ratio.

— Create competitive situations in the fitness drills to maintain intensity, e.g. relay races.

H. Cool-down

— Allow players to slow down gradually to avoid cramps, the result of lactic acid build-up in the muscles.

— If time permits, have players work on individual skills.

— In ending the practice, share a final positive message.

1.8   Practice Planning: A Diagnostic Approach

The on-ice practice session is the fundamental building block of coaching/teaching. Athletes may have a number of opportunities to learn the game of hockey by playing, observing, discussing and reading about the game, but a well-organized practice remains the most important setting in terms of training and preparation. It is for this primary reason that a practice should be extremely well planned and organized according to the needs of the athletes.

The practice planning model (see Figure 1.4) illustrates our thoughts on and approach to this topic. This model describes both the *planning* phase and the subsequent on-ice *interacting* phase, two closely interrelated components.

FIGURE 1.4   Practice planning model (adapted from Fisher *et al.*, 1980 and Trudel, 1987)

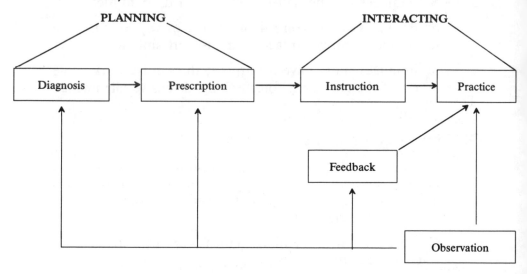

1.8.1   The planning phase

The first step in planning a practice, whether at the beginning, middle or end of the season, is to assess the present needs of the participants (Fisher et al., 1980; Andrews, 1983; Trudel, 1987). This is what we have labelled as the diagnostic phase in the model. This phase is primarily accomplished by the coach and assistants observing the players in a series of practices and games, followed by an accurate interpretation of their present level of ability. The video (VCR) can facilitate diagnosis by affording the coach unlimited opportunities to review the actions of the players. Other methods of assessment may include evaluation of abilities through the use of standardized tests, information from previous coaches and, if appropriate, an open dialogue with the player (Chouinard, 1982).

Following an accurate diagnosis of the players' skills, a prescription, remedy or plan is prepared on paper. This prescription should contain all the specific learning activities and drills under the various components of a practice that will enable the athletes to improve systematically. Some refer to this plan as the design (content) of the practice — the different exercises and drills that will be used during the practice. Once you have completed these planning steps — a diagnosis of needs and prescription based upon these needs — you are ready to "step" onto the ice and face the challenge of running the practice.

1.8.2 The interacting phase

The object of most practices is to teach the players something new, whether individual or group skills or a playing principle, and to let the players experience these new skills or plays in action. This often requires a review of acquired skills, which may act as a lead-up drill, and a gradual phasing-in of the new skill or principle to be learned in the form of some group activity. This represents the core of a practice — learning by doing.

While the players are active, the coach must now assume a very important function, becoming an observer. An effective teacher/coach should always remain perceptually alert, play the role of an observer, and provide the necessary individual and group feedback to the players when appropriate. Feedback — the communication of perceptions — has a number of effects on the learner, the main effect being to guide the player onto the proper track. Without feedback, the learner formulates his own set of assumptions, sometimes correct, other times incorrect, regarding the manner of execution. This element of doubt must be avoided and replaced with timely feedback that is positive, specific and meaningful to the player. In short, observation and feedback are essential functions of any teacher/coach in the learning process.

Information as a result of observation by the coaches, however, does not always have to be used as feedback in the form of a message to the players. Observation and the resulting information processing can be used, first, as a means of *regulating* the practice at hand and, second, in terms of *preparing* the next practice session. Regulating essentially implies adjusting the content of the practice to more accurately reflect the needs of the players. This adjustment may take the form of repeating the objective of the exercise, modifying the drill, selecting a totally different drill or even moving on to the next component of the practice sooner than anticipated. As a coach, you must always be ready and prepared to adjust the practice plan as you see fit.

It is crucial to select the appropriate drills to develop the skills of the players. Equally important is monitoring the drill to see whether it is meeting your practice objectives. If not, then the necessary adjustments must be made. Chambers (1985) reinforces this message:

> The key to using drills properly is knowing what you want to achieve. If there is a particular problem or skill that you feel should be dealt with, then this should be the basis for selecting your drill. If the drill can also be made to simulate game conditions, it will eliminate one further problem of transferring what has been learned to how it will be used in a game. Done with game intensity, it will also add a spirit and enthusiasm to your practice similar to what is expected during a game.

> Besides setting up drills that are skill and game-specific, note what kind of learning is taking place. This is the mark of a good coach. Knowing the detail of what is required and comparing it with what is actually being demonstrated by the player(s). Evaluating the outcome and offering constructive feedback is essential in the proper use of drills (p. 35).

Closely related to this point of how players are actually practicing is what physical educators have been referring to as "time on task" (Metzler, 1979; Rate, 1980; Rushall, 1980; Trudel, 1987). Time on task, that is, the amount of time players truly spend working on the appropriate task(s) or drill objectives, is extremely important to maximize learning. Many studies (Rate, 1980; Rushall, 1980;

Trudel, 1987) have shown the low amount of actual learning time spent during practices in many sports, particularly in ice hockey. Coaches need to learn the various pedagogical skills, methods and techniques before, during and after practices that will enable players to increase their time on the appropriate task (Naylor and Howe, 1990).

An effective method of accomplishing this is to:

1. State *specific* learning objectives prior to drill.
2. Identify *concepts and learning cues* (key words) for the players to focus on.
3. Offer a *visual* demonstration, both on a blackboard and on-ice.
4. *Reinforce* learning cues during practice to promote time on task.
5. Provide *effective feedback* by referring back to drill objectives and related concepts (Chouinard and McKenzie, 1990).

Your observations should also be the source of information in planning the next practice, a sort of extension of the above process whereby you made adjustments according to the needs of the participants. However, in this case, the information you acquired through your observation of the players in action is used to plan for the next practice. For example, as a coach you have observed that the players have a tendency to favor the forehand pass, consequently neglecting the backhand pass. Logically, in the next practice you communicate your concern and introduce a drill that specifically forces the players to use the backhand pass. It may take more than one practice to correct the bad habit, but with appropriate, challenging drills, players will soon develop a sense of confidence and purpose in the proper technique.

This planning practice model is not intended to highlight the principles or favorable characteristics of a practice, nor the components of a practice, both of which have already been described. Instead, the model offers a new perspective on how to *plan* and *adjust* a practice according to the needs of your hockey players and the team.

2

The Nature of Team Sports

2.1 Introduction

In his popular book "Road to Olympus" (1969), Tarasov shared insights, methods and strategies that were used to build the Soviet hockey dynasty. One of the underlying themes found in his autobiographical book — with which we have since become familiar through many international events — is their strong emphasis on collective or team play. The Soviets' concept of team play is a total commitment to the overall well-being of the team. The central focus is an unshakeable "what's best for the team?" For the individual athlete, the question becomes "What's the best way I can help our team?" For some, this may be viewed as a form of altruism; for others, a socialist regime, a way of life. Whatever sociological term we use, the end result remains the same if we look closely at the player's actions during a game — unselfishness, discipline and concentration, maximum effort at all times and total support for team play. All individual efforts are channelled towards one very specific end — boosting team performance within a detailed system of play. To accomplish this objective, coaches and athletes must first understand the general nature of team sports.

2.2 Hockey, a *Team* Sport

Hockey, like basketball, soccer and football, is a team sport. But what exactly is meant by the word *team*? For many, a team is "good," "average," or "bad," depending on the quality of the players on the team. For others, especially as the season progresses, statistics become the measuring stick. A particular club is considered a solid "team" because they are leading in their division. Unfortunately, this is a far cry from the true notion of a team (Caron and Pelchat, 1974, 1975).

A team is also more than the sum of its parts. We may say of a team that "they are a good squad on paper" (meaning that they have the individual talent) but when it comes to executing, the team falls short of the public's expectations. The true notion of a team implies that each and every athlete has a vital role to play in determining the nature and character of the team. It also implies that the players have a sense of belonging and mutual respect as they channel their individual efforts to achieve the team's objectives.

For a group of players to come together and form a "real" team, a number of elements must be present: organizational effectiveness, coaching expertise, highly motivated and dedicated athletes and sound preparation in the four areas of training. From a tactical perspective, team play occurs when players execute the various actions/skills taking a cooperative, systematic and rationalized approach while leaving sufficient room for creativity and improvisation. The basis that makes team play at all possible rests on two extremely important concepts, which we would now like to explore – the *perceptual-motor process* and the *communication network* among the players.

2.3 The Perceptual-Motor Process (Reading and Reacting Skills)

The perceptual-motor process is the mechanism by which an individual athlete receives information from his environment and, through a series of complex brain functions, executes the appropriate action. This entire process essentially deals with a player's ability to perceive, decide and react to ever-changing on-ice situations during the course of a game. King (1985) has referred to this process as the "reading and reacting" skill, which is so important to the modern hockey player. The late Lloyd Percival, a pioneer in his own right, advanced a similar notion back in the early 1950s in his *Hockey Handbook* (1951):

> By taking a look and using his head, the puck carrier can take full advantage of any poor positional play on the part of the opposing team or his own particular check (p. 119).

> If he develops the habit of analyzing the opposing player when on the bench and at every opportunity, he will soon have a remarkable store of knowledge that will enable him to react instinctively (p. 117).

> Therefore the player who does not learn to plan his movements will probably remain a headlong player who, though he may do well in the lower categories of hockey because of his industry and determination, will probably find that the going gets tougher as the class of hockey in which he is playing improves (p. 116).

His book was revered by the European hockey community, especially by the Soviets during the coaching era of Anatoli Tarasov.

In hockey, we receive information about our playing environment mainly through our sense of vision, but hearing and feeling also play an important role. The modern approach to hockey requires each and every player to act and react judiciously and precisely to various playing situations. The athlete is not a robot. He relies on his intellectual processes to scan the specific playing situation, make a decision in relation to the on-going play and execute the action accordingly. Given the speed at which the game is played, the number of players on the ice and the necessity of almost instantly integrating all the situational elements for that moment, this becomes a very complex task. Yet in the context of fostering total team play, this issue must be addressed comprehensively. First, let us examine this perceptual-motor process in some detail.

As in many sub-disciplines under the umbrella of sport and physical activity, psychomotor learning has made an enormous contribution to the understanding of movement. Many of its tenets have had a direct impact on how we teach and practice sports. To define the term psychomotor learning, we must first define motor learning. Motor learning is a relatively permanent change in the performance of a motor skill resulting from practice or past experience (Kerr, 1982). Adding the prefix "psycho" implies that the performance of the skill involves more than muscular activity. The actions represent only observable behavior. As Kerr (1982) suggests: "Behind this behavior there is a large central control operation that not only supervises the specific muscle commands regarding 'how' to move but also supervises the specific decisions of 'why,' 'when,' 'where,' and 'how far' to move" (p. 6). Briefly, psychomotor learning is concerned with the controlling processes that initiate, guide and produce the movement or behavior. To understand these processes represents an initial step towards grasping the nature of tactical actions and how they apply to the field of hockey.

Several authors (Gibson, 1969; Kerr, 1982; Mahlo, 1974; Schmidt, 1982; Whiting, 1969) have identified three main components in the processing of information: *perception*, *decision-making* and *response mechanism* (see Figure 2.1).

FIGURE 2.1   Information-processing model

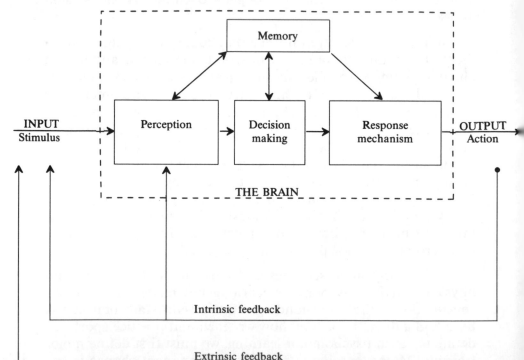

PERCEPTION involves the identification and integration of information that enters our brain through the various senses. It represents the first step in the process of executing an action. Based upon the interpretation of sensory stimuli emanating from our environment, we make decisions and coordinate our actions. Similarly, in hockey, athletes are continually bombarded with information from their playing environment, intellectually challenged to make the correct decision and required to execute the appropriate tactical action. The exact and appropriate tactical action depends on the quantity of the information perceived and on the quality of this perception or "display," a term used by Whiting to represent "that part of the external environment which contains information which is likely to be of use — or in some cases necessary — in the performance of a skill." To broaden this idea, two other terms must be introduced, "selective attention" and "pattern recognition."

Perception is selective by nature. *Selective attention* (Whiting, 1969) refers to an athlete's ability to select from the environment or display those specific cues which are relevant to the performance of the skill. Experience and training obviously play a significant role in this process of identifying and integrating only the stimuli that will guide the player to execute the quality tactical skill. There is so much information, and so little time to react, that the rate of selection becomes extremely critical, especially in hockey, where speed is virtually the determining factor. *Pattern recognition* refers to the ability to recognize or extract a pattern from the mass of information. The experienced player has the ability to assimilate pertinent cues from the playing environment and instantly form an image or pattern that will enable him to act intelligently in the situation. For example, in a one-on-one situation in hockey, the offensive player must first recognize the backward speed of the opposing defenseman before deciding whether to stickhandle or use sheer speed to get around him.

Intelligence and anticipation, experience, memory, and the kinesthetic sense or body awareness all facilitate this process of selective attention and pattern recognition. The kinesthetic sense, sometimes referred to as the sixth sense in athletics, is an extremely important attribute to develop in young hockey players. Many hockey schools in Europe, for both on- and off-ice programs, stress the development of this kinesthetic awareness (Persson, 1981).

Finally, perception is not a passive reception of information. It is an active search. We don't just see, we look; we don't just hear, we listen; and we not only feel, we touch. Indeed, as experienced and mature athletes, we learn what to extract from our playing environment since so much is happening all at once. We come to recognize certain "situations" as typical play patterns necessitating a specific action or intervention. However, for this exploratory process to occur, the player must in a sense know what he is looking for, have a framework or system upon which to base his decisions, and finally, operate under the same principles and rules of action as his teammates. All of this comes only after the athlete has acquired sufficient tactical play experience and knowledge of the game. We will come back to this later. For now let us examine the second component — decision-making.

DECISION-MAKING as part of the information process model deals with the choice and timing of responses. Having received and screened the information from the playing environment through sight, sound and touch, the brain must now decide on the appropriate action. Knowing "what to do" and "when to do it" is closely associated with experience, memory, tactical savvy, sound judgement and mental creativity. Furthermore, psychological factors such as motivation, desire to win and level of aspiration all have a bearing on the decision. The resulting movement or motor action is thus based on a reflected, sophisticated and voluntary decision. It is not simply a reflex movement.

RESPONSE MECHANISM is responsible for the control and coordination of one or more movements. This represents the final mental process before the skill is actually executed, commonly referred to as the reaction time. Having perceived the playing situation and decided on the required course of action, the brain coordinates the signals to the muscles that will perform the movement. *Input*, in the form of stimuli, has now been transformed into *output*, the energy for action.

Finally, a few words on feedback. FEEDBACK refers to the information that the athlete receives while performing a task or as a result of performing a task. Although there are many ways of classifying the various types of feedback, one common division is *intrinsic* and *extrinsic*. Intrinsic feedback refers to all the information hockey players are constantly receiving from the different senses as they move in either a practice or game situation. For instance, a player skating with the puck may suddenly shift to the left to allow himself more space because he feels a stick check coming from the right side. Or, a player stickhandling towards the net on a break-away senses an opponent back-checking, which indicates that he should hurry, "protect" the puck and opt for a quick wrist shot. Extrinsic feedback is most commonly associated with knowledge of performance and/or knowledge of results. The classic example is the coach sharing his opinion regarding a particular skill executed by a hockey player. For instance, whether or not a player has scored a goal on a particular attack (knowledge of results), the coach may still choose to provide valuable feedback on how he performed the technical and/or tactical actions (knowledge of performance). In the world of coaching, we often focus on correcting athletes' mistakes or identifying areas of weakness, but our feedback should always be in a spirit of encouragement, understanding and optimism. Attempt to provide positive feedback as much as possible.

This is obviously an extremely simplified explanation of the information processing system, but it does explain how athletes "read and react" to specific playing situations as the game evolves. It also offers both coach and athlete a theoretical framework to enhance their understanding of the importance of the intellectual processes associated with the execution of individual and group tactical actions or skills.

A direct and practical application of this reasoning process is the use of the videotape machine, which lets coaches and players analyze specific playing situations. Coaches can point out certain situations, but the player is the one who lived the moment of play. Only the player can truly explain why he "reacted" in such a way; only he can provide the reason for his decision, based upon what he "read" at the time. This video experience, if properly utilized, can be an invaluable learning tool for coaches. It helps coaches recall situations and players, see their own moves and analyze the technico-tactical decisions they made. It serves as a useful mechanism for feedback, both positive and negative.

To complete this discussion on the importance of hockey players being able to "read" the specific playing situation and "react" appropriately, a final but important point must be made: "reading" and "reacting" is not the sole responsibility of the puck carrier, but should be performed by all the players *simultaneously*. Tarasov (1969), in his wisdom, expressed this idea by stating that in North American hockey four players depend on the puck carrier, whereas in Soviet hockey the puck carrier depends on the other four players for what we now call "support." If our objective is to offer total support to the puck carrier, thus creating a collaborative tactical pattern of attack or defense, then it becomes apparent that all players must simultaneously and continually "read" and "react" as the play evolves. This relatively new way of thinking about the role of the non-puck carriers challenges us to reexamine the game of hockey within the context of a team sport. This concept will be analyzed later and in greater detail in a later chapter.

To facilitate and extend this perceptual-motor process in terms of team play, i.e., coordinate all the individual decisions, some sort of pre-established communication network must be present among the players.

2.4 Communication Networks

Closely associated to the perceptual-motor process, especially as it relates to team sports such as hockey, is the area of communication. Perception, decision-making and executing group tactical skills are the result of a sophisticated communication network among the players interacting on the ice. Effective communication implies that there is a message, a sender, a receiver and an appropriate response to the message (see Figure 2.2). Experienced hockey players,

FIGURE 2.2   Communication model

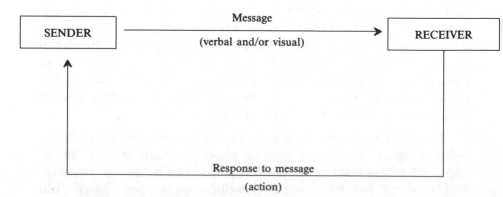

especially those who have played together for some time, are constantly communicating with one another, both verbally and non-verbally. Verbal messages, such as calling the name of your defensive partner, indicating that you are "open" for receiving a pass, are evident throughout the game. However, non-verbal and more subtle messages common to the players represent the underlying communication network which is critical to the execution of group tactical skills. Non-verbal messages or cues are in a sense a form of sign language belonging to the players, communicated through certain individual gestures, movements and patterns of play that the receiver recognizes and which require a specific response. To recognize these cues or patterns, such as a raised stick or slapping stick on the ice, suggesting the player is open for a pass, and respond accordingly takes time and experience, but is mainly a series of learned group tactical patterns familiar to all the players on the team. To be able to make the proper individual and collective tactical decisions, it becomes imperative to establish a form of language of intentions that will enable players to coordinate their actions (Caron and Pelchat, 1975; Caron, 1985). To illustrate this subtle communication system, let's analyze the well known "give-and-go" group tactical skill.

Figure 2.3 depicts the total scenario, playing situation and probable effect of a "give-and-go" in the neutral zone; however, it does not explain precisely what has happened between players 2 and 4, the key actors in the execution of the play. This does not imply that the other players were not instrumental in carrying out the play; rather, they facilitated its development by their timely movements, camouflaged the counterattack and accelerated towards the opponents' blue line. But let's resume the analysis by developing a series of pictures that will progressively illustrate what actually transpired. In Figure 2.3a, we see that player 4 has possession of the puck and is anticipating opponent 6 as a potential checker. He therefore scans the immediate area looking for an outlet pass to an open player, and sees players 2 and 5. He opts to pass to player 2, since he is available for a pass, unlike player 5, as shown in Figure 2.3b. When player 4 realized that player 2 was open, communication had begun. In other words, player 2 sent a message by shouting, tapping his stick on the ice or simply being there completely open. Whatever signal player 2 used, 4 received the message and responded with a direct pass − "the give." But what triggered the return pass — "the go"? First, player 4 skated to an open area — his cue or intention — while at the same time player 2 noticed his displacement, although player 6 was about to crisscross between the two (see Figure 2.3c). Second, player 2 looked at the alternatives before him and felt that in the situation, the return pass — "the go" — to player 4 was his best decision, tactically speaking (see Figure 2.3d).

FIGURE 2.3   Give-and-go

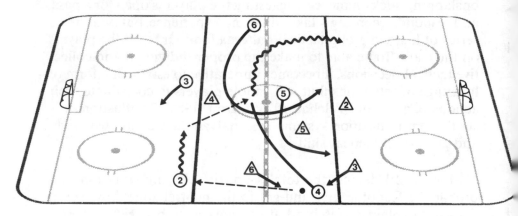

FIGURE 2.3a   Kinogram: give-and-go

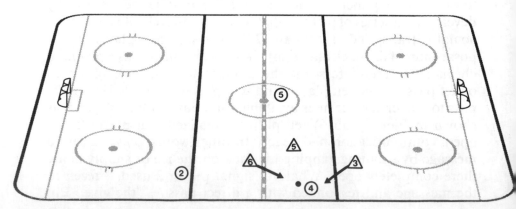

FIGURE 2.3b   Kinogram: give-and-go

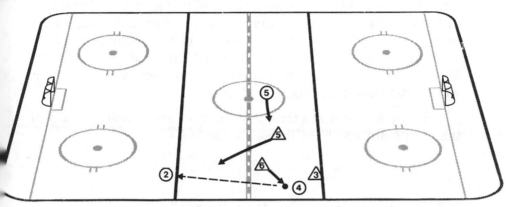

FIGURE 2.3c   Kinogram: give-and-go

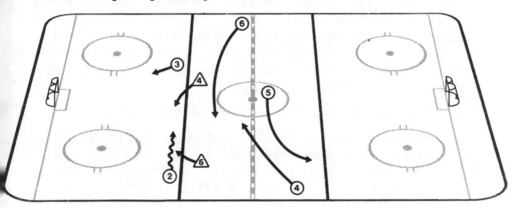

FIGURE 2.3d   Kinogram: give-and-go

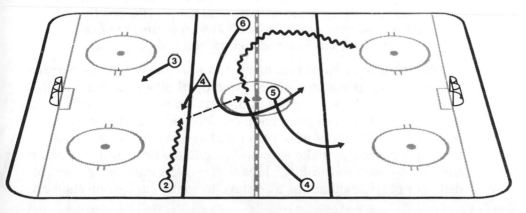

This brief analysis of a typical "give-and-go" combination play has helped us appreciate the importance of the "reading and reacting" skills, as well as the subtle communication network that must exist among the players to produce team play. However, another critical element remains to be considered in order to produce a collective form of play and not a haphazard one – a "system of play." This will be the subject of our next chapter.

Finally, let's look at a term that captures or symbolizes many of the points discussed – "hockey sense."

2.5 Developing "Hockey Sense"

The one element that sets star hockey players apart from others playing in the National Hockey League is hockey sense. Think of the superstars of past and present. What extra or special ability did/do they possess? Most hockey scouts, coaches and reporters have referred to this special magic as "hockey sense" — a combination of skill, intellect and judgement.

Meagher (1975) wrote a fine essay on this topic.

> When one sits down to make a list of the so-called professional superstars the single most important criterion is that thing we call "hockey sense" ... Call it what you will – anticipating, "guesstimating," reacting before the fact or reading the play, all of these superstars show us an uncanny ability called hockey sense (p. 47).

> The intelligent hockey player is the one who understands the flow of the game – and the impact of that flow on the lines, the boards, the rules. He is the one who has identified the very limited number of alternatives that can exist at any one time and has then reduced them to the first and second best choices (p. 52).

But what does all of this mean to the aspiring hockey player? What can we as coaches do to develop this special trait called hockey sense? The answer lies in the way we both teach and coach the game. As we saw in the section on "Principles and Components of a Practice," coaches *must* select and create drills that will challenge our players to make wise and intelligent decisions. Practices should be conceived with the idea that players must be exposed to different playing situations and have to make choices on the best solution in this particular context of play. Games must also be used to stretch a player's intellectual ability. During game-time, coaches should not only reinforce what players are doing right and identify mistakes, but also encourage creativity and improvisation. Players must be taught the importance of using their thinking skills during practices and games to prepare mentally, anticipate, read, select the best alternative and execute the action. This is how coaches can develop the Wayne Gretzkys of tomorrow.

2.6   The Role of a Coach

As a coach, you have certain responsibilities, not only to your athletes, but also to their parents, the local hockey organization, the school, college or university and the community at large, depending on the coaching situation. These responsibilities require that you "wear many hats" or assume various roles to effectively get the job done, on and off the ice. This is what makes coaching such a dynamic and challenging occupation, whether as a professional, amateur or house-league coach.

Recognizing the multifaceted nature of the coaching job and the various roles a coach must play, we would like to briefly expand on two of these roles which we feel deserve special attention. These are: the coach as an *educator* and *leader*.

The most important responsibility of a coach is to teach the players the game of hockey within the context of the four areas of preparation — technical, tactical, physical and psychological. If a coach perceives himself as an educator first and foremost, we believe that many positive things will occur for the players and the coaching staff, both on and off the ice. To be an effective teacher/ coach implies seasonal planning; individual and team goal setting; establishing teaching objectives; organizational effectiveness; and, but most of all, creating a positive learning environment. We strongly believe that coaching is teaching —communicating new and innovative ideas.

Coaches must also be leaders. Effective leadership embraces many characteristics, but we believe that it all begins by acting as an exemplary role model for these developing athletes. Studies have shown that coaches have a tremendous influence on young athletes just as teachers in schools. Players do form attitudes and values based on the behavior of coaches. Wayne Gretzky had this to say about his first coach:

> Thanks dad. You taught me to play hockey, yes, but that wasn't the half of it. You taught me to be fair, to do the right thing, to respect people and, most of all, to be a man. Not that it was tough to learn. All I had to do was watch (p. 248).

As an amateur coach, you have the responsibility of teaching the technical and tactical skills of the game and, more importantly, making these learning experiences enjoyable for the player and yourself. Don't rush the process. As an instructor, you must exercise patience and progress according to their needs as developing children and students of the game. A quote, taken from Murray Costello, President of the Canadian Amateur Hockey Association, captures this message extremely well.

> Don't attempt to make them [the players] specialized too soon by throwing too much information at them all at once. It takes the fun out of playing the game; it will make it seem like work at a time when they should be experiencing the positive feelings that come from playing a sport.
>
> Make sure *you* [italics added] are enjoying the game yourself. Pause and enjoy, laugh a little, and the kids will be more relaxed and likely to have fun too! (p. i)

Coaching is an art and science. The art is the human relations, communication, teaching and leadership skills; the science is the knowledge, new technologies and methods of coaching the game.

3

A System
of Play

3.1 Introduction

The word "system" has been used, even abused, in the world of
hockey to refer to many different aspects of the game. Today, there
is still some confusion as to its proper meaning, use and interpretation. As in many other fields of study, the word "system" seems to
have become extremely popular. Take anatomy or physiology,
where the discipline is broken down into the respiratory system, the
circulatory system, etc. Even in the social sciences, in fields such as
politics and economics, we commonly refer to the "political system"
or the "economic system." Closer to home, we often refer to the
"postal system," "heating system" and even "music system." But
what are we really trying to say?

The word system refers to a number of elements working separately *and* together for the overall purpose of the whole. To explain
this definition, let's look at how a typical music system works. The
essential components are a receiver or tuner, an amplifier and
speakers. It goes without saying that no one element can produce a
single note; even two might only give you a hum. The point is that
each individual component is essential *and* they must all work
together to produce sound — hence a music "system." Unfortunately, the music system becomes more complex when we look at the

various parts within the individual components, in other words the parts that make up the receiver, amplifier and speakers. Academics commonly refer to these as sub-systems. The analysis could also be extended to include the broadcasting station — the supra-system — which transmits the radio waves. But for common usage, the word system suffices. It becomes even more complicated when we attempt to understand how the radio waves are transmitted from the broadcasting station to the home receiver, from the receiver to the amplifier and in turn to the speakers.

In hockey we have a similar situation. We use the word system in many different ways to avoid getting too technical — and with good reason. However, it is still important to understand the full meaning of the word when used in hockey terms. For example, the phraseology and system of play include all the various elements that make up the offense and defense. Since this is an extremely large area of study, we divide the pie into offensive and defensive systems. But again, we can further separate the defensive system into forechecking and penalty-killing systems, etc., and similarly separate our offensive system into power play and breakout systems, for instance. This is certainly an acceptable usage of the word "system." The fact remains, however, that when we refer to a particular system, it is critical that all the elements contained in that system be identified *and* related to one another rationally and comprehensively. Only then is the word "system" given its fair and correct meaning. This form of analytical thinking is called a *systems or integrated approach*.

3.2 A Systems or Integrated Approach

There are many ways to teach and coach the game of hockey. For instance, some coaches, believing that you must first develop a sound defensive system, will devote most of their initial practices to that theme. Some coaches place a stronger emphasis on defense than on offense throughout the season. Other coaches stress the development of technical and individual tactical skills slightly more than group tactical skills, even at higher levels of competition. Still others place a great deal of emphasis on having the best power play and penalty killing units in the league. Occasionally, you may meet a coach who dedicates a relatively enormous amount of time to developing the goaltenders compared to other aspects of the game. In short, coaches have their own personal preferences and approaches to teaching and coaching the game of hockey.

Traditionally, most coaches have also approached the game in sections, teaching breakouts, neutral zone play and various attacking plays on offense and forechecking, backchecking and defensive zone play on defense. This approach was not totally inappropriate, but we submit that it was incomplete.

While we concede that coaches have their own personal methods, approaches and philosophy regarding the teaching and coaching of the game, and that many have been trained, influenced and accustomed to a particular style, one very important fact remains that forces us to reexamine our overall manner of coaching. *Athletes have changed as learners.* Hockey players now have a need to know the reasons why they must act or react to a particular playing situation. Athletes need to understand the rationale behind the çoach's decision to choose a particular system of play in order to be totally committed to the coach's methods and approaches. Hence, if our objective is to teach our players how to play the game rationally, then we must also teach them the underlying and interacting reasons — the *principles* and *concepts* — behind our coaching decisions. To teach and coach the game through the application of these principles and concepts is to use a *systems or integrated approach.*

For example, in describing how to execute a breakout system, we must first *identify* the main elements (principles and concepts) that produce an effective breakout, such as flow, acceleration, width, depth, movement of players, support, etc., and second, *integrate* all of these into a complete framework or system of play. This will help the players better understand and assimilate the breakout system, and in turn prepare them to execute under varied situations. Neilson and Smith (1978) also held this belief, stating:

> I think two things happen if you establish a thorough understanding of the concepts of team play:
>
> — the players will definitely learn faster
> — your players and your team in the future will have a lot more flexibility. They'll be able to switch into another style more easily. During a game you'll be able to change your forechecking etc., more quickly. They'll be less stereotyped, and will be more natural in their approach to the game (p. 187).

Neilson and Smith advocated a three-stage system of play consisting of general concepts, zone play and specific patterns. They firmly believed that general concepts must be taught first so that the players know the reasons or rationale behind their actions or specific patterns. Incidentally, it was also Roger Neilson who pioneered the idea of using the video as a teaching and coaching tool in hockey. Others may have used film or video-tape replay before him, but he was the one who popularized the concept among many ice hockey coaches, especially at the higher levels.

Gagnon (1982, 1989) developed a system of play model consisting of three parts: fundamental principles, rules of operation and structures (alignment or formation). According to Gagnon, fundamental principles refer to the *what*, rules of operation to the *how* and structures to the *where* in terms of the various actions of the players. This system of play represents a global form of group tactics.

In summary, a systems or integrated approach is a global way of looking at all the main elements within a particular system of play and the way these interact with one another. It is a way of thinking about these various interacting elements in a logical, creative and thoughtful manner by expressing them in the form of principles and concepts to gain a better understanding or "conceptualization" of the game of hockey.

3.3   Elements and Relationship within a System of Play

The overall purpose of using a "true" system of play is to organize and coordinate all the individual techniques and tactics into a synchronized, collaborative form of play — team play. More specifically, the effects of a common system of play will be:

1. To improve the quality of decision-making by each and every player in any given situation;
2. To decrease their reading and reaction time; and
3. To facilitate and coordinate their decisions in group tactical plays.

Whether you are describing a backchecking system, a forechecking system or a power play system, certain specific elements and the relationship between these elements must first be understood and analyzed. Because "a picture is worth a thousand words," we offer this model, which represents what we believe should be contained in a complete system of play (see Figure 3.1). This model depicts a certain number of elements, some of which are familiar to us while others have not yet been fully explained.

FIGURE 3.1   System of play model

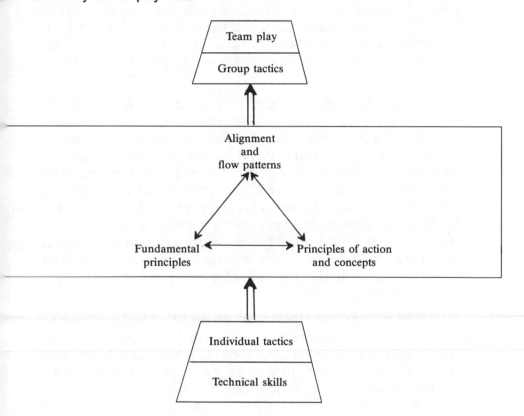

3.3.1 Technical and individual tactical skills

Technical and individual tactical skills are the individual actions/skills performed by the players. These actions/skills are simply building blocks for group tactical skills. These individual skills must now be channeled or directed towards a collective and coordinated effort, hence the need to identify guiding principles and concepts.

3.3.2 Fundamental principles, principles of action and concepts

The function of these principles and concepts is to coordinate the individual actions of the players into some form of harmony. *Fundamental principles* represents the foundation upon which tactics and systems of play are developed (adapted from Caron and Pelchat, 1975; Kingston, 1981). *Principles of action* are guidelines for players' individual and collective actions. Some authors refer to these as rules of play; others, as principles of play. *Concepts* are ideas closely associated with the fundamental principles and principles of action.

The point of all these principles and concepts is that they let players play under a similar set of guidelines, and help them make individual and collective action decisions necessary for the proper execution of group tactical plays without stifling improvisation or creativity. As we will discover later, the principle of support and the concept of overload, for example, are extremely critical in the execution of most breakout plays. This fact does not, however, dictate specific player movements, but rather a general framework which, if followed, will augment the success of the play. In other words, various options for a particular breakout play can be conceived while still respecting the principle of support and the concept of overloading an area of the ice.

Principles and concepts give general direction and guidance for actions. The coach stresses the need for certain plays over others based on his particular beliefs, the fabric of his team, and the strengths and weaknesses of the opposition. However, players must remember that the application of these various principles and concepts must always be balanced with good judgement based on the specific playing situation (Ratushny, personal communication, September 5, 1988).

3.3.3 Alignment and flow patterns

The *alignment* is the formation or arrangement of the players on the ice, usually in reference to a specific zone and a particular playing

situation. It acts as a general framework or starting point to facilitate the various patterns of movement and the permutations needed to
maintain a certain balance among the players. *Flow patterns* are the
general patterns of movement by the players on the ice. Traditionally, we have used numbers (e.g., 2-1-2) or expressions such as
the "box" formation on defense to refer to an alignment. Flow patterns
are a little more difficult to describe in words because of the dynamic
nature of flow, but easier and clearer to depict by illustrations.
Certain illustrations in Chapter 5 describe various flow patterns.

We know from our previous discussion that fundamental principles, principles of action and concepts guide the players in their
action-decisions. For instance, the fundamental principle of puck
control, the concept of creating time and space and the action principle of supporting the puck carrier will direct and guide all the
players towards a common objective. The element of alignment
and flow pattern simply adds more clarity and precision to players'
movement-decisions as they implement the various principles and
concepts. Both the fundamental principles, principles of action and
concepts, and the alignment and flow patterns facilitate individual
and collective decisions. Both are indispensable in terms of directing the players towards coordinated group tactics and team
play.

3.3.4 Group tactics and team play

Group tactics are collective actions used consciously by two or more
players to gain advantage over one or more opponents, whether
offensively or defensively. In group tactics, we are usually referring
to 2 on 1, 2 on 2, 3 on 1 and 3 on 2 situations of play. *Team play* is the
sum of individual and collective actions by all the players on a
team, organized, coordinated and unified rationally with the objective of winning the game (adapted from Théodoresco, 1965). Team
play should also be perceived as a series of group tactical actions
over a certain period of time. Group work by two or three players is
most often the basis for effective tactical maneuvers. At one particular moment, it might be two forwards and a back engaged in
group tactics, while the following play may involve a different back
with the same forwards. And there is a reason for this. Coordinating the actions of two or three players at the same time is easier,
more practical and more natural given the speed of the game than
coordinating the actions of all the players on the ice. Despite the

fact that all players should contribute towards team play, in practice, winning the individual and small group battles is what makes the difference. On offense, this means capitalizing on a 2 on 1, for example, and on defense, it may mean stopping a dangerous 3 on 1 attack by the defenseman making the big play.

Putting all these various elements together – technical and individual tactical skills, fundamental principles, principles of action and concepts, alignment and flow patterns, group tactics and team play – produces an entire system of play. The main ingredients of a system of play, however, are those within the circle, the fundamental principles and related concepts along with the alignment and flow patterns.

II

MOVEMENT AND PUCK CONTROL

A successful offense or attack in hockey depends on a team's ability to move the puck under control towards the opposition's end, shoot from an optimal location and score a goal. Part Two will describe the first two fundamental principles of offense: movement and puck control. These basic principles will be examined in terms of the puck and non-puck carrier for both individual and group tactical actions.

4

Introduction

4.1 The Object of the Game

The object of any game is to win. In hockey, this basically means that you must score more goals than your opponents in order to win the game. Stated slightly differently, the team's objective is to score goals *and* to prevent the opposition from scoring (or at least limit their scoring). Based upon these general objectives we should be able to derive, or at least suggest, the best approach to attain these objectives. In other words, what should coaches emphasize to their athletes to accomplish these objectives? What general guidelines should players follow to make the correct action-decision? The answers to these questions lie in the fundamental principles and their related factors.

4.2 Fundamental Principles of Offense

A team is on the attack or offense when they have definite possession of the puck. *Offensively*, four fundamental principles should guide the decisions of players on the ice (see Figure 4.1). These are:

1. *Movement*
2. *Puck control*
3. *Progression of attack*
4. *Optimal shooting*

FIGURE 4.1   Fundamental principles of offense

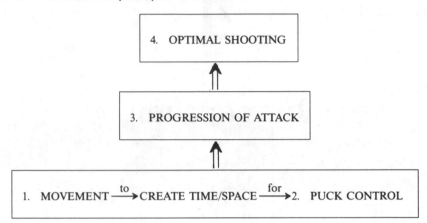

Movement by all the players is absolutely essential to effective play. All players must be active. Puck control enables a team to be in charge or in control of its actions. And a concerted attack must advance or progress towards the opponents' net, planning to set up a shooting play from the best possible location.

All four fundamental principles are essential to produce a successful offense. However, movement and puck control form the basis, while progression of attack and optimal shooting are the intermediate and final objectives respectively.

4.3   Factors Relating to Fundamental Principles

As we saw in the previous chapter, there are a number of principles of action and concepts associated with the fundamental principles. In most cases, these are interrelated; they work together to produce a common effect. In some instances, these principles of action and concepts are more the result or consequence of applying the fundamental principles themselves rather than the cause. But in most cases, the fundamental principles are enhanced by certain principles of action and concepts. For instance, the fundamental principle of puck control is enhanced by the principle of support and the concept of flow.

The principles of action and concepts are more specific and concrete. They allow us to more fully understand, respect and apply the four fundamental principles. They also help us to explore the meaning of the fundamental principles under various playing situations.

Depending on the term or expression, we will use either the word "principle" or "concept," whichever seems more natural, appropriate and in vogue with popular terminology used by coaches. For instance, "support" is usually referred to as a principle; in our examination, therefore, we have identified it as the principle of support. Similarly, "flow" is more commonly referred to as a concept; hence, we have called it the concept of flow.

Before we begin our analysis of the fundamental principles and their related principles and concepts, we must first introduce some terms that will be used to describe the fundamental principles of movement and puck control. This will help us communicate our thoughts more clearly and precisely and reduce the possibility of misunderstanding.

4.4 Terminology of Movement and Puck Control

The terms that need to be defined and developed can be grouped into two categories:

1. The *way* (manner) a player skates versus the *direction* a player moves.
2. The *way* (manner) a player passes versus the *direction* of the pass.

Hockey players can skate in three different ways : *forward*, *backward* and *laterally*. Here we are not referring to the direction of the moving player, e.g. towards his own net, but the manner he chooses to get there. A player can move from point A to point B by skating forward, backward or laterally, or a combination of the three. The symbols used to represent these ways of skating are illustrated below. They also appear in the front of the book under "Symbols."

Forward skating   ⟶

Backward skating   〜〜〜〜〜⟶

Lateral skating   ‖‖‖‖‖‖‖‖‖‖‖‖‖‖⟶

The way or manner in which a player chooses to skate, forward, backward and on occasion laterally, is totally independent of the direction in which he moves. Direction refers to movement in relation to the ice surface. For example, it is quite obvious that a player may choose to skate forward or backward while returning to his own end. But players are not limited to skating directly towards or away from their net, perpendicular to the goal line or parallel to the length of the boards; they can also choose to move in as many directions as there are degrees in a circle. However, it would be far too technical and quite impractical to describe the movement of players in terms of specific degrees from 0 to 360. In the teaching of hockey, we believe that three terms suffice when describing the *direction* in which a player moves (see Figure 4.2). These are:

Longitudinal   A direction parallel to the length of the boards. Skating the length of the ice or up and down the ice is an example of longitudinal movement. Many coaches refer to this direction as *linear*.

Lateral   A direction parallel to the blue lines, goal lines or the width of the boards. Skating along one blue line or skating from side to side is an example of lateral movement.

Diagonal   A direction in between the lateral and longitudinal axes.

There are other directions or patterns of movement that players typically use during competition. Game analyses reveal that players skate in many different directions and patterns. Virtually any type of skating pattern can be used in hockey by puck or non-puck

FIGURE 4.2   Three directions of movement : 1) longitudinal ; 2) lateral ; 3) diagonal

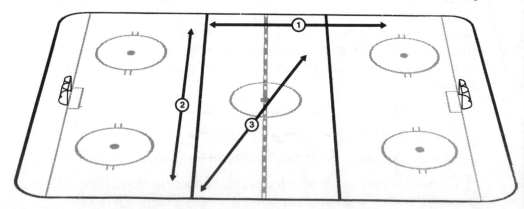

carriers. Again, for communication purposes we feel that two terms are sufficient in describing various *patterns* of movement (see Figure 4.3). These are :

1. *Circular* : a skating pattern in the form of a circle.
2. *Curvilinear* : a skating pattern in the form of a curved line.

FIGURE 4.3   Two patterns of movement : 1) circular ; 2) curvilinear

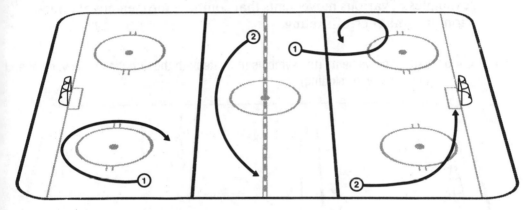

FIGURE 4.4   Longitudinal movements (the symbols indicate both the *direction* of movement and the *manner* of skating)

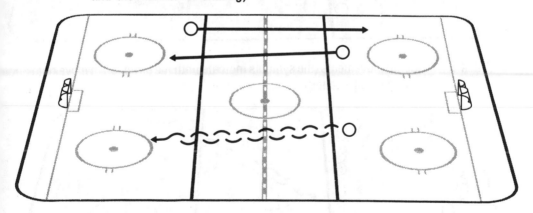

At times, when describing a particular action of a player, it becomes necessary to combine both elements for clarity's sake, the *manner* in which the player skates and the *direction* in which he moves. To simply state, for example, that a player is skating laterally leaves the reader open to two possible interpretations. Is the player *moving* in a lateral direction or is he *skating* laterally? We highlight this point because we found in our review of the literature that the use of these terms was frequently ambiguous. Fortunately, the use of diagrams and appropriate symbols makes the task of explicitly describing the actions of one or more players much easier. For our purposes, when a distinction needs to be made we will use the word "move" to refer to the direction or pattern of movement and the word "skate" to refer to the manner in which the player chooses to skate. Figures 4.4, 4.5, 4.6 and 4.7 offer some examples of various movements that combine the element of direction and manner of skating.

FIGURE 4.5   Lateral movements (the symbols indicate both the *direction* of movement and the *manner* of skating)

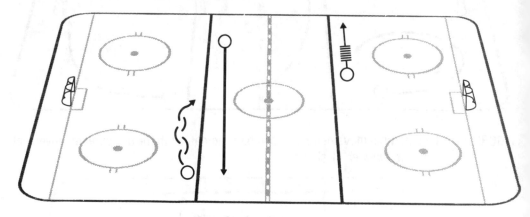

FIGURE 4.6   Diagonal movements (the symbols indicate both the *direction* of movement and the *manner* of skating)

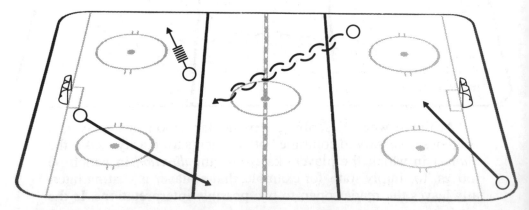

FIGURE 4.7   Circular and curvilinear movements (the symbols indicate both the *direction* of movement and the *manner* of skating)

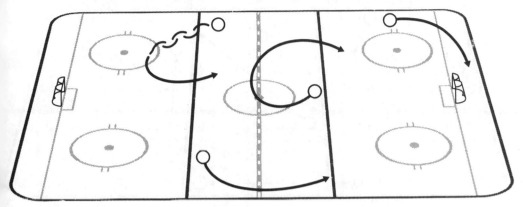

With regard to passes (see Figure 4.8), the terms most commonly used to refer to the direction of a pass are:

1. Forward or lead pass
2. Backward or back pass
3. Lateral pass
4. Diagonal pass

As with the movement of the players, where direction and manner represent two separate classifications, the above terminology is used strictly to denote the direction of the pass. It does not refer to the manner or technique used to execute the pass. A lateral pass, for example, could be performed by using a backhand sweep pass or a forehand flip pass. In hockey, because the playing surface is surrounded by boards, two other types of passes are possible − the "board" or "off the boards" pass and the "around the boards" pass. We also refer to these as "indirect" passes. Depending on the playing situation, these passes can be a very effective means of reaching an open player, which otherwise would have been impossible with a "direct pass" (see Figure 4.9).

Because player and puck movements happen on the ice surface, it is also necessary for the sake of accuracy to describe the various divisions of the rink.

FIGURE 4.8   Four directions of passes : 1. forward pass ; 2. back pass ; 3. lateral pass ; 4. diagonal pass

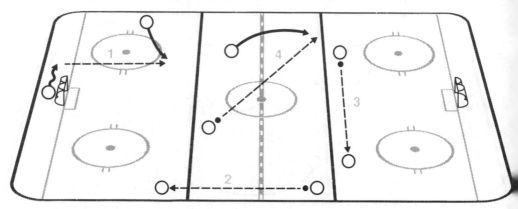

FIGURE 4.9   Board pass and around-the-boards pass

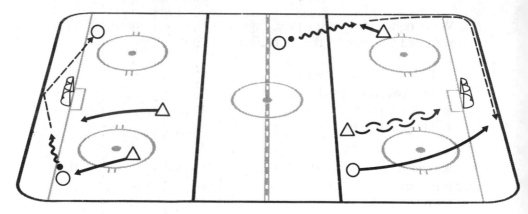

4.5 Rink Divisions — Zones, Lanes and Areas

Since movements of both players and puck occur on the ice surface, it is essential to pinpoint the various zones, lanes and areas of the rink. This will also help us to describe the movements and direction of the players and the passes with greater precision.

Almost all North American hockey rinks measure 200 feet in length by 85 feet in width. If there is a discrepancy, they are usually slightly smaller. European hockey rinks, on the other hand, measure 200 by 100 feet, with a greater distance between the goal line and the board. This additional width, along with the extra space behind the goal lines, allows or encourages players to make it more of a "skating" game rather than a "hitting" game. Some hockey experts have even suggested that it is because of this larger ice surface that European hockey has evolved differently in terms of team play. We bring this to your attention because it was the Europeans, especially through the influence of the Soviets, who developed a radically different approach to movement. Nevertheless, we should not for an instant believe that our rinks in North America are too small to allow the full use of the principles of movement which we will discuss in the next chapter. Incidentally, with the increased number of international tournaments played abroad at various levels of hockey – national, junior, university, midget – we are building more European-size hockey rinks in Canada.

Traditionally in hockey, we have divided the rink into three main parts: defensive, neutral and offensive zones. We personally do not like this terminology, since it seems to imply that the team is on offense, defense or something in between, depending on which zone you are playing in – and, as we all know, this is far from the truth. Moreover, except for the neutral zone, which remains the same for both teams, the defensive zone for one team is the offensive zone for the other, and vice versa. This only increases the confusion; however, we must respect certain conventions and accepted customs.

For the purpose of this book, we will have the defensive zone on the left side, as illustrated in Figure 4.10. This, we feel, is the appropriate convention to illustrate actions by the players on one team, since we are writing in the same manner or direction. Hence, the direction of the attack will be from left to right. When we need to represent the respective actions of two teams, then Team A will move from left to right and Team B will move from right to left (see Figure 4.11).

From a teaching and/or coaching standpoint, further divisions of the ice surface are absolutely necessary for the sake of clarity and precision. Various terms have been used by coaches to meet this need over the years as the tactical aspect of the game has evolved, but today, there is still no standard terminology. After an extensive review of the literature and consultations with various coaches, we chose terms which were clear, simple and logical as well as familiar to most in the field. Figure 4.12 illustrates the divisions and terminology used for the respective zones : *low*, *mid* and *high* area for the defensive and offensive zones, and *bottom*, *middle* and *top* area for the neutral zone. We have purposely selected slightly different words for the neutral zone to clearly distinguish it from the defensive and offensive zones. For many coaches the words *low* and *deep* have the same meaning; we have adopted this convention as well. Finally, as we shall soon discover, these areas also relate directly to the *depth concept* — the degree to which players take advantage of the length of the ice within the rules of the game.

FIGURE 4.10   Rink orientation: one team

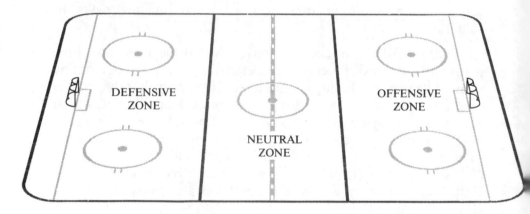

FIGURE 4.11   Rink orientation: two teams

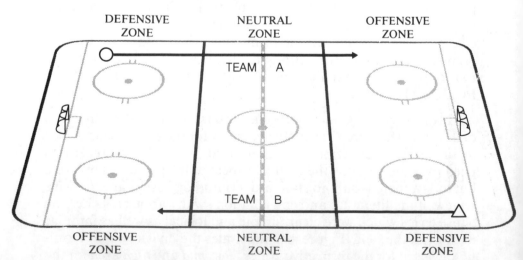

FIGURE 4.12   Zone divisions

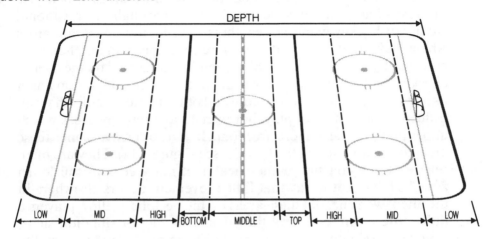

Figure 4.13 shows the rink sectioned longitudinally into three lanes : *left*, *middle* and *right*. This separation is closely linked to the *width concept*, that is, the degree to which players use the full width of the ice. Both the width and depth concepts will be discussed at length below.

FIGURE 4.13   Lanes

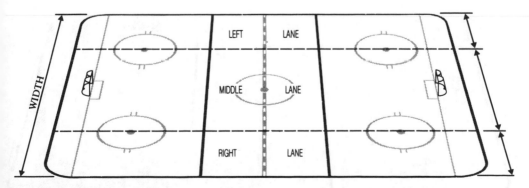

Other areas of the rink identified are those areas which give players slightly more space and time. Through observational studies of hockey games, researchers have identified certain areas where individual puck control is more common than in other more congested areas. Obviously, this depends a great deal on the overall checking style of the opposing team and other considerations such as power play situations, the score and other related factors that can influence the system of play, but in general, there are areas which allow puck carriers more freedom. In the offensive zone, these areas are mainly along the boards (see Figure 4.14). They are often referred to by coaches, paradoxical as it may seem, as the "quiet zone." This is not to say that little movement occurs elsewhere in the offensive zone, but these areas on the periphery allow players a little more room to control the puck. This fact or situation stems from the very nature of the game. The team on defense will tend to closely protect their slot, leaving the team on offense more freedom of movement away from the primary scoring area. In their defensive end, a team on offense will exhibit a similar pattern of behavior. Afraid of a critical give-away in the slot area, the puck carrier under heavy checking pressure will try to avoid skating throught the slot area; passes in general should also keep away from the slot. These conditions of play are also common to other team sports such as basketball, ringette and soccer.

In the neutral zone, it is more difficult to generalize. The area along the boards seems to favor many North American players,

FIGURE 4.14   Quiet zone

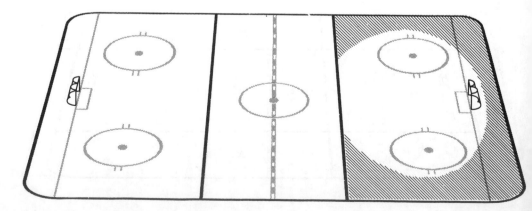

especially the "grinders," "diggers" or "muckers." This is also a symptom or result of our linear pattern of play, in which the wingers tend to remain on their own side. In European hockey, we find more circular and curvilinear patterns, with an emphasis on more extensive use of the entire neutral ice area for passing and stick-handling. This again depends to a large extent on what the opposition "gives" you, as dictated by their neutral ice system of play.

Finally, one other area has received some attention over the past few years — the "extended zone" located in the high area of the defensive zone (see Figure 4.15). The basic idea is extending the neutral zone to your advantage on offense by creating more space and depth in the attack. The usual play situation where we see teams using the extended zone is when the defensemen recuperate the puck around their own blue line and move backwards, passing the puck to each other while they wait for the forwards to get in the open. It is also particularly useful when forwards decide to regroup for a second attack passing the puck back to their defensemen, or simply when preparing for the classic quick counterattack. This subject will be discussed further when we consider attacks through the neutral zone.

Having introduced these terms as a base for our discussions, we will now proceed to analyze the first two fundamental principles of offense — movement and puck control.

IGURE 4.15   Extended zone

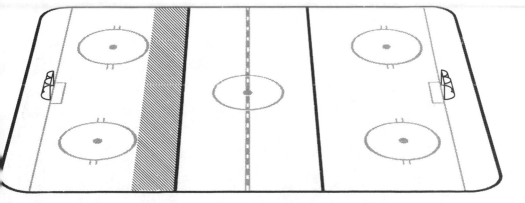

CHAPTER

5

The Fundamental Principle of Movement

5.1 Introduction

Many time-motion studies have confirmed the importance of movement for effective puck control in both North American and European hockey (Boulonne et al., 1976; Korolov, 1978; Boulonne, 1986). Basically, these studies have established the link between the length of puck control and the likelihood of winning. This relationship also exists in other team sports such as football, basketball and soccer, where time of possession, along with proper movement patterns, is a major factor in determining victory

Movement and puck control form the basis of any successful offense. They are also closely related; that is, puck control is enhanced through movement by all the players, commonly referred to as five-men active. To advance and ultimately score goals, you must first be in control of the puck, although some goals are obtained through indirect methods such as aggressive forechecking or waiting for the opposition to commit a mistake and capitalizing on that error. But even in such a situation, puck control is necessary before shooting.

There is also another facet to puck control in terms of the effect it has on the team not controlling the puck. A team not in possession of the puck for some length of time can become "rusty" because the players are not stickhandling, passing, receiving and shooting as often as they should to keep their individual offensive skills sharp. Over an extended period of time, this can become rather frustrating, especially for players who need to "feel the puck" to "remain in the game." In the absence of the puck, the opposition is also limited to a reactive rather than proactive role, and its chances of scoring a goal are virtually nil. Hockey players need to feel the puck to "stay in the game." In short, puck control fosters a sense of confidence among the players which in turn translates into a positive attitude about team performance. Feeling confident and positive are vital mental ingredients to playing the game.

5.2   Movement with a Purpose and Creating Space

Hockey players must move with a purpose, which means that they must have an immediate or imminent reason for skating to a certain point following a particular pattern. This principle of *movement with a purpose* applies equally — as we shall discover — to both puck carriers and non-puck carriers or players off the puck.

Closely associated with this principle of purposeful movement is the *concept of locating and creating space*, again for both puck and non-puck carriers. Before an attack can out-maneuver a presumably well-organized defense, some thought must be given to creating space. Only by looking for space and moving into open space will an attack progress and upset zone or man-to-man defense. Hockey requires players to move constantly in all directions to enhance the creation of space. The players off the puck determine the shaping of the play; the puck carrier, searching for and attempting to create time/space to maintain puck control, relies immensely on his teammates for support (Lodziak, 1966; Batty, 1969; Gratereau, 1970; Hughes, 1973; Waiters, 1984).

Successful European and North American teams maximize the movement principle by stressing two points. The first is that all players should be in constant motion; the second, that players should vary their speed. Perpetual movement and change in speed by all five players will facilitate a number of related principles and concepts on offense, such as:

1. Creation of time and space
2. Collective puck control
3. Interchanging of positions
4. Offensive support
5. Area overload
6. Options in attack, creativity and improvisation
7. Progression of attack
8. Pressure on defenders
9. Increase in scoring opportunities

These principles and concepts will be discussed as we explore the fundamental principles of movement, puck control, progression of attack and optimal shooting. For the moment, however, let's focus our attention specifically on the nature of player movements.

Figures 5.1 and 5.2 illustrate respectively the difference between significant movement (flow) and very limited motion (linear pattern) by players away from the puck in a regrouping play. Which scenario produces more speed and acceleration? Which counterattack is more difficult for the opposition to cover? Which style of play is likely to be more enjoyable for our young hockey players?

FIGURE 5.1   Regrouping with flow and interchange

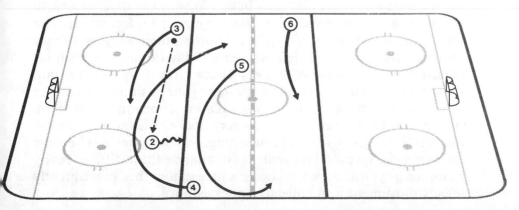

FIGURE 5.2   Regrouping with limited movement

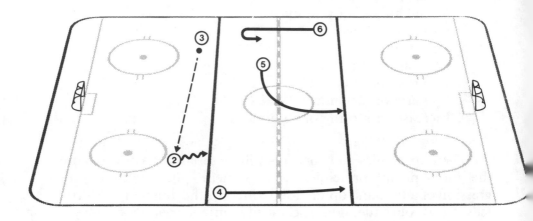

5.3 The Nature of Movement

As we have seen, skating can be analyzed from a movement perspective, that is, the direction and patterns used by players during the game. Here again, credit must be given to the Europeans for having altered our outlook and approach on the movement of players on the ice. This change in attitude has significantly influenced the way we now teach and coach the game. Linear patterns of movement up and down the ice have given way to curvilinear and circular skating patterns. Moreover, players must now learn to interchange with other players, whether forwards or defensemen, to maintain a certain balance in the alignment or formation. The long-standing tradition of coaches exhorting their wingers to "stay on their side" and their defensemen to "stay home" has been replaced by a new wave of hockey characterized by the constant movement of *all* the players. Maintaining your position is no longer the credo used to guide the player's skating direction and pattern. As a result, the task of each and every hockey player has become much more challenging and interesting, and the game has become an even more spectacular event. Let us analyze these differences by examining typical play situations and see how this subsequently affects movement and collective puck control.

The first outcome of this new wave or approach to movement is in the area of *speed* (Perron, 1986). Allowing players more freedom or space on the ice by not restricting them to lanes and positions offers them greater potential to build up speed. Furthermore, because of the off-side and two-line pass rules, players must have the latitude to leave their lanes in search of more space and distance to build up speed and acceleration. It's a fact of physics, a law of motion: speed and acceleration are a function, in part, of the distance and time available.

In many playing situations, another important element results from curvilinear skating: enhanced potential for passing and receiving, especially when the player is moving in a lateral direction (note that it is difficult to speak of direction when the pattern of movement is curvilinear or circular; however, we can identify the intended direction in most curvilinear patterns). Lateral or diagonal movement, many times as a result of curving towards the middle, will maximize the time of pass reception, followed by more time to the receiver once the pass is completed. We are all too familiar with the "suicide" pass, which is typically the longitudinal pass to a player who is skating in the same direction as the passer − crunch! By moving laterally or diagonally towards the middle lane, players are *usually* more open for a pass − and more than once − with more space and time during and after puck reception. Figures 5.3 to 5.6 highlight this distinction.

IGURE 5.3   Limited passing time and space due to linear skating

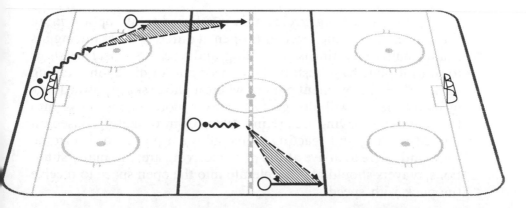

FIGURE 5.4   More passing time and space due to curvilinear skating

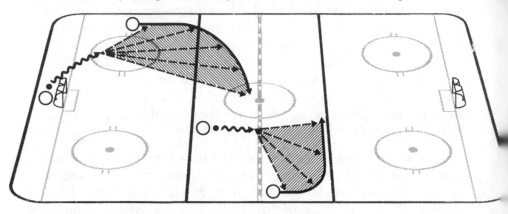

FIGURE 5.5   Linear versus curvilinear skating by player 6 (note the number of passi options created by curvilinear skating)

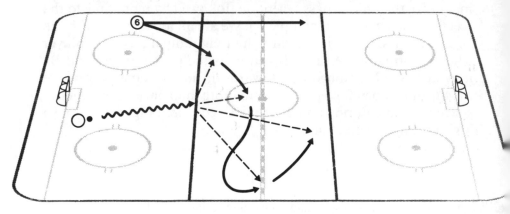

In many coaching circles, this is referred to as "option more than once," that is, the receiver is open at different times during his skating pattern. Timing is everything, and receivers must learn how to control skate by adjusting their speed and/or direction. "Taking back ice" — a movement pattern where a player skates towards his own end first — will also give the player more time to move into the potential receiving area (King, 1989). Control skating, based on refined reading and reacting skills, allows a player to determine *when* and *where* to arrive at the pass-receiving area. In many situations, players should also accelerate into the open space to receive the puck with speed.

FIGURE 5.6   Linear versus curvilinear skating by player 6 (note the number of passing options created by curvilinear skating)

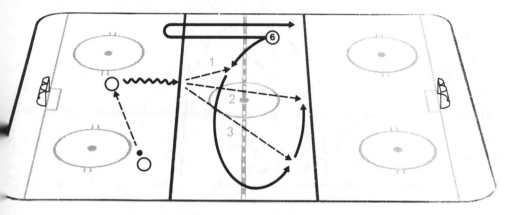

Another effect of this type of movement is what a number of coaches have referred to as *flow*. A flow pattern occurs when a certain number of players turn in the same direction in a coordinated manner, creating an eventual overload or numerical advantage in that area, lane or side of the ice (see Figure 5.7). This we refer to as the *primary flow*. Since it is usually difficult for all players – and not recommended from a tactical viewpoint – to be moving or curling in the same direction, we can consequently identify a *secondary flow* in most instances (see Figure 5.8). A secondary flow can also be conceptualized as a reverse flow or a flow pattern that goes counter to the primary flow (see Figure 5.9). Either type of

FIGURE 5.7   Flow pattern on a breakout play

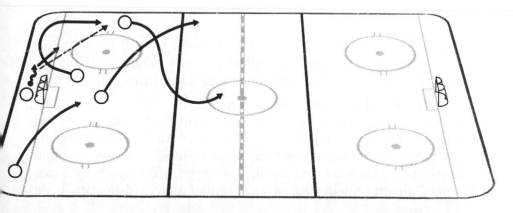

FIGURE 5.8   Flow pattern on a counterattack (note secondary flow by player 4)

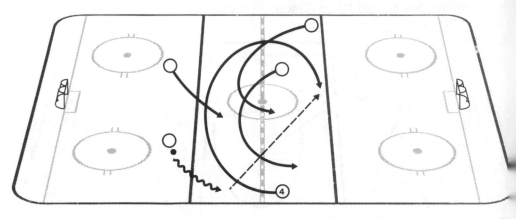

FIGURE 5.9   Secondary flow or reverse on a breakout play

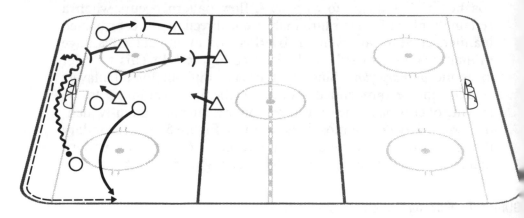

flow can be used to generate the attack: the primary flow allows for a concerted attack − at least initially − while the secondary flow offers a more unexpected single charge away from heavy traffic.

Multiple directional flows have additional effects on the opposing team. First, they create an element of uncertainty or confusion, since the different flow patterns make it difficult for the defense to read accurately without some hesitation. Flows also tend to give an attack *width* and *depth*, again leaving the opposition in a state of uncertainty in terms of the point of attack. Moreover, as we have seen, curvilinear patterns of flow add speed to the attack. These various factors produce a more dynamic and multifaceted attack, which is difficult for any team to defend against effectively. Having all five players in constant motion, using curvilinear patterns, changing lanes and interchanging positions makes it extremely difficult for the opposition to read the attack, let alone attempt to check the puck and non-puck carriers. And because the checkers are unsure about the direction of the attack, they tend to act cautiously, retreating instead of challenging. Their defense is now a passive structure, ready to be exploited. Furthermore, this makes man-to-man defense virtually impossible, especially in the neutral zone.

Maximizing movement has a number of positive effects on defense. The most significant effect is to enhance puck control by creating time and space for both puck and non-puck carriers. In Chapters 6 and 7, we will focus our attention on the individual technical and tactical skills of non-puck carriers and puck carriers respectively in maintaining puck control. Chapter 8 will analyze the group tactical skills required for puck control.

6

The Role of the Non-Puck Carrier in Movement and Puck Control

6.1 Introduction

The new wave in coaching the game of hockey has been marked by a much stronger emphasis on the role of non-puck carriers or players off the puck. In the past, the puck handler carried most of the burden in terms of maintaining team puck control. For example, the puck carrier often had to make the "perfect" pass to a teammate who was just barely in the open and, if he was unsuccessful in the passing/receiving play, most of the blame would fall on his shoulders. Today, it is generally recognized that the puck carrier and players off the puck share responsibility for executing group tactical actions required for collective puck control. Coaches have now recognized, and players, for the most part, have accepted, this new role or function of the non-puck carriers − the role of "support." In an address to coaches at a national symposium in 1985, Dennis McDonald, Technical Director of the Canadian Amateur Hockey Association, reiterated this point: "four playing for one rather than one playing for four."

The result of this new wave has been to give puck control a different dimension. Puck control must now be viewed as a collective effort provided by both puck and non-puck carriers. With this in mind, we have identified three player skills required for collective puck control :

1. *Individual tactical skills* of puck and non-puck carriers
2. *Group tactical skills* of puck and non-puck carriers
3. *Reading and reacting skills* based upon the fundamental principles of movement and puck control by both puck and non-puck carriers

All three skills are interrelated and interdependent. All are equally important in achieving collective puck control. Another critical dimension, as we have seen, is that these skills apply equally to puck carrier and non-puck carriers.

The skills of reading and reacting were covered in Chapter 2. In this chapter, we will identify the individual tactical skills required of non-puck carriers for collective puck control. In the next chapter, we will analyze the individual tactical skills required of the puck carrier.

6.2 Individual Tactical Skills of Non-Puck Carriers

The role of the non-puck carriers is to provide support to the puck carrier in enhancing and maintaining puck control. The primary individual tactical skill required to accomplish this support role is *skating agility*; there are others, but this is the primary skill required to play an effective supporting role. Now let's take a brief look at skating agility before addressing the principle of offensive support.

The characteristics of an excellent skater have changed radically over the years as the game of hockey has become more sophisticated and players more highly skilled and specialized. Under the strong influence of international hockey, North American coaches and other technical experts have modified their outlook and analysis of what represents excellence in skating ability and proper movement by all the players. Several studies and presentations, by King (1985) and Kingston (1978, 1981) to name just a few, have provided valuable information for coaches in Canada on many new European trends in skating and movement, from both the technical and tactical standpoints.

The proficient skater in today's game of hockey is able to perform "magic" on ice. Forward, backward and lateral skating are only the basic rudiments of skating dynamics. Agility, change of speed, pivoting, tight turns, accelerating and running starts are just a few of the technical skills in the new wave of skating ability. Good skaters, with or without the puck, have the ability to move with lightning speed, forward, backward and laterally, change direction quickly and break away from their checkers by using refined skating skills. A player's ability to skate (in the broad sense of the word) will determine his overall effectiveness as a total hockey player. A team filled with dynamic skaters will enhance and facilitate all the technical and tactical actions required for collective puck control. The skating agility of the non-puck carriers is the main individual tactical skill that provides "support."

6.3   The Principle of Offensive Support

Offensive support refers to the activity or movement of the non-puck carriers (players off the puck) designed to assist or "support" the actions of the puck carrier. This activity by the non-puck carriers is extremely important, and can take various forms. As Larsson (1985) stated: "the player without the puck creates the conditions for play " (p. 65).

The main forms of offensive support to the puck carrier can be accomplished by:

1. Players making themselves *available* or open to receive a pass
2. *Clearing* an area to allow space for the puck carrier to execute the required action
3. *Screening* an opponent or potential checker
4. Offering *proximal support* or close assistance to the puck carrier
5. *Decoying* to stretch or spread the defensive formation

If you as a player perform any of these activities, you are by definition providing support to your teammate in possession of the puck. Now let's explain and develop the main form of support, the ability of the players to be truly available for a pass.

6.3.1   Support by availability

The concept of availability is closely tied to the concept of "open or free" space, that is, a player must move to a space or area on the ice where he will be able to successfully receive a pass (within the limits of the rules of the game). Moreover, the player who is potentially available must be recognized by the puck carrier if a successful pass is to be made. This highlights the importance of communicating your intentions − making the puck carrier aware that you are open using visual or verbal cues, as we have seen in an earlier chapter. However, given the total number of players on the ice, the multi-directional movement of the players and the speed of execution of the various actions, it is not always possible for all the players to be what we would call "truly and immediately available" for a pass. As a player, you must constantly strive to support, if not for the immediate moment at least for upcoming action. This requires a fine sense of judgement and anticipation of what is likely to happen. King (1984) discussed anticipation :

> To be effective in the support role, a player must anticipate the puck carrier's intentions and read the checking pressure being applied onthe puck carrier. He must be willing to adjust his position in relation to the puck carrier and open a passing lane by moving to open space. As you realize, this requires the ability to "read" the game and be aware of movement of one's teammates on the ice. (p. 1)

Depending on the location of the player in relation to the puck carrier, we can distinguish three types of support by availability:

1. Support *behind* (below) the puck carrier
2. Support *in front* (above) of the puck carrier
3. Support *to the side* (lateral) of the puck carrier

Now let's look at a few examples that illustrate the three basic types of support by a player moving to an open space and being available to receive a pass.

Figure 6.1 is an example of a defenseman (no. 3) moving laterally to provide support below to his left winger (no. 6). If the defenseman had not moved, he would not have been available for a pass from his winger since opponent no. 5 stood between the two players. By moving, the back opened the left passing lane, allowing the team to maintain control of the puck. Figure 6.2 is another example of support behind the puck carrier, this time in the offensive zone. The puck carrier (no. 5) has managed to penetrate deep into the opposition's end; however, he is running out of room or space and is therefore looking for support, an outlet − someone to pass the puck to. Enter player 2. Moving rapidly enough to be available − also

FIGURE 6.1   Support below by availability

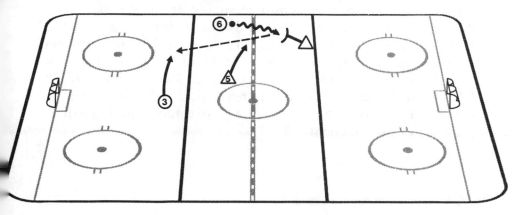

FIGURE 6.2   Support below by availability

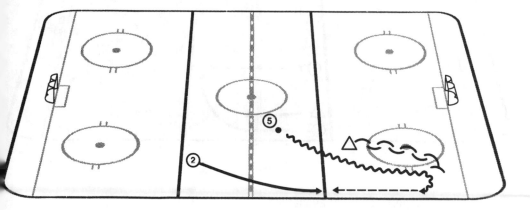

referred to as "closing the gap" — the defenseman has provided support below the puck carrier in the right passing lane.

Figures 6.3 to 6.6 give examples of high and lateral support. These illustrations highlight the importance of forwards moving to an open space to become available for a pass, often requiring the players to switch lanes.

Although there is a relationship between finding an open space and being available, the former does not always guarantee the latter. We must consider the element of timing and whether the space will still be "truly" open once the pass has reached the receiver. Open spaces in hockey are constantly changing as players skate and develop plays from zone to zone and area to area. A space may be free or open for a short time, only to be occupied by an opponent seconds later. To illustrate this point, let's look at a few examples of "truly" open spaces and "not truly" open spaces (see Figures 6.7 to 6.10). A "truly" open space is an area which makes the potential receiver "truly" available to accept a pass without the immediate presence of an opponent.

FIGURE 6.3   Support above by availability

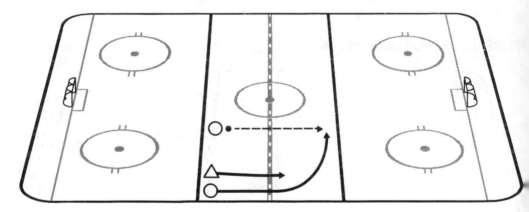

FIGURE 6.4   Support above by availability

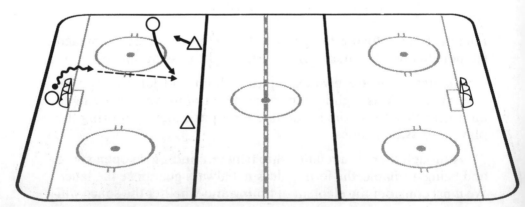

FIGURE 6.5   Lateral support by availability

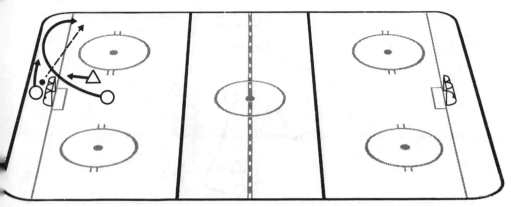

FIGURE 6.6   Lateral support by availability

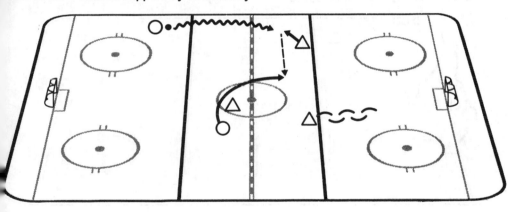

FIGURE 6.7   Truly an open space

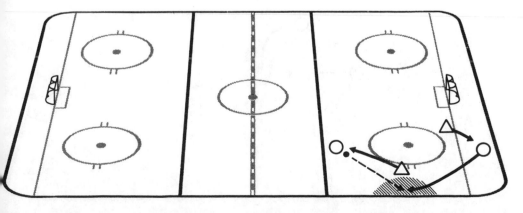

FIGURE 6.8   Truly an open space

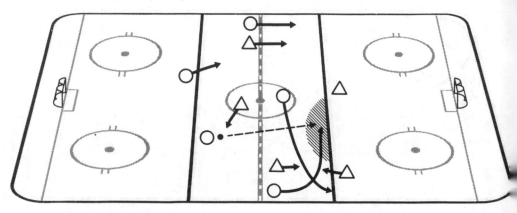

FIGURE 6.9   Not truly an open space

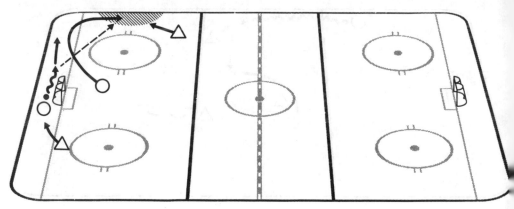

FIGURE 6.10   Not truly an open space

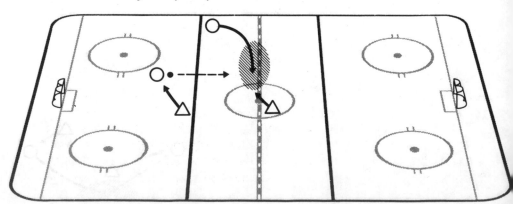

This point highlights the importance for players of developing the skills necessary to locate "truly" open spaces so as to provide support to the puck carrier. This requires a great capacity for anticipating both the immediate and longer-term intentions of the puck carrier and the entire play. Great anticipation, reading the developing play, astute decision-making and timing are the key ingredients for offering the necessary support to your teammates. This applies to support by availability as well as to support by other means.

In this category of support, we should also include the player who is truly open to take a shot on net. Depending on the situation, the open player might elect to one-time the puck rather than controlling followed by shooting. This is still supporting the puck carrier by availability. In a sense, it represents the ultimate form of support.

6.3.2 Support by clearing an area

Occasionally, by moving away from a specific area, you allow more space for the puck carrier to maneuver and execute the appropriate actions, technical and/or tactical, thereby assisting the puck carrier's actions. Conversely, in selected situations, if you remain in a certain area, you would be hindering rather than facilitating the puck carrier's immediate task. Moreover, in clearing the congested area, you are also attempting to move into an open space to make yourself available for a pass, thus playing a dual support role. Figures 6.11 to 6.13 illustrate these principles.

By having player 6 in Figure 6.11 clear the anticipated crowded area and skate to the middle lane, he has created space for player 5 and has moved into a better position to receive a pass than had he stayed in the left lane. In Figure 6.12, we see player 4 clearing the top area of the neutral zone to allow room for the puck carrier to stickhandle, switching lanes to avoid an off-side and positioning himself for a possible lateral pass. Figure 6.13 depicts player 5 clearing the middle slot area and drawing the right defense (no. 2) low in the zone to let player 6 move into the newly created space. In all three examples, the player who cleared the area assisted or supported the puck carrier's intentions and the accomplishment of the group tactical play.

FIGURE 6.11   Clearing an area and switching lanes

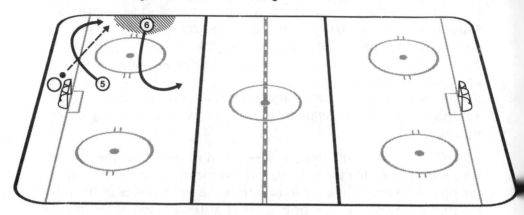

FIGURE 6.12   Clearing an area and switching lanes

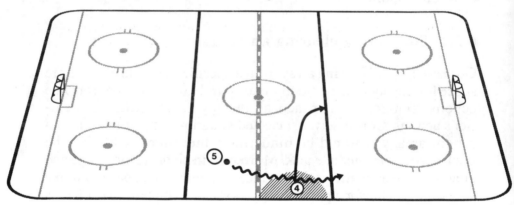

FIGURE 6.13   Clearing an area to draw opponent 2

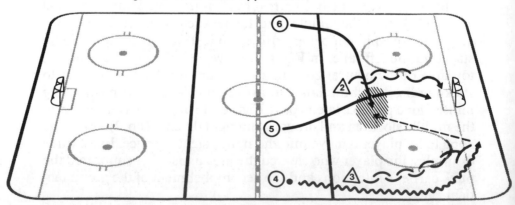

6.3.3 Support by screening

Before delving into the subject of support by screening an opponent, we would like to clarify any possible misconceptions about the use of the word "screen," as well as other terms frequently used to describe a similar action. First, we make a distinction between screening a goaltender and screening a player, meaning a forward or a back. *Screening a goaltender* is the action by which a player will position himself between the shooter and the goaltender to basically try to obstruct the goaltender's vision of the oncoming puck. This type of screen can result in the goaltender not seeing the puck − at least partially obstructing the puck's trajectory − with a good chance of a goal being scored. *Screening a player* is the action by which a player will restrict, interfere with or hinder (within the rules of the game) the movement of an opponent to give a teammate more space and time. Screening is an offensive technico-tactical skill and an effective means of freeing a player who is up against a man-to-man checking or defense. The use of screens is not only an effective way of fending off checkers attempting to reach the puck carrier, but also a technique for freeing non-puck carriers from their checkers. In summary, screening an opponent is a very effective means of supporting a teammate's actions for better collective puck control.

The term "blocking" is also commonly used to refer to the act of screening a player as well as in the sense of "blocking a shot." Recognizing that it is common in some circles to use the word blocking to describe the action of actually screening an opponent, in this text we will use the word blocking exclusively to refer to the action of blocking shots − by either the goaltender or a player.

Screens can be executed in different ways, depending on the nature of the playing situation. We distinguish three basic types of screens:

1. Stationary screen or pick
2. Moving screen
3. Shunting screen

In the *stationary screen*, commonly referred to as a "pick," the actions of the screener are directed towards one specific area on the ice. The player performing the action selects the particular opponent, the anticipated location of the pick, then moves towards the opponent and executes the picking screen. The pick per se occurs at a very precise area, suddenly and usually with a relatively short time of actual contact between the two players. The key word, suddenly, captures the essence of this type of screen. Figures 6.14 and 6.15 illustrate typical examples of the stationary screen or pick. Occasionally, a puck carrier will take advantage of an already established screen by simply moving towards the "protected" area. In this situation (see Figure 6.16), the potential screener plays a relatively more passive role since he already happened to be at that spot while the puck carrier chose to move and use the playing situation to his benefit. It is a question of degree. Obviously, in either case both players must collaborate: the screener must be present and the puck carrier must take advantage of the screen.

Face-off picks are also extremely important ploys, especially when the center wins the draw in the offensive end. The screening of the appropriate players lining up at the face-off circle will allow the shooter additional time to release the puck (see Figure 6.17).

The *moving screen*, as the words imply, is characterized by the player moving or screening the opponent over a certain distance. The duration of the moving screen or the time of "contact" between the screener and the opponent is thus relatively longer compared to the stationary screen. It is not as sudden and the intent of the moving screen is more to delay or obstruct the potential player from reaching the puck carrier. There is less of an element of surprise than in the typical stationary screen or pick. Common situations in which moving screens can be effective are shown in Figures 6.18 and 6.19.

The *shunting screen* is quite different from the other two. In this case, it is more the puck carrier who initiates the action of screening by forcing or "dragging" the immediate checker towards an undesirable path. Usually, the puck carrier will force or drag the checker towards a player or group of players, forcing the checker to delay or abandon his action of checking the puck carrier (Barnes, 1980; Boulonne et al., 1976). Figure 6.20 shows an example of a shunting screen.

FIGURE 6.14   Stationary screen or pick

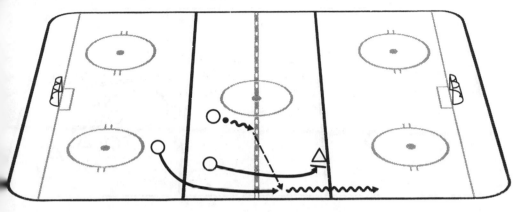

FIGURE 6.15   Stationary screen or pick (power play situation)

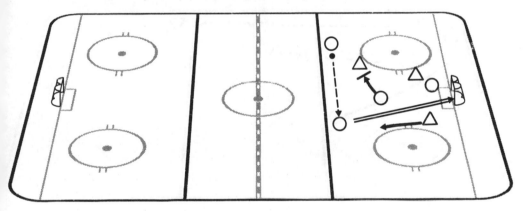

FIGURE 6.16   Potential screen : puck carrier taking advantage of existing screen set by player 3

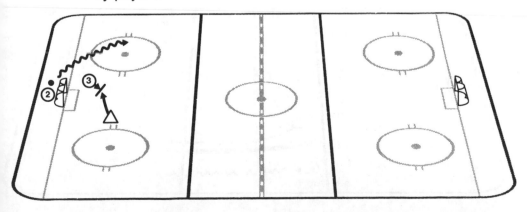

FIGURE 6.17   Screening from a face-off situation

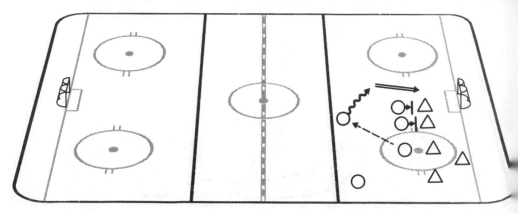

FIGURE 6.18   Moving screen : player 3 screens for partner 2 to gain puck control

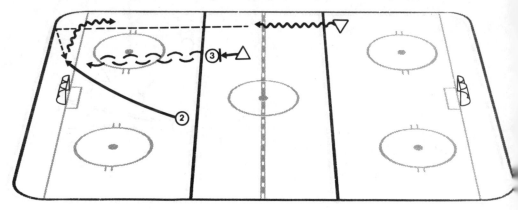

FIGURE 6.19   Moving screen : player 5 sets moving screen for partner 4 to maintain puck control

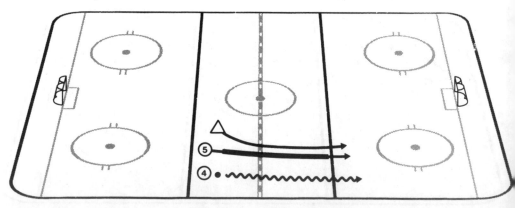

IGURE 6.20   Shunting screen : puck carrier 3 draws checker 5 into player 6

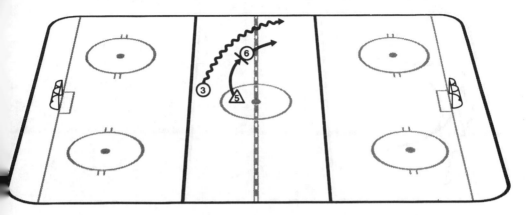

Another example of a shunting screen is when a defenseman uses his own net to shunt an opponent, forcing the immediate checker to take the undesirable path. This action can be combined with a passive or unassertive pick provided by a teammate to allow the puck carrier even more space and time (see Figures 6.21 and 6.22). The goaltender can also assist in the screening process by moving towards the top of his goal crease. In the offensive zone, the puck carrier can use the net to force the opponent off his preferred checking path (see Figure 6.23).

Screens can also be divided into two other categories:

1. Screens that support the puck carrier
2. Screens that support a non-puck carrier

Screens that support the puck carrier are the most common in hockey; these are also referred to as screens "on the puck" or close to the puck, since they are used to support the actions of the puck carrier. But screens can also be performed to help a non-puck carrier free himself from his check to become available for a pass; we refer to these as screening "off the puck" or "away from the puck carrier." The latter is common practice in both basketball and football. In contemporary hockey, coaches should use off the puck screens more often as part of their tactical arsenal on offense, since these screens are a relatively underused means of enhancing collective puck control. Figures 6.24 to 6.26 offer examples of screening "off the puck" for a non-puck carrier attempting to locate open space for the eventual pass.

FIGURE 6.21   Shunting screen

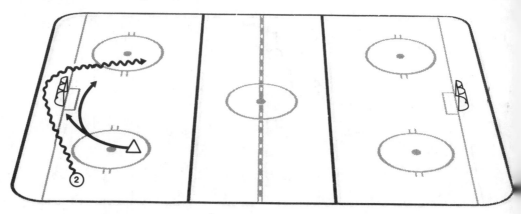

FIGURE 6.22   Shunting screen

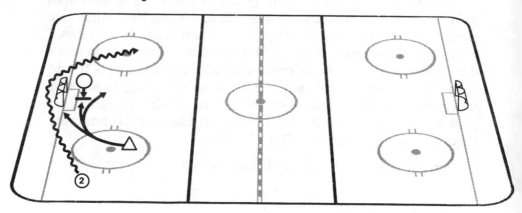

FIGURE 6.23   Shunting screen

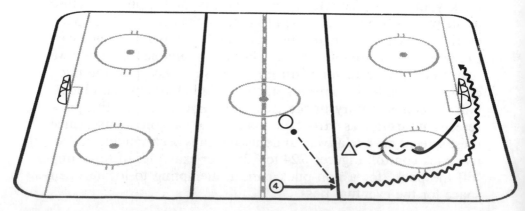

IGURE 6.24   Screening "off the puck" by player 5

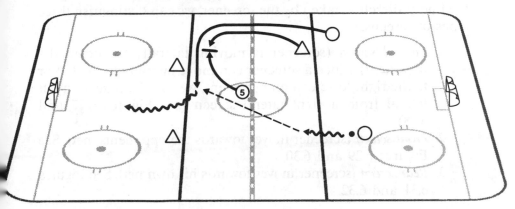

FIGURE 6.25   Screening "off the puck" by player 6

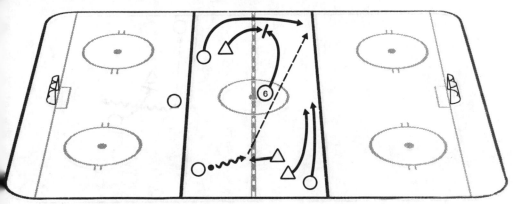

FIGURE 6.26   Screening "off the puck" by player 5 (power play situation)

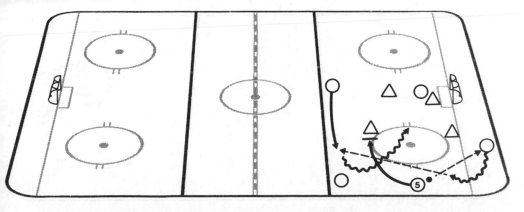

There is yet another way of classifying screens. Depending on the line of direction taken by the screener, we can distinguish three types of screens.

1. *Lateral screen* (screener is moving laterally to screen the opponent). Since a screener can move laterally to the left or to the right to screen an opponent, we can distinguish a left lateral from a right lateral screen (see Figures 6.27 and 6.28).
2. *Front screen* (screener moves towards the opponents' net). See Figures 6.29 and 6.30.
3. *Rear screen* (screener moves towards his own net). See Figures 6.31 and 6.32.

FIGURE 6.27   Left lateral screen

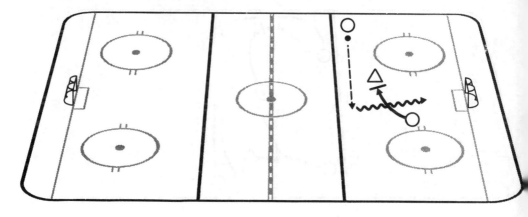

FIGURE 6.28   Right lateral screen

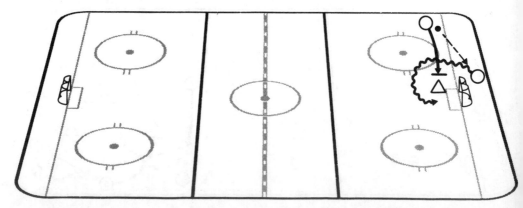

FIGURE 6.29   Front screen

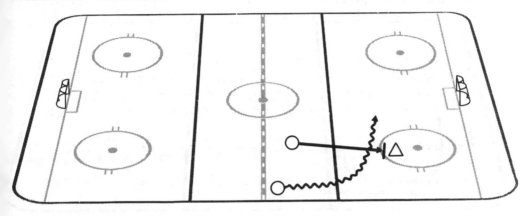

FIGURE 6.30   Front screen

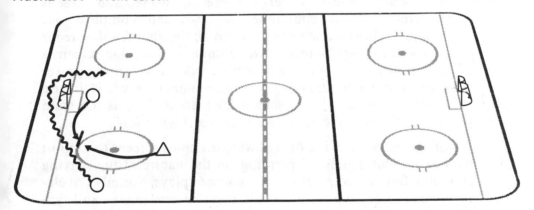

FIGURE 6.31   Back or rear screen

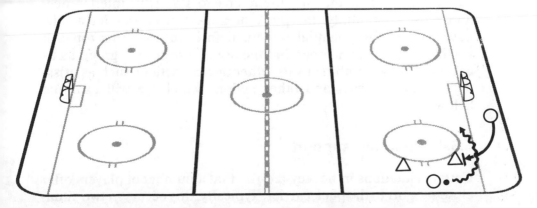

FIGURE 6.32   Back or rear screen

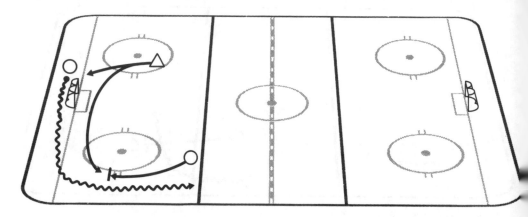

And finally, because players can execute two separate screens on different players simultaneously, we can complete our discussion or classification of screens by stating that *double* screens exist as well as *single* screens. An example of a double screen is often seen when attacking the blue line, especially during a power play situation (see Figure 6.33). More common, however, is the use of *successive* screens — one screen after another — as the team progresses through the various zones (see Figure 6.34).

In summary, there is a host of ways to deploy screens to support various tactical actions, depending on the nature of the playing situation. But to successfully execute screen plays, a number of elements, as in all group tactical skills, must be coordinated and synchronized. The teammate receiving support from the screener must read or anticipate the play, the screener must time his move in a subtle way (so as not to alert the referee to a possible interference) and most importantly, the puck or non-puck carrier must take advantage of the potential screen. Before we leave this topic, it would be wise to remember that the use of screens as a group tactical skill can be combined with other tactical actions such as crisscrosses, drop passes and other actions which we will examine below.

6.3.4 Proximal support

Certain situations in hockey require that a number of players offer close support to the puck carrier. Typically, this occurs in two situa-

FIGURE 6.33   Double screen (power play situation)

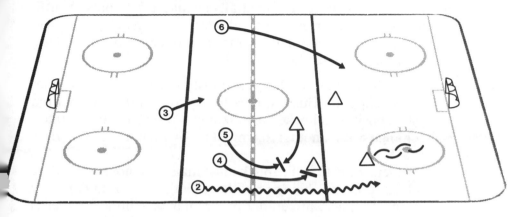

FIGURE 6.34   Successive screens by players 3 and 5

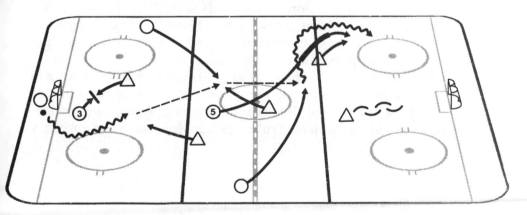

tions : first, when the puck carrier is being closely checked, usually along the side of the boards or in the corners, and second, during the undetermined possession phase of the game when neither team has definite control of the puck. In both of these situations, close support, preferably coupled with a numerical advantage, would offer the best tactical approach to maintain or regain possession of the puck (see Figures 6.35 and 6.36).

Since puck control is the primary objective in most playing situations, players must move and orient their actions towards that end. When a teammate is struggling to gain possession of the puck, it makes absolutely no sense for all the players to be removed from the play, even if they are all potentially available for a pass. A sufficient number of players must provide close support at least equal to the number of opponents in the same area. To accomplish this task, certain principles must be followed:

1. The closest man to the puck must be the first man to offer close support. This requires that players break away from stick positional hockey so that they can switch lanes or interchange with another teammate, whether a forward or a back.
2. Players away from the puck must maintain movement while close support is being provided by others. Movement away from the puck, preferably in circular or elliptical patterns (figure-8 pattern, for example), will provide the best preparation for adjusting back to defense or offense.
3. Strive for numerical superiority. The chances of winning the battle for possession are relatively slim if the opposition outmans you in the area of the puck. There is little use in players being distantly available for a pass if your teammate does not gain possession of the puck.
4. Finally, since there is always uncertainty as to who will obtain possession of the puck, defensive responsibilities must still prevail. Be ready to adjust to offense or defense, but as a general rule, make defense your primary concern.

FIGURE 6.35   Close support during a 1 on 1 battle

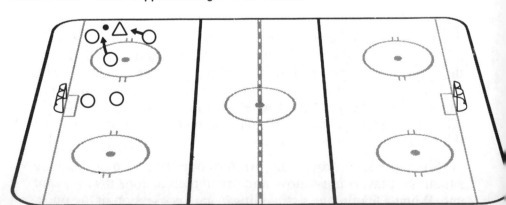

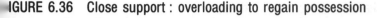

IGURE 6.36   Close support : overloading to regain possession

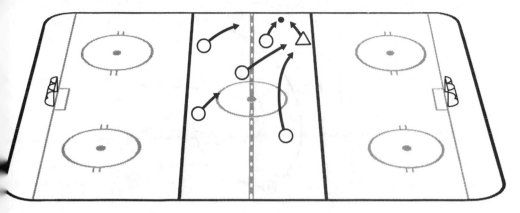

6.3.5 Support by decoying

A player who acts as a decoy is creating another form of support for the entire attack. By his mere presence, he forces the defensive formation to back off or be stretched. This creates more space for the puck carrier, and more openings for potential receivers. A player acting as a decoy also gives the attack a certain width and depth. A decoying player may or may not be immediately available for a pass, but his presence keeps the opposition "honest" by forcing them to retreat. The defensemen are in a sense annoyed or preoccupied by having to keep an eye on the decoy skater (see Figures 6.37 and 6.38).

In summary, the role of support or assisting a teammate's actions during a particular play is certainly not an easy one to accomplish. It takes a great deal of hockey experience, reading and reacting skill and technico-tactical skills to decide on the best support role in all playing situations. It also requires players to play and practice together regularly to refine the different group tactical plays resulting from the various support roles. What makes the choice even more complicated is the fact that in most playing situations, players must select different roles. It would be rather foolish if every player chose to support by screening. Similarly, not all players should provide close support. Ideally, players choose different support roles from moment to moment depending on the nature of the play.

FIGURE 6.37   Decoy skater 4 stretching the defense

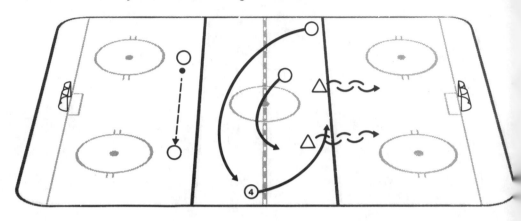

FIGURE 6.38   Decoy skater 4 stretching and spreading the defense

As a general rule — and this really depends on the specific playing situation — one player should provide close support to the puck carrier, at least one but preferably two players should be available to receive a pass, another player should be thinking of a possible screen and occasionally yet another player should be acting as a decoy.

Although the principle of availability is an extremely important support role and probably the first that should be taught, in many situations, as we have seen above, other forms of support must override the principle of support by availability. Sometimes you must provide a screen, at other times simply clear the area. In certain situations, you need to offer close support — it depends on the circumstances. The ability to select the optimal role for each and every moment is what makes a total and mature hockey player. As coaches striving to enhance our group tactical play or dynamics, we must emphasize to our players the need to understand each and every support role. Reading the playing situation accurately is the first step in selecting the appropriate support role; reacting in a timely manner is equally important, and adjusting your role as the play evolves will enable you to make a most effective contribution to maintaining puck control and progression in the attack.

7

The Role of the Puck Carrier in Movement and Puck Control

7.1 Introduction

As we saw in Chapter 6, collective puck control rests on individual tactical skills, group tactical skills and reading-reacting skills of both puck and non-puck carriers. In this chapter, we will identify and discuss the individual tactical skills required of a proficient puck carrier.

A competent puck carrier is one who can carry the puck with speed and agility, stickhandle and fake past opponents at the opportune moment, "protect" the puck from potential checkers when required, and make the next correct action-decision. Spassky (1981) described the role of the puck carrier:

> It is not enough to merely dribble [stickhandle] the puck. You have to dribble it with a great speed, executing sharp turns, making abrupt stops and by-passing an opponent. Because dribbling will be followed by your next move: passing the puck to your partner, shooting for goal, or by-passing, it is essential to learn to control the puck and at the same time see what is happening on the rink (p. 67).

7.2 Individual Puck Control

Collective puck control depends to a great extent on the individual puck control skills of each and every player. To be aware of your playing environment, make the greatest possible contribution to the developing attack and make the correct decision, you as a puck carrier must be in full control of your actions and in particular the puck. A skilled puck carrier is constantly considering various options: should I carry the puck, stickhandle past an opponent, pass the puck or shoot? To make the proper choice, the player must first and foremost feel so confident about controlling the puck that it is instinctive or second nature to him. If too much effort is devoted to maintaining the puck on the blade, the player will not be able to make the correct decision in terms of the developing play. This in turn will affect the overall objective of collectively maintaining control of the puck.

There is no doubt that this individual ability or knack of controlling the puck can and should be developed, particularly during the early years of training. The various techniques that constitute sound puck control require a tremendous amount of individual practice, some of which can be acquired through off-ice training programs, especially in a gymnasium. Marcotte and Chapleau (1959), hockey pioneers in their own right, were among the first Canadians to suggest practicing various hockey skills in a gymnasium, because of the high cost and lack of availability of ice-time in indoor rinks. Thanks to their influence, many dry-land programs now include various exercises that develop individual skills, such as stickhandling, deking and protecting the puck.

Players who demonstrate excellent individual puck control have mastered very specific skills. These skills can be grouped under four general headings, all of which are interrelated in producing a skilled puck carrier:

1) Skating agility with a puck
2) Body and head positioning
3) Stickhandling and faking
4) Puck protection

7.2.1 Skating agility with a puck

Although many hockey players, even at the professional level, possess excellent skating skills, when the puck is introduced, their level of skating ability drops off sharply due to the added task of keeping the puck on their stick. The additional task of carrying the puck, let alone stickhandling, limits their skating ability. They are "dynamic" skaters, but unfortunately, not with the puck. A developing hockey player is not expected to learn this combined task of skating and puck-carrying overnight. This requires a tremendous amount of practice under the guidance of an experienced coach. Eventually though, the aspiring player must demonstrate that he can skate and perform equally well with or without the puck if he hopes to advance further. The skating ability and agility of proficient hockey players do not drop off when they are in possession of the puck. They are natural skaters *and* natural puck carriers. This is an extremely important point.

Skilled puck carriers also facilitate many group tactical plays. Because they are in "full control," they are able to read the developing play and make the best decision for the given situation. They are not limited in their movements and patterns because they have the puck on their stick. Rather, they relish the opportunity, anticipate the play and select the most appropriate option. One such option which we would like to mention at this point is creating space. Up till now, we have placed the onus on the non-puck carriers to locate open spaces to be available for a potential pass. We are now stating, however, that the puck carrier himself plays a pivotal role in creating space for his teammate(s). Figures 7.1 and 7.2 illustrate the point. There are obviously many other situations where the puck carrier determines the eventual success of an individual or group tactical action; our objective in this illustration was to highlight just one of the many important roles a skilled puck carrier can play. At a later point, we will reexamine this and other interplays between puck and non-puck carriers when we discuss group tactical skills.

7.2.2 Body and head positioning

Body positioning is an extremely important element in almost every facet of the game, whether the player is on offense, defense or in the period of transition. The position or attitude of the body, including the head position, in relation to the playing context has a significant impact on the eventual or anticipated outcome of the developing play. Proper body and head positioning allows the player to more accurately perceive the playing environment by providing the player with the necessary information to assist in the decision-making process. The common "keep your head up" or "play with your head up" slogans are often used by coaches to refer to the importance of players seeing what is ahead of them. More recently, coaches have used the expressions "look over your

FIGURE 7.1   Creating space : puck carrier 5 moves diagonally to the left to create space fo
player 4

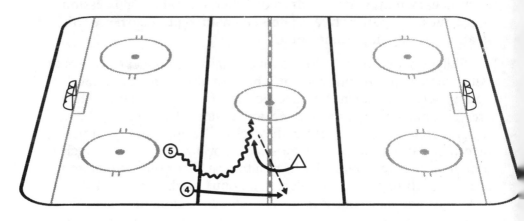

FIGURE 7.2   Creating space : puck carrier 3 creates space for player 5

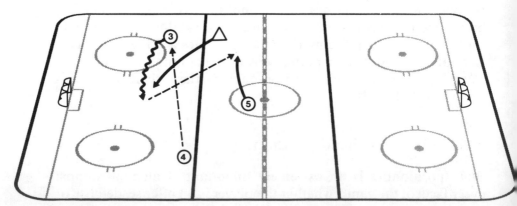

shoulders," "look up and down, down and up" and "head on a swivel" to stress the importance of players being aware of what is in front, on the side and behind them simply by moving their heads. The intent is really to develop players' peripheral vision rather than tunnel vision, thus increasing the quality of their perception and the likelihood of a good decision. Total awareness and accurate perception form the basis upon which creative and improvised plays can occur.

Along with skating ability, proper body and head positioning represent the building blocks for effective handling of the puck. Too often, we see in young as well as more mature hockey players the tendency or habit not to look or "read the play" as they carry the puck. Ideally, the puck carrier should attempt to have his body and head in such a position so as to maximize his vision, both peripheral and straight-ahead, recognizing that this is not always possible in tight playing situations. Skilled puck carriers have a knack for finding open spaces because they constantly try to "face the play" or place themselves in the best possible position in relation to their teammates and opponents.

Once a player has learned the skill of controlling the puck on his stick — without looking at the puck too often — he will then be able to look ahead and increase his scope of vision. The proper inclination or attitude of the head also makes it easier to pivot the head for added peripheral vision. As Watt (1973) explains: "When you are handling the puck on your stick, it is important that you keep your head up and gently nurse the puck on your blade from side to side. Feel the puck on your stick. Although you shouldn't look down, your eyes will nevertheless catch a glimpse of the puck on your stick from time to time " (pp. 19-20).

7.2.3 Stickhandling and faking

Good puck carriers also show proficiency in the area of *stickhandling* or *puckhandling*. Stickhandling refers specifically to the refined hand and stick movements that enable a player to deke an opponent and maintain possession of the puck. However, deking an opponent must be viewed in a broader context of which stickhandling is only one aspect. Deking, faking or feinting an opponent may only require that you take advantage of your present speed or simply the space around you for proper directional movement away from the checker. Although the ability to stickhandle is affected by such elements as speed, space — and other factors — it nevertheless rests upon some very specific techniques that must be perfected. Furthermore, the effectiveness of a stickhandler is closely related to the fine tuning of these various techniques as well as the number of techniques a player has at his disposal.

A slick puckhandler is also a very good indication of excellent individual puck control, a prerequisite for sound passing and receiving skills for group play. The ability of a player to stickhandle with speed and grace without sacrificing any skating ability lets him make an effective contribution to team play. For coaches, puckhandling ability is also one of the most important yardsticks for gauging the potential of players, particularly at a young age. A challenging stickhandling test on-ice combined with skating speed and ability can prove to be extremely revealing of a player's present and future ability. Tarasov himself endorsed this concept, placing tremendous importance on the ability to stickhandle when selecting prospective players for his hockey school — the training ground for future Olympians. In his book *Tarasov's Hockey Technique* (1973), he stated, "A player who is merely fast on the ice but who has no stickhandling technique is like a 'horse without reins.' The faster you skate and the quicker the tempo of the game the more stickhandling technique is needed"(p. 19).

Any discussion of stickhandling must also address the matter of *faking* your opponent. Faking essentially boosts a stickhandler's power or ability to deceive an opponent. A player can resort to pure stickhandling *or* faking technique to get by an opponent; however, in many situations a combination of stickhandling and faking makes the puck carrier most effective. As a matter of fact, it is often quite difficult to determine during the course of a game whether a puck carrier beat the opponent through the use of a fake or through a slick stickhandling technique. The reality is that both skills go hand-in-hand.

King (1989), in a video produced by Hockey Canada in cooperation with the Canadian Amateur Hockey Association, offered several faking tips to augment the success of deceiving a defender. In order, these are:

1. Execute fake away from checker
2. Move the puck laterally and quickly

3. Move yourself laterally and quickly
4. Accelerate as you go by the defender
5. Protect the puck as you go by

Faking and stickhandling should be viewed as mutually reinforcing techniques. Good stickhandlers regularly use fakes to further confuse or deceive their opponents. Whether you use fakes, stickhandling techniques or both, your objective remains the same — to free yourself from your immediate checker and to maintain puck control. To describe the various techniques involved in the art and science of stickhandling and faking, we have developed separate classifications. Please keep in mind, however, that on many occasions the two — stickhandling and faking — form one integrated action.

A. Stickhandling skills

We classify stickhandling skills as follows:

1) Dribbling
2) Forehand shift
3) Backhand shift
4) Slip through the skates
5) Slip between stick and skates
6) Pulling in the puck
7) Stick-skate-stick (faking puck loss)
8) Using the boards (pass to yourself off the boards)

B. Faking skills

We classify faking skills as follows:

1) Body fakes (head, shoulder and/or hips)
   — Single body fake
   — Double body fake
   — Avoiding the "hit" or body check first, usually by a move to the side, moving puck slightly to the side or in front (e.g. between the legs) and then picking up the puck

2) Skating fakes
   — Change in speed
   — Stop and start
   — Pivots

3) Fake pass (fake look or look away)
   - Fake pass and shot
   - Fake pass and carry
   - Fake pass to one player with a pass to another

4) Fake shot (fake look or look away)
   - Fake shot and pass
   - Fake shot and carry

7.2.4 Puck protection

In many playing situations, it is necessary for the puck carrier to focus on protecting the puck in order to maintain puck control. Puck protection also allows you to "buy time" until a teammate arrives to provide support. What is puck protection? Puck protection is a technico-tactical action in which the puck carrier keeps his body between the checker and the puck. Some coaches use the term "setting the wall" as a teaching concept. It is most commonly used in tight checking situations such as in the corners or along the boards, but is also deployed in open-ice situations, such as when a defenseman makes a turn-up with a checker on his back.

In certain situations where you do not now have the puck but will soon gain possession, the idea of puck protection should start before you get to the puck. Again, this is accomplished by placing your body in between the puck and the eventual checker. At times, as you get closer to the puck, you may elect to lift the opponent's stick and use your feet to control the puck. This is all part of puck protection.

The main technical elements involved in puck protection are:

1. Constantly reading your opponent's position and adjusting your body position accordingly
2. Assuming a flexed body position for additional strength
3. Making the best possible use of your arms to fend off the checker; legs should also be spread apart.

Players driving for the net should also shield the puck. Here, the technique is slightly different. While still keeping his body between the checker and the puck, the carrier will often hold the puck in one hand and push off the checker with the other.

Although the primary focus of this book is the tactical dimension of the game, we have purposely chosen to expand on various stickhandling and faking techniques for two fundamental reasons. First, if we compare ourselves to the Europeans and especially the Soviets in the area of individual puck control, we still have a long way to go before reaching their level of ability. Certain North American hockey players have attained the level of proficiency found in the Soviets and many European players, but in general there is still a great deal of room for improvement. Second, and in light of the first reason, we felt that there was a clear need to explain in detail all the various techniques related to stickhandling in the hope of helping coaches provide proper instruction for their players. There is no question in our minds that a stronger emphasis must be placed on these foundation skills, especially at the budding stage of a player's development.

Tarasov (1986), describing the ability of the late Valeri Kharlamov, brilliantly captured the message and relevance of this point. "What Kharlamov did was master the three speeds of hockey — the acceleration and change of tempo skating speed, the speed of the stickhand and eye coordination, and the mental speed of knowing instinctively where to go. Any one of these speeds can be found separately in hockey players, but the combination of the three was typical only of Valeri" (p. 10).

Skating agility with a puck, stickhandling and faking, puck protection and anticipation (reading and reacting) are all interrelated and interdependent skills in individual puck control. How many players do you know who possess all these skills?

7.3 Individual Tactical Actions

So far in this chapter, we have elaborated on the skills required for individual puck control. These skills, like other skills in hockey, have technical and tactical dimensions, that is, a player must first master the technique before attempting to use it tactically against an opponent. Together, these combined skills let the puck carrier fully exploit the opposition, especially in one-on-one situations. Consequently, when we described the various skating, stickhandling, faking and puck protection skills, we could have easily referred to these as *individual tactical actions or skills*.

Regardless of the nomenclature, we would now like to share with you *some* specific playing situations where these combined individual puck control skills can be used as an offensive tactic. At the same time, we will also introduce some new words or terms that are part and parcel of hockey jargon. These selected playing situations will highlight the importance of individual puck control skills – the skills that let a puck carrier take advantage of his opponent.

The individual tactical actions and playing context we have chosen are the following:

1. Turn-up towards the middle lane (Figures 7.3 and 7.4)
2. Turn-up towards the outside lane (Figures 7.5 and 7.6)
3. Defense skating behind the net followed by a sudden stop and change in direction (Figure 7.7)
4. Rushing defense using a fake pass (Figure 7.8)
5. Defense dragging to the middle (Figure 7.9)
6. Accelerating winger driving to the net and protecting the puck (Figure 7.10)
7. Sudden stop by the center (Figures 7.11 and 7.12)
8. Delay with turn-away pivot (Figure 7.13)
9. Fake pass and shoot (Figure 7.14)

FIGURE 7.3   High turn-up (note outside fake)

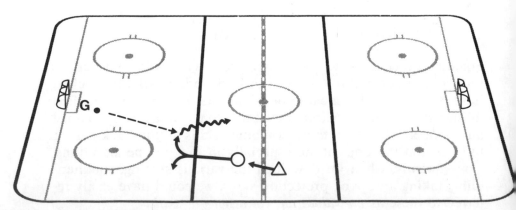

IGURE 7.4   Low turn-up (note outside fake)

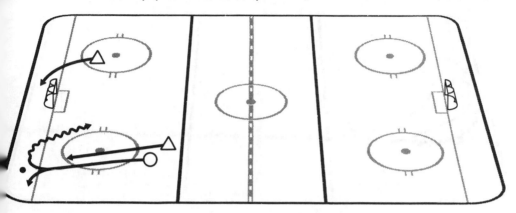

FIGURE 7.5   High turn-up (note inside fake)

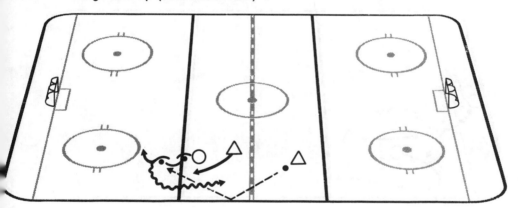

FIGURE 7.6   Low turn-up (note inside fake)

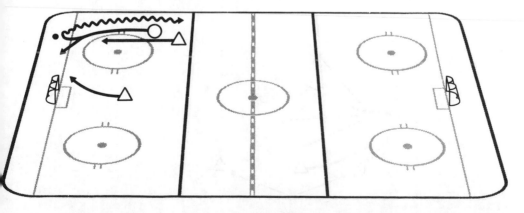

FIGURE 7.7 Stop with quick change of direction

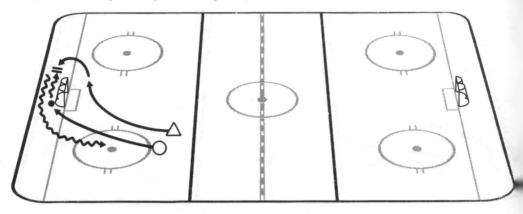

FIGURE 7.8 Fake pass by rushing defenseman

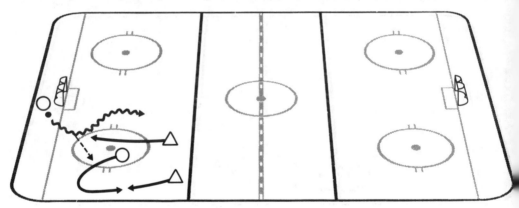

FIGURE 7.9 Drag to the middle : defense moves to the middle to open passing options

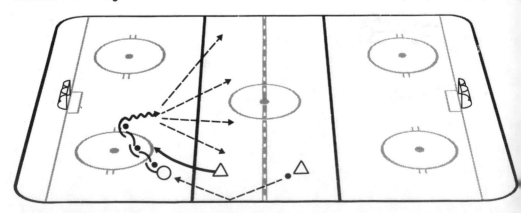

■IGURE 7.10   Driving to the net

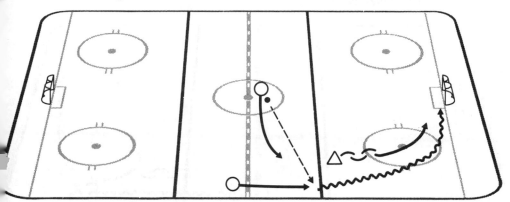

■IGURE 7.11   Sudden stop to avoid check

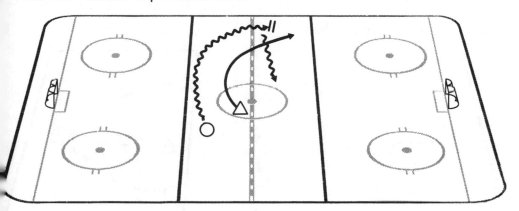

■FIGURE 7.12   Sudden stop and pivot

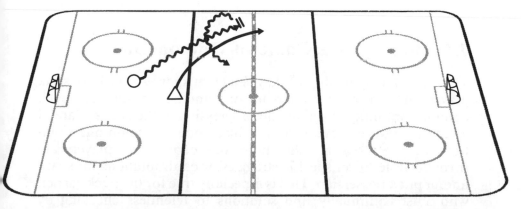

FIGURE 7.13   Turn-away pivot

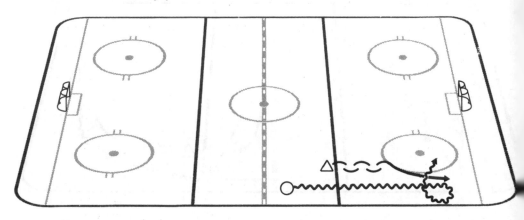

FIGURE 7.14   Fake pass and shoot

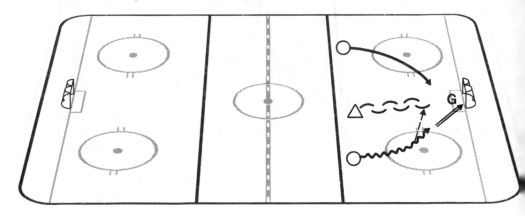

7.4   Hockey Is a Game of One on One

There is no denying that hockey is a team sport. As we have seen, players must provide support for one another to maintain puck control, continuity of action and progression in the attack. Careful analysis, however, reveals a high incidence of one-on-one situations during the game, situations where only two players are involved in terms of specific struggles or confrontations for space and/or puck possession. This is especially true for the puck carrier, who must continually find solutions to relentless checking by opponents, but it is also a reality for the non-puck carriers in their attempt to provide the ideal support role.

By the very nature of the game, the puck carrier is constantly being harassed by his opponent. He must consistently face this intense challenge of "beating his opponent" via either purely individual actions such as stickhandling, faking, accelerating speed or sheer strength, or by a collective action such as passing. However, the nature of the specific playing environment quite often prohibits, or at least limits, the puck carrier from using a pass as a means to maintain possession; the puck carrier must therefore resort to his own individual abilities to safeguard the puck. There is a time and place for an individual action, and the situation usually dictates such an approach. This principle of choosing an individual skill over a collective approach (e.g. give-and-go) to puck control follows the same line of thought as the catch phrase "don't give up the puck." In short, there is a time to pass and a time to hold on to the puck. In time, experience, a sense of anticipation, confidence and poise will allow you to select the correct option or tactical action.

Recognizing this fact, many coaches have placed a greater emphasis in their regular practices on "winning the individual battles." New drills have been formulated to develop this aspect, covering many different one-on-one situations commonly encountered in a game. We support this trend. We do not mean to suggest that a swing towards developing individual talent should be at the detriment of a more collective approach, but instead prefer to accept the reality that each and every player must fully develop the necessary technical and individual tactical skills for a strong collective game. As we have said, individual technico-tactical and group tactical actions are inextricably linked and interdependent. And the success of the overall play depends on the level of interaction between these actions. We believe that a dynamic and potent offense is created by a swarming front of both individual talent and highly coordinated group action.

8

Group Tactical Skills in Movement and Puck Control

8.1 Introduction

In Chapter 6, we noted that collective puck control depends on three factors: individual technico-tactical skills, group tactical skills and sound judgement on the part of the players. We then discussed the responsibilities of the non-puck carriers in providing necessary support for the puck carrier. Although the main emphasis was on the role of the non-puck carriers, we also took a look at group tactical actions. Now, it's time for a more detailed examination of the interplay between the puck carrier and non-puck carriers — the group tactical actions that generate the vital punch on attack.

Because group tactical actions or skills depend to a large extent on the passing and receiving abilities of the players, let us first examine the key individual technical and tactical elements that promote excellent passing and receiving.

8.2 The Art of Passing and Receiving

There are obviously some purely technical elements involved in the skills of passing and pass-receiving, such as the types of passes, ways of receiving a pass and the correct bio-mechanical factors associated with the proper execution. Many other writers have addressed this aspect of passing-receiving skills. Our focus here is to study the skills of passing and receiving from a more game-like point of view.

To successfully execute a passing-receiving play within the context of the game, certain elements must be kept in mind. Here we refer to factors such as passing unexpectedly or not "telegraphing" the pass, combining certain fakes when passing and using the most appropriate pass given the playing situation, to name just a few. These factors basically augment the effectiveness and success of a passing-receiving play, especially at the higher levels of competition, where speed, finesse, creativity and the element of surprise make the big difference. Let's look at the various factors that affect the outcome of a passing-receiving play.

8.2.1 The passer

Certain behaviors are typical of our passing game in North America. One which we are quite familiar with is that we do not pass as often as the Europeans, especially the Soviets. This has been confirmed time and time again by game analyses, although in recent years, we have narrowed the gap. Upon closer examination, we can also detect a related or associated behavior − North American players quite often do not pass the puck until they are absolutely forced to do so, meaning that they will carry the puck until they are checked by an opponent (Tarasov and Persson, 1973; Horsky, 1983). This common habit among our players should be addressed seriously by our hockey experts and associations, especially in the formative years of players' careers.

Passes are made for various reasons, but in general we can classify them in two categories:

1. Passes to maintain puck control
2. Passes to gain advantage over the opposition

Passes are often made to maintain puck control, with no immediate purpose of progressing the attack. Classic examples are back passes to regroup and lateral passes to delay the attack or escape pressure. On the other hand, passes are also made to gain territorial or numerical advantage, forcing the opposition to readjust its alignment. In the latter case, Tarasov (1969) referred to these as "active" passes, passes "to the man who is in the best position for developing the attack" (p. 8). This type of pass will force the defense to retreat or modify their defensive coverage. But aren't some passes a mixture of the two? Absolutely. In many instances, the purpose is to maintain puck control as well as pressure the opposition to retreat or adjust to the pass. In reality, most passes accomplish both purposes. However, the more a pass is "active," the more tactically dangerous it can be for the opposition.

With this in mind, we present four important points on passing. Remember that these points relate more to the tactical than to the technical aspects of passing.

POINT NO. 1: _TIMING_. *A PLAYER MUST PASS AT THE APPROPRIATE MOMENT AND NOT WAIT UNTIL HE HAS NO OTHER OPTION BUT TO GET RID OF THE PUCK.*

In other words, there is a "perfect" time to pass the puck and this should not be solely contingent upon the puck carrier being checked by an opponent and no longer having the choice of carrying the puck. Furthermore, it is best to pass the puck before you get *body* checked; this will allow you to continue in the developing play. Obviously, this requires excellent puckhandling skills, confidence in your passing and receiving abilities, and the willingness to change to a more collective game. Again, we believe that this rule of action should be instilled by coaches early in players' careers.

POINT NO. 2: _CAMOUFLAGING_. *WHENEVER POSSIBLE, CAMOUFLAGE YOUR PASS.*

The success of a pass depends to a significant degree on deceiving the opposition into believing that the pass is intended for a certain player when in fact it is designated for another. Too often when making a pass, the puck carrier will clearly give away or "telegraph" the direction of the pass rather than truly camouflaging it. This facilitates checking by the opposition and leaves the receiver (now the puck carrier) with little time or space. Drop passes, crisscrosses, flow patterns and various fakes are excellent ways to conceal the direction of a pass.

Camouflaging a pass is also linked to technique, that is, using the appropriate passing method. Whether it is a new wave in passing, a lack of practice or the influence of the curved stick, the fact remains that most players do not use the backhand pass as often as they should. In many situations, this affects the possibility of camouflaging the pass, simply because the player utilized his forehand when the natural, quicker and more efficient pass should have been his backhand.

The quick or one-touch pass is also related to camouflage. This technique essentially consists of passing, actually redirecting the puck instantly rather than truly receiving the pass (holding on to the puck). This quick redirection of the puck is another form of camouflaging passes, which leaves the opposition little time to adjust. Given the speed of today's game, hockey players are using this form of passing more frequently as another means of gaining advantage over the opposition. We will return to the importance of the one-touch or redirected pass when discussing the various group tactical actions.

POINT NO. 3: ACCURACY. CONCENTRATE ON MAKING AN ACCURATE PASS.

Accuracy in passing is primarily determined by the ability of the passer to read the speed and intended direction of the receiver in relation to his own speed. Then, and only then, can the passer determine the speed of the pass to be made. Given these passing-receiving conditions or variables, it is crucial for the passer to first gauge the difference, if any, in their speeds before attempting to pass the puck. After making a quick assessment of this speed differential, the passer is then able to judge or adjust the speed of the pass. Generally, it is recommended to pass the puck at a good speed to minimize the risk of interceptions, reduce the time for the opposition to adjust and maximize the time for the receiver to handle the puck for his next move. However, certain conditions require a pass to be "soft" or slow. This is especially true when you are passing to an area rather than to a player. Soft passes are also commonly used when making flip and drop type passes, or when the distance between passer and receiver is relatively short.

On-ice drills should be selected so as to enable the players to adjust to all the passing situations, using different types of passes and executing at various differential speeds between the passer and the receiver. Players on a team that has developed a high level of passing-receiving ability are well on their way to achieving successful group tactical plays.

Finally, we cannot overemphasize the importance of concentrating, if only for a brief moment, when attempting to pass the puck. Reading the situation, deciding on the type of pass, adjusting to the skating speed of the receiver and focusing on making the pass directly on the stick are all elements that require the passer to concentrate. If just one of these elements fails, the pass will be unsuccessful.

POINT NO. 4: _JUDGEMENT_. PASS THE PUCK TO THE MOST APPROPRIATE RECEIVER.

A player executing a pass can be compared to a quarterback in football. Defensemen in hockey are often referred to as such; however, the analogy should be extended to all players. The passer must decide who he chooses as receiver. This can make or break the entire group tactical play. This is not an easy task, since making the decision as to who should receive the pass requires a mature judgement based upon a vision of the developing attack, recognized patterns of play with the various options, the ability to read and quick decision-making. As we have said, the passer must decide whether the pass should be "active" in nature or more for the purpose of maintaining puck control. Of course, a lot of these decision-making abilities come with practice and experience. Nevertheless, in a game situation where players are under pressure to perform, this is a very important and critical task.

8.2.2 The receiver

It would be a serious omission not to identify the specific duties of a receiver in the successful completion of a pass. As discussed in earlier chapters, there are various support roles or options for the non-puck carriers: support by availability, by clearing the area, by screening and by proximal support. Assuming that a player has chosen to support the puck carrier by making himself available for a pass — which is the most common support role — there are certain tactical points a receiver must observe to be truly effective. Let's examine those points now.

POINT NO. 1: _DECEPTION_. THE RECEIVER MUST TRICK HIS OPPONENT AND LOCATE SPACE.

In many situations, non-puck carriers are checked (watched) by an opponent, either closely or at a distance. To locate open space and become available for a pass, a potential receiver often needs to trick or deceive his checker. He accomplishes this by body fakes, changing direction or simply accelerating. Just as a passer needs to avoid "telegraphing" his pass, a receiver must also attempt to camouflage his moves. Once again, movement patterns such as flow and counterflow and interchange will facilitate this task.

The receiver must also perform all these preliminary actions at the perfect moment, which makes the task even more complex. The role of the receiver is to accommodate the passer, that is, the receiver must be available at the passer's convenience. The receiver must time his actions based upon the needs of the passer. Too often, we hear receivers (quite often forwards) complain to the passer (quite often a defenseman) that they were open for a pass. Yes, the receivers were open, but the passer may have been unable to make the pass at that particular moment. Coordination between passer and receivers is critical, but the responsibility of being open for a pass at the right moment falls primarily on the receiver. As mentioned earlier, the principle is "four playing for one" not "one playing for four."

POINT NO. 2: *TIMING AND COMMUNICATION*. AT THE PERFECT MOMENT, THE RECEIVER MUST GIVE A CLEAR SIGNAL THAT HE IS OPEN FOR A PASS.

Receivers also have the responsibility of indicating to the puck carrier whether they are open or not open for a pass. This signal or message should be made at the opportune time to accommodate the passer. Of course, the puck carrier should look first to see if the receiver is available before making the pass; however, in many situations the passer is often pressed, leaving little time to read the entire play. In such cases, a signal to the puck carrier can make the difference. In other easier situations, a signal may reassure him as to his intended decision. Receivers should also indicate where they would like to receive the pass by having their stick on the ice. For shooters waiting for the puck, especially in one-time shots, this can make or break your chances of scoring.

This communication or signal to the passer can be either verbal or non-verbal. For verbal signals, we suggest the most simple words such as "yes" or "no." Calling the player by his first name can also be effective, but bear in mind that opponents may know your name, even your nickname. Non-verbal cues can be audible, such as tapping your stick on the ice or the board, or silent, as in raising your stick.

Messages to a puck carrier can also be sent by other players besides the receiver. Goaltenders, for instance, may say to a defenseman, "two men on you," suggesting that he should make an around-the-boards pass. Or a defenseman may tell his partner "up the middle."

POINT NO. 3: OPTION MORE THAN ONCE. THE RECEIVER MUST KEEP SKATING, LOCATE OPEN ICE AND BE OPEN FOR A PASS MORE THAN ONCE TO TRULY SUPPORT THE PUCK CARRIER.

A potential receiver must never give up trying to get into the open, even though the passer may have missed him the first time around. Receivers must appreciate the task faced by the puck carrier in attempting to make the perfect pass, given the forechecking pressure and the speed of the game. This is why receivers need to be patient and keep trying to find open ice. Timing your arrival by controlling your direction and/or movement pattern (direction) is the key to successfully supporting the puck carrier. Support by availability also means supporting the puck carrier more than once.

POINT NO. 4: CONTROL THE PUCK AND ANTICIPATE. THE RECEIVER MUST QUICKLY CONTROL THE PUCK AND ANTICIPATE THE NEXT ACTION.

Many passes are not perfectly on-target. It would be foolish to expect every pass to land on the stick without the receiver having to make some type of adjustment, such as reaching for the puck or slowing down. Quite often, passes must be completed by the receiver using his skate to redirect the pass onto his stick. The point is that receivers must accept the fact that many passes will be imperfect, and be ready to make the adjustment to bring the puck under control as quickly as possible. In many situations, this also means that the receiver must protect the puck. Controlling and protecting the puck from your opponents will allow you more time to execute your next move, whether it be passing, stickhandling or shooting.

Even before the pass is completed, the receiver should have some idea of his next move, such as driving for the net, passing, shooting or carrying the puck. Anticipating the next action is the cornerstone for successive group tactical plays. All great hockey players have the ability to anticipate the plays ahead.

There are many points to consider in the execution of a passing-receiving play during the course of a game. Almost every skill comes into play — skating, individual puck control, passing and receiving skills, as well as the constant ability to read and react quickly and accurately. As mentioned earlier, we have highlighted the more tactical points rather than the purely technical ones. This was a deliberate choice — and consistent with the general thrust of the book.

After looking at these main points which affect the success of a passing-receiving play, we will now turn our attention to the various types of group tactical plays in hockey.

8.3 Group Tactical Plays

As we saw in Chapter 1, a *group tactical skill* is the collective action used consciously by two or more players to gain advantage over one or more opponents, whether offensively or defensively. The word *group* implies that two or more players have come together for the purpose of coordinating certain actions, and *tactical* signifies that the action has had the effect of deceiving or "beating" the opponent. This chapter will explore the various combinations or group tactical actions commonly used on offense.

The passer and receiver are obviously the key actors in any group tactical play — they must precisely coordinate their actions to execute flawlessly. However, movement of the other players is also vital. They must provide additional support by such actions as decoying, screening or close support while readying themselves for the next group play. There should be no passive players. If the player is not the passer or the receiver for this first group action, he must still play some support role and anticipate that the next pass may be sent to him. Consequently, although we intend to focus primarily in our analysis of these group tactical actions on the passer and receiver, we must remember that all the players have a role to play — *during* the action and in anticipation and preparation for the *next* play. Normally, various combinations of players execute the various group tactical actions as the play advances and develops.

Our approach will be to explain each group tactical action. However, a thorough understanding and application of these group plays must also be considered within the overall developing play. Typically, an attack consists of a series of group tactical actions that should eventually lead to a good scoring opportunity (unless the opposition successfully interferes). Therefore, it will become necessary at times to link the various group tactical actions to the broader playing context.

We must also bear in mind that the illustrations used to describe these various group actions are only snapshots of a series of successive and integrated actions by the players. This, to say the least, poses certain limitations when we attempt to give accurate, precise explanations of the continuous and interrelated movements typical of group plays. A picture (diagram) may "be worth a thousand words," but a movie "gives you the story."

Let's begin by sharing the list of group tactical actions before looking at each action separately.

1. Forms of passes
   - direct
   - bank
   - around-the-boards
   - lob
   - open area (spot pass)
   - one-touch (redirected pass)
   - drop
   - skate
2. Give-and-go
   - with return pass
   - without return pass
3. Pass and follow
4. Interchange or weave
   - pass and interchange
   - interchange and pass
5. Shuttle
   - with drop pass
   - without drop pass

    6. Reverse
    7. Crisscross
       – with drop pass
       – without drop pass
    8. Screen
       – pass and screen
       – screen and receive
    9. Cycling

Group tactical actions on offense are almost always characterized by some form of passing play. The speed and change in direction of an attack by rapid puck exchanges is the backbone of any successful group tactical play. Since puck movement is usually faster than player movement, passing must be perceived as the premier mode of upsetting a balanced defense. And passing-receiving must be understood as the main ingredient in group tactical actions. Let's begin by examining forms of passes that can be used to beat the opposition.

8.3.1 Forms of passes

There are many types or forms of passes in hockey, each serving a unique purpose in terms of catching the opposition off-guard. Complete hockey players should be familiar with each type of pass, and the time and place to use these various passes.

A. The direct pass

Most passes that occur during the game are direct. These passes, as we have already seen, can be longitudinal, lateral or diagonal. They are usually the quickest way of passing the puck to your teammate (see Figures 8.1 and 8.2).

B. The bank pass

Although the bank pass depends on a passer's good judgement, timing and strict accuracy, it is an extremely safe and effective means of "reaching" a teammate when the normal passing lane is blocked. In the end zones, it also allows you to pass from one side to another without hitting the net or having to pass the puck through the slot area when in your end (see Figures 8.3 to 8.5).

FIGURE 8.1   Direct pass

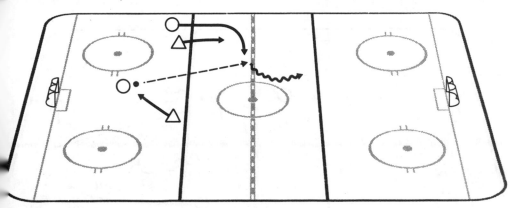

FIGURE 8.2   Direct pass

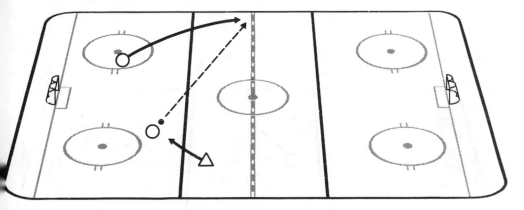

FIGURE 8.3   Bank pass

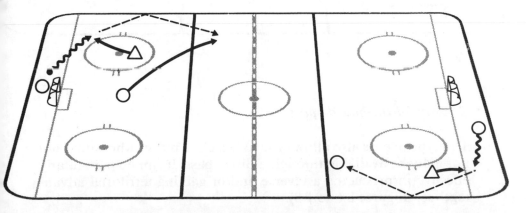

FIGURE 8.4   Shoot-in pass

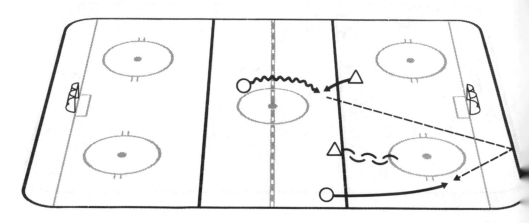

FIGURE 8.5   Bank pass

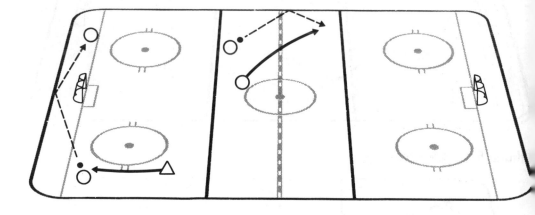

C. *Around-the-boards pass*

This type of pass also allows you to "reach" a player who would not normally be available through a direct pass. It can be particularly effective in producing a reverse and/or gaining territorial advantage (see Figures 8.6 to 8.8).

FIGURE 8.6   Around-the-boards pass

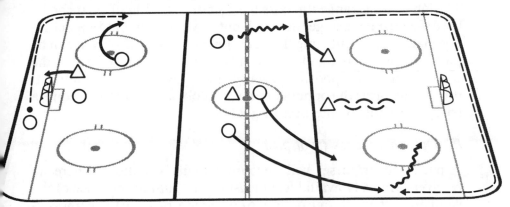

FIGURE 8.7   Reverse

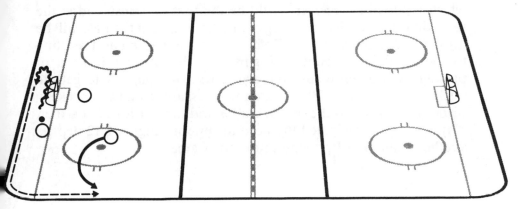

FIGURE 8.8   Around-the-boards pass

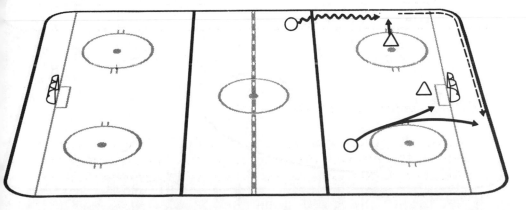

D. The lob pass

The lob or long-range flip pass has its purpose in hockey. It can be used, for instance, to get the puck out of your own end in a definitive manner without icing the puck. On a "dumping" play, it can be particularly effective in letting a speedy winger gain control of the puck before the opposing defense (see Figures 8.9 and 8.10). If directed towards the opponents' net, the lob pass can also become a tricky lob shot for the best of goalies.

E. Open area pass (spot pass)

A puck carrier/passer will encounter many situations where no receivers are truly available, at least in the traditional sense of the word. In such cases, one option to consider is passing to an unoccupied space. Passing to an open area requires a keen sense of reading and reacting – the passer reading that the area is an open space which a potential receiver would be the first to access and at the same time, the receiver reacting or anticipating that the pass will be directed into the open area. Both players are reading and reacting to coordinate their actions. Figure 8.11 illustrates this form of passing by a defenseman interacting with his partner to get the puck out of their end. Player 2, under pressure from two checkers, pivots and passes to the open area behind the net for his partner, player 3, who anticipated the need to support. Figure 8.12 depicts another example of passing to an open area.

FIGURE 8.9 Lob pass

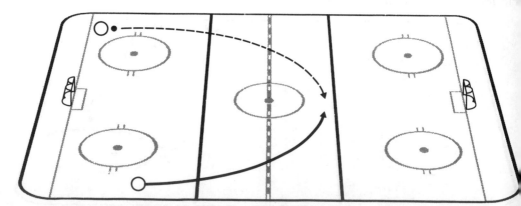

GURE 8.10   Lob pass

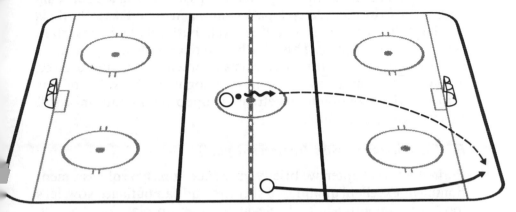

FIGURE 8.11   Passing to an open space

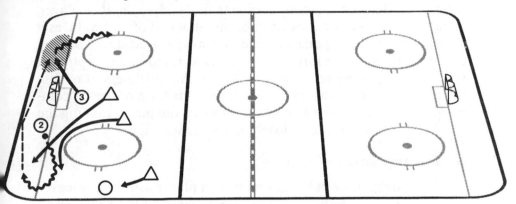

FIGURE 8.12   Passing to an open space

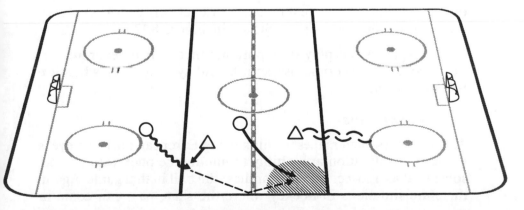

The shoot-in pass, where a player dumps the puck in the opposing end, can also be considered a pass to an open area. The scenario is similar. The receiver is not there yet, but will be to maintain possession of the puck. This North American style of play can be successful if good coordination exists between passer and receiver. Today, many European teams have recognized the value of this play as a viable option to penetrate the opposition's end while still maintaining puck control.

F. The one-touch pass (redirected pass)

Earlier in this chapter, we briefly introduced this type of pass, mentioning its excellent qualities of surprise and camouflage. Now, let's look at its importance and relevance in group plays.

The one-touch or redirected pass has one central tactical advantage. Because it *quickly* redirects the puck to another player, changing the point and location of the attack, it often produces a situation where the opponents are unable to adjust, creating a scoring opportunity. No other form of passing is as rapid and deceptive. It is as effective as the one-time shot where the quickness of release offers no chance for the goalie to adjust. This form of pass is commonly seen in a give-and-go situation when the player making the return pass finds himself closely marked (see Figure 8.13).

G. The drop pass

The term "drop" pass in hockey refers to a player who simply leaves the puck or very softly passes the puck behind him a very short distance to one of his teammates. As illustrated in Figures 8.14 to 8.16, most drop passes are back passes, but they can also be "pure" or real drop passes, where the puck carrier clearly deposits (leaves) the puck for the receiver, as shown in Figure 8.17.

Drop passes also play an important function in other group tactical plays, such as crisscross, shuttle and cycling plays, which we will look at later.

H. The skate pass

The skate pass often makes us think of the European hockey player's foot-eye coordination and ability to handle the puck with his feet somewhat as a soccer player "handles" the ball in that game. Again, there are situations in hockey where the skate pass can come in

FIGURE 8.13   One-touch pass

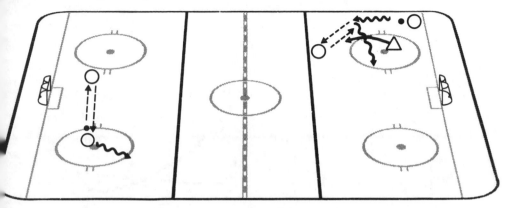

FIGURE 8.14   Drop pass on a breakout play

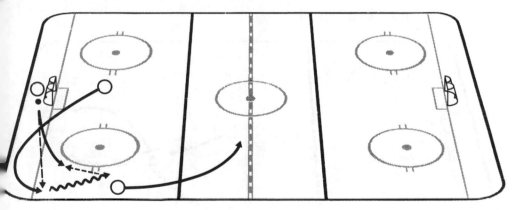

FIGURE 8.15   Drop pass on a breakout play

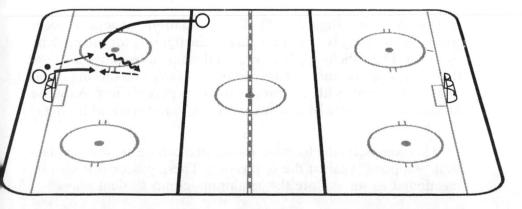

FIGURE 8.16   Drop pass to trailing player

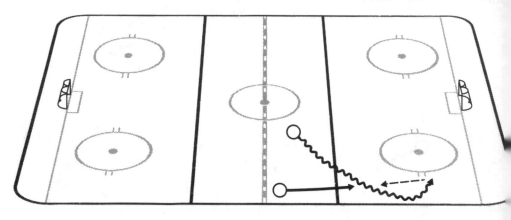

FIGURE 8.17   "Pure" drop pass

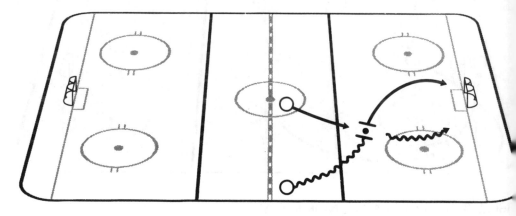

quite handy (see Figure 8.18). These situations generally occur when the checking is close and players are fighting for the puck by their feet. Their sticks are "tied up," so the only alternative is to use their feet to move and/or pass the puck. Many one-on-one situations can be won with the proper use of a player's feet. As we've already seen, the use of feet/skates in puckhandling and faking is also important.

This completes the forms of passes that can be deployed as tactical "weapons" against the opposition. These passes will also be mentioned as we explore the remaining group tactical plays.

FIGURE 8.18   Skate pass

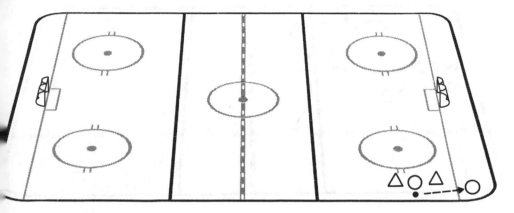

8.3.2   The give-and-go

A.   With return pass

The "give-and-go" is the most commonly referred-to group tactical or combination play, not only in ice hockey but also in other team sports such as basketball, soccer and field hockey. This play is a very effective means for a puck carrier to beat his opponent(s) by passing the puck at the appropriate moment to get around his immediate checker and receive the puck later when he is open for the return pass. In general, the give-and-go is most effective when working on a 2 on 1 situation.

In hockey, there are many areas on the ice where this play can be used successfully. We have isolated two examples of such plays in Figures 8.19 and 8.20.

B.   Without return pass

This play requires both offensive players to play the situation as a typical give-and-go, except that there is no return pass. Instead of obtaining the return pass, the passer acts as a decoy, taking the checker with him, or forces some other player to check him (Figure 8.21). The intended receiver can also follow up with a pick to create more space for the puck carrier (Figure 8.22).

FIGURE 8.19 Give-and-go

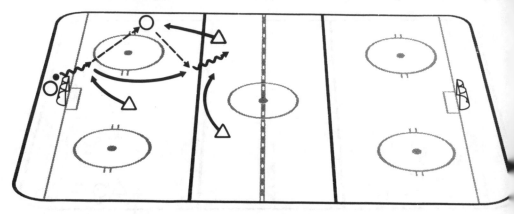

FIGURE 8.20 Give-and-go (power play situation)

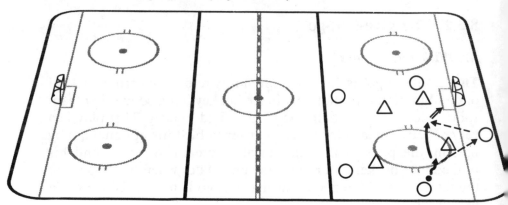

FIGURE 8.21 Give-and-go with no return pass

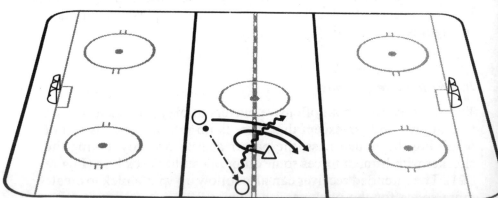

FIGURE 8.22   Give-and-go with no return pass (note pick set by player 4)

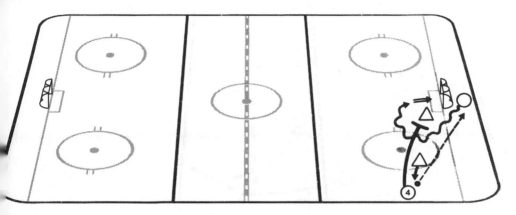

8.3.3 The pass and follow

With the advent of more circular movements by both puck carrier and non-puck carriers, the pass and follow play has become increasingly popular and effective as a means of maintaining puck control. In this play, the passer follows his pass and consequently provides low support for the puck carrier. Because it is sometimes very difficult for a player who has just passed the puck to find open ice ahead of or at the same level as the puck carrier, this particular play offers the passer an opportunity to support the puck carrier from behind. To put it another way, you could say that as a general principle it's wise to follow your pass, especially if you do not have the speed to move ahead of the play. Furthermore, when following you should stay relatively close to effectively provide low support — a very important outlet for many attacking forwards. Figures 8.23 and 8.24 show examples of the pass and follow group tactical play.

8.3.4 The interchange or weave

A. Pass and interchange

The pass and interchange is accomplished by first making a pass followed with a change in lanes or corridor between the passer and the receiver. The passer cuts across and *behind* the receiver (Figure 8.25). An even more basic play would be for the puck carrier and a teammate to weave or interchange without passing (Figure 8.26). That would also be a type of tactical play, since it would have the effect of confusing the opposition.

FIGURE 8.23   Pass and follow

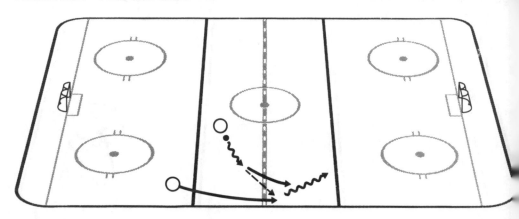

FIGURE 8.24   Pass and follow

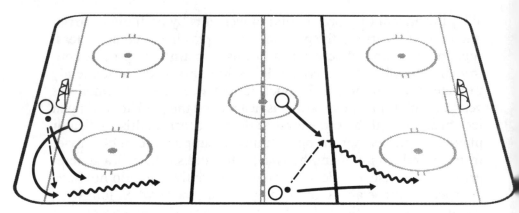

FIGURE 8.25   Pass and interchange

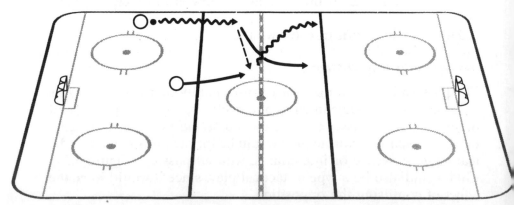

GURE 8.26   Interchange

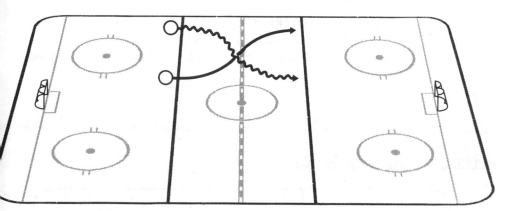

B. Interchange and pass

Another option is to interchange by switching lanes first and then
follow with a pass. Here the puck carrier would initiate the play by
moving laterally, indicating to his teammate to cross over behind
him and switch lanes (see Figure 8.27). The receiver coming slightly
from behind gives the play a camouflaged effect. The puck carrier
must move and stickhandle in such a way as to make both defensemen move to one side and quickly pass to the other, at times to the
area (spot pass) where the receiver is intending to move. The interchanging or crossing-over is what makes this play tactically effective. A play consisting of only a lateral pass without two players
switching lanes would reduce the tactical effect on the defensemen
(see Figure 8.28). Such a play would be read by the defense as a
classic 2 on 2 with each defenseman taking a man. However, in the
case of the play illustrated in Figure 8.27, the defensemen are
uncertain about the eventual direction of the attack and are therefore hard pressed to read the play clearly and adjust accordingly.

Many types of weaves or permutations exist in hockey, some of
which involve more than two players. With the new wave in hockey
placing more emphasis on moving to open spaces rather than stay-
ing on your wing, these forms of tactical plays have become essential. Jeremiah (1942), who was then head coach at Dartmouth
College, supported the idea of forwards changing lanes and weaving
with other players, which he referred to as the "crossing wing style

of play." For Jeremiah, the crossing wing style of play had three big advantages:

1. Got rid of backchecking "cover"
2. Wings could break into "open ice" for passes
3. Playmaking possibilities at the defense would be increased (p. 41)

FIGURE 8.27   Interchange and pass

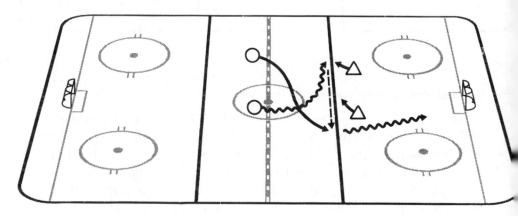

FIGURE 8.28   No interchange

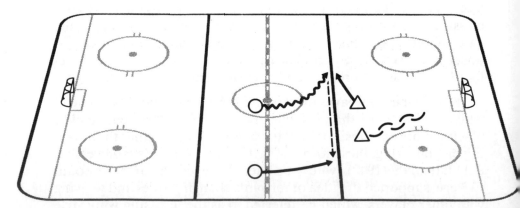

8.3.5 The shuttle

A. With drop pass

A shuttle play involves two players — one of them the puck carrier — coming from opposite directions and moving on a parallel
course towards each other. The puck carrier, slightly in front or
goal-side (depending on the area of execution), drops the puck to
his partner. We refer to this play as a "shuttle" play because the net
effect of the two players skating in opposite directions and exchanging
the puck is a back and forth movement of the puck. Figures 8.29
through 8.31 illustrate some examples of this type of play. Note that
the receiver is actually providing close support to the puck
carrier.

With a slight variation in the direction of the skating players
— more curvilinear instead of linear — this play can be extended
to other areas of the rink, particularly the corners and near the top
of the offensive zone. The essence or tactical dimension of the play
remains the same, except for the small change in the movement
patterns of the players (see Figure 8.32).

B. Without drop pass

With or without the drop pass, the skating pattern between the two
players remains the same. In both situations, it is the puck carrier
who must make the split-second decision whether or not to leave
the puck behind, depending on the reaction and positioning of the
defenders. If the immediate checker follows the puck carrier, then
the drop pass is the correct play. If, however, the opponent anticipates
the drop pass, then the puck carrier must opt to keep the puck. The
potential receiver in the latter instance plays the role of decoying or
tricking the defense (see Figure 8.33).

Essentially, this shuttle play allows the puck carrier more space
and time to make a pass or another play. When attacking the blue
line, a puck carrier quite often does not have the speed or angle to
beat a defenseman; the alternative is to buy time by skating parallel
to the blue line, which makes it difficult for the defense to adjust.
This adjustment is difficult because the defensemen must cope
with the following elements:

1. Who will check the puck carrier, me or my partner?
2. Will there be a drop pass? And if so, do we switch our man-to-man coverage?
3. Technically, the defense must eventually stop skating backwards and move forward and laterally.
4. The decision time is rather short, with very little opportunity to recover.

The effectiveness of this play can be greatly enhanced by the puck carrier faking the drop pass followed by acceleration, the receiver pretending to pick up the puck, and as always the speed, timing and location of execution.

FIGURE 8.29   Shuttle play with drop pass

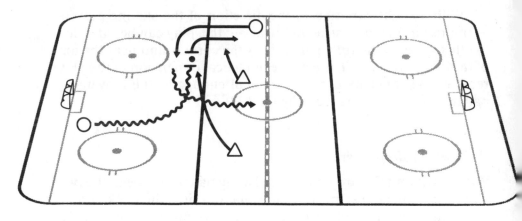

FIGURE 8.30   Shuttle play with drop pass

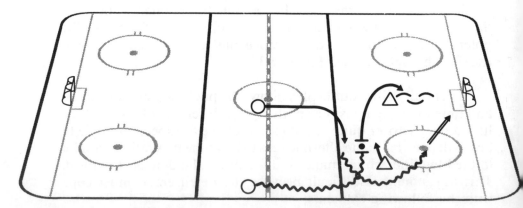

FIGURE 8.31   Shuttle play with drop pass

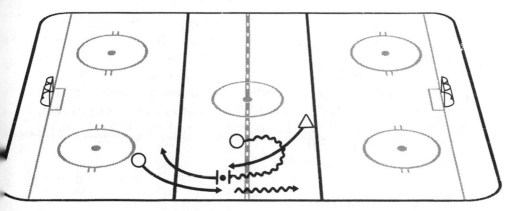

FIGURE 8.32   Shuttle plays with drop pass

FIGURE 8.33   Shuttle plays without drop pass (note fakes)

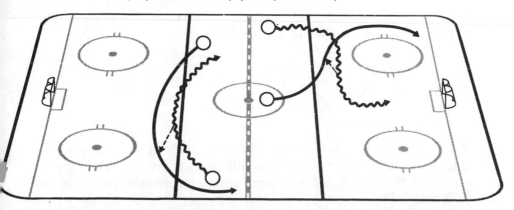

8.3.6 The reverse

The reverse play is a very effective play to use when the puck carrier is under close checking pressure. The reverse relies heavily on close support by one player to be successful. The classic reverse play is seen by two defensemen behind their goal line, but all sorts of player combinations are possible. The reverse usually implies using a bank or around-the-boards pass, but a direct back pass can also be used to complete the play. Figures 8.34 and 8.35 offer some examples of reverse plays.

8.3.7 The crisscross

A. With pass

To some extent, the crisscross resembles shuttle play. However, as the word implies, the two players actually intersect while moving towards each other. In the shuttle play, the players move on a parallel course towards each other while in the crisscross the players skate more at an angle towards each other, forcing them to eventually intersect in their paths. Figure 8.36 illustrates the fundamental difference.

Usually, the puck carrier will crisscross in front of his partner and make the drop pass, but the opposite is also possible, that is, the puck carrier passes first and then crisscrosses behind the receiver. Figures 8.37 and 8.38 show these two unique plays.

B. Without pass

A crisscross without an immediate pass is basically an interchange play as described earlier in Figure 8.26.

8.3.8 The screen

A. Pass and screen

After a player has made a pass, he can assist the receiver by screening. As in most screen plays, this will give the receiver more space and time to execute the next appropriate maneuver (see Figures 8.39 and 8.40).

IGURE 8.34 Reverses

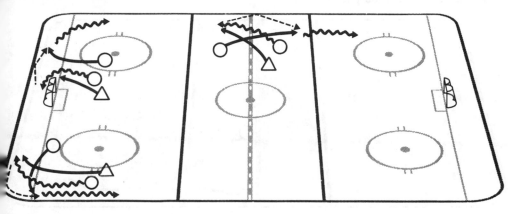

FIGURE 8.35 Reverses

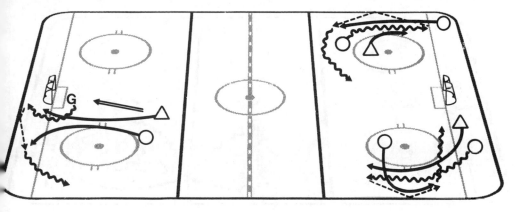

FIGURE 8.36 Crisscross versus shuttle

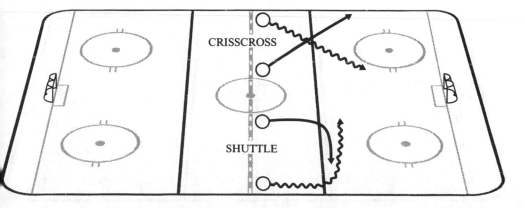

FIGURE 8.37   Crisscross play

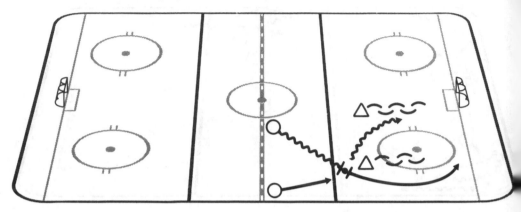

FIGURE 8.38   Crisscross play

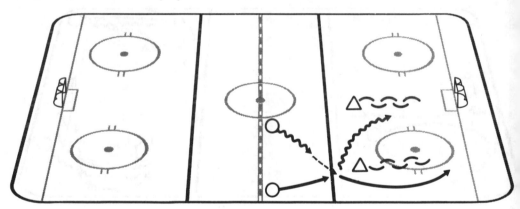

FIGURE 8.39   Pass and screen

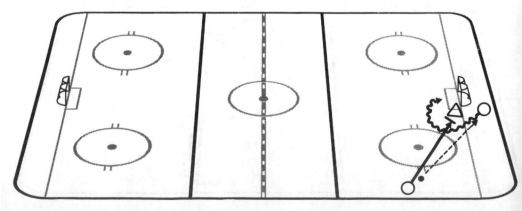

IGURE 8.40   Pass and screen

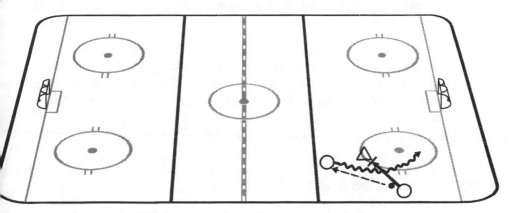

B. Screen and receive

This play is similar to the pick and roll in basketball. The player screens first for the puck carrier, then frees himself by moving into the open for a pass. The basic idea here is to provide two successive types of support: screening for the puck carrier first and later moving into an open area to receive a pass (see Figure 8.41).

C. Pass and screen the goaltender

Occasionally, after the puck carrier has made a pass, his best support role is to screen or block the view of the goalie by moving between the goalie and his teammate/shooter. This play usually develops by having the puck carrier make a drop pass and skating towards one of the defenders in line with the anticipated shot from his receiver. The object of this play is to screen the view of the goalie and create time and space for the shooter by pushing the defender toward his own net (see Figure 8.42).

8.3.9 Cycling

A. Two-man cycling

Cycling, as the term implies, is a circular pattern of skating by two or more players, usually executed in the offensive zone. Cycling creates a dynamic numerical advantage, allowing players to maintain puck control in restricted areas by a series of drop passes. The main teaching point is to constantly provide close support behind the puck carrier.

In two-man cycling, the puck carrier leaves the puck to his teammate and immediately skates in a circular pattern to assume a support position behind him. In short, they keep alternating between being the puck carrier and providing close support (see Figure 8.43).

FIGURE 8.41   Screen and receive

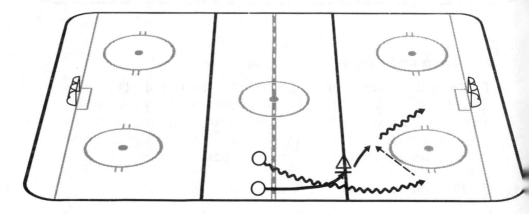

FIGURE 8.42   Pass and screen the goaltender

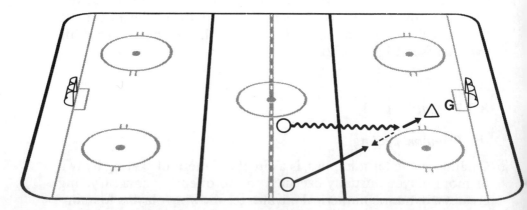

FIGURE 8.43   Two-man cycling

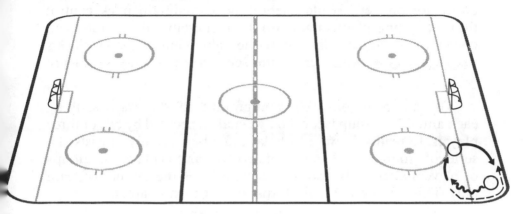

B. *Three-man cycling*

The concept in three-man cycling is the same as in two-man. At times, a third man is necessary to create a numerical advantage and enhance the chances of maintaining puck control (see Figure 8.44).

Both two-man and three-man cycling can be performed clockwise or counterclockwise. Although most cycling occurs in the offensive corners, it can also be performed on other areas of the ice, including around the opponents' net and in the defensive zone.

FIGURE 8.44   Three-man cycling

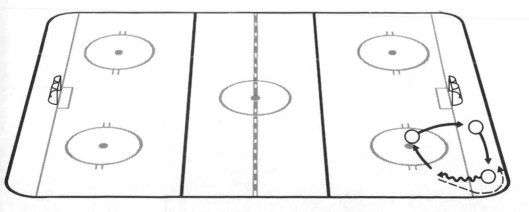

In the offensive end, cycling is only a means (puck control) to an end (shot on net). While attempting to maintain puck control through cycling, players must also think of establishing a pass to an open man moving into the slot. In the right offensive corner, players need to cycle *clockwise* to create this scoring opportunity (see Figure 8.45).

This completes our section on group tactical plays, describing each and every group tactical play usually executed by two or three players. In reality, however, a balanced attack usually consists of a series of group tactical plays that involve various players or groups of players alternately and/or successively — the essence of team play. This will be the main thrust of our next chapter.

FIGURE 8.45   Cycling followed by a shot on net

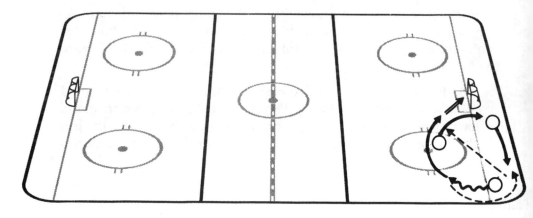

PART # III

TEAM PLAY

Any successful attack must advance or progress towards the opponents' end, penetrate the optimal shooting area, and release a high percentage shot on net. In Part Two, we examined the roles of both puck and non-puck carriers in various individual and group tactical actions. Guided by the fundamental principles of movement and puck control, these individual and group tactical actions form the basis of offensive team play — the five-man unit of attack. In Part Three, we will examine the fundamental principles of progression of an attack and optimal shooting within the context of team play.

9

Introduction

9.1 The Phases of the Game

According to our study and analysis of hockey, we have identified four phases during the course of a game:

1. Offense
2. Defense
3. The "undetermined possession" phase
4. The transition phase

Hockey games have traditionally been divided into two main parts, offense and defense, a practical division for analyzing the various aspects of the game. A team is on offense when they are in control of the puck. A team is on defense when the other team has possession of the puck. Notice that we did not say, a team is on defense when they do not have puck control. In our minds, this would have been inaccurate, because we believe that there are moments during the game when neither team has puck control. When both teams are struggling to obtain possession of the puck, it is impossible to determine which team is on offense and which is on defense. A typical example of this phase, which we will refer to as the phase of "undetermined possession," is when players are fighting for the puck in the corner, usually in a 1 on 1, 2 on 2, or even 3 on 3 situation. This phase may not last long, but it is still a very important phase of the game considering what actions are required by your players to obtain puck control.

Recently, hockey experts have identified a fourth phase – the transitional period – as another important aspect of the game to study. This phase is the time or period of adjustment that teams must undergo between the offensive and defensive phases of the game. This phase is extremely short but it occurs frequently and must be taken into account as we attempt to fully understand and analyze the game. Let us now explore the "undetermined possession" and the transition phases of the game.

9.2 The "Undetermined Possession" Phase

Coaches, we believe, have traditionally alluded to this phase as the "fighting for the puck" phase, and with good reason, because the main observable characteristic is players attempting to regain possession of the puck, either in tight quarters or in a loose puck situation. According to our analyses, which include recent NHL and international games of prominent junior and national teams, this phase can occupy anywhere from twenty-six to forty-eight percent of the game, not including the time during man-advantage situations. Smaller ice surfaces seem to have the effect of increasing the time of "undetermined possession." Other reports suggest that there is a loose or free puck situation in over half the game (King, 1990).

It is relatively easy to identify the "undetermined possession" phase during a game – neither team is in control of the puck and some players are striving to regain possession while others wait to see the outcome. Two pertinent questions come to mind: what principles or rules of action should players follow to guide their movements during this phase of the game? And, are these principles of action different from those during the offensive, defensive and transition phases of the game?

In an attempt to answer these questions, we must first return to the perceptual-motor process, that is, the importance of reading and reacting. We mentioned earlier that players must not only read the actions of the opposition but also those of their teammates. Now, we want to emphasize that players need to read the particular phase of the game before reacting, bearing in mind this new phase, the "undetermined possession." Players must first become conscious of this phase during play to be able to adequately judge (read) the situation.

Secondly, players cannot assume during this phase that they are on offense or defense. They are in neither situation, and to pre-judge the outcome of the battle of possession is to take an un-necessary risk, especially if you prepared yourself offensively when in fact the contrary occurs. Essentially, players away from the puck must support differently during this unique phase. They must react with a slightly different set of principles in mind.

Since the primary objective, with some exceptions in the defensive zone, is to regain puck control, we believe that players should maximize their efforts towards that end during the "unde-termined possession" phase. Their actions should be guided by the following principles:

1. Have your mind set on winning the fight for possession of the puck rather than on offense or defense, except in one very specific situation. This situation revolves around protect-ing the slot area in your own end. This means that in a loose puck situation, the closest man should make the maximum effort to get to the puck before the opposition.

2. Players away from the puck should in general create numerical superiority (overload) by having more players attempting to regain control than the opposition. In other words, don't sit back hoping your partner will win the battle; instead, offer close support by being ready to jump in, screen or retrieve the loose puck. Adhere to this approach even more rig-orously in a power play; in penalty killing, it depends on the situation.

We have observed on a number of occasions that the Soviets will often apply this principle during a short-handed situation. Specifically, during the second game of Rendez-Vous 1987, we observed in a one-man-short situation that the Soviets were battling for the puck on the side of the boards with three players to Canada's two, while only one Soviet back stood guard in front of the net. We concluded that this was part of their tactical play, even while short-handed and in their own end. Actually, their approach during this "undetermined possession" phase was a combined defense − a man-to-man defense close to the puck plus one close support player trying to regain possession, and a zone defense in front of their net.

3. Maintain movement during the struggle for puck control. While some players are battling for the puck, the other supporting players should still maintain an adequate skating speed close to the puck. Movement will always help you to recover in the event that your team does not win possession of the "loose" puck.

4. Finally, use your better judgement and keep watching the puck to determine your next support role. You might be back to offense or defense − don't take any unnecessary risks by predicting the outcome. Of course, the specific playing context or situation should have some bearing on your actions. If, for instance, you are leading by one goal and the battle for the loose puck is along the side of the boards inside your blue line, then reason would indicate that you select the most prudent action. Obviously, all sorts of scenarios are possible, and each will dictate how prudent or daring you are willing to be.

In summary, we believe that in the future, coaches will pay more attention to this "undetermined possession" phase of the game. In the next decade, we may see specific drills developed around this theme to help players select the appropriate support role. In the past decade, we have seen professional coaches place a stronger emphasis on the transition phase of the game along with specialty teams (power play and penalty killing), at least as reflected in their on-ice practices.

9.3 The Transition Phase

In a typical game of hockey, teams make frequent swings between offense and defense. Add to these frequent transitions moments occupied by the "undetermined possession" phase, and you begin to understand the complexity of trying to "read" the situation accurately to choose the proper action-decision. Adjusting as players to this ever-changing directional play is an extremely important dimension of the game. However, players must learn to adapt quickly as the play switches from one phase to the next or face the inevitable consequences of not adequately supporting the offense or defense. Again, a player's ability to make the transition from one playing situation to another depends on his reading and reacting skills, anticipation and sound judgement.

Studies on transition (Pelchat et al, 1980; Kinding, 1990) have shown the importance of reacting quickly to take advantage of your opponent. An overwhelming number of successful counterattacks occur within the first ten seconds after recovering the puck. Furthermore, excellent scoring chances compared to poor ones also occur within this period. If players are to counterattack effectively, they must minimize the transition period to take advantage of their opposition, positionally and/or numerically. Failure to do so allows the opposition to recover defensively, and diminishes the essence of a counterattack. "Offense transition hockey" is actualized through counterattacks. Kinding (1990) emphasized this point by saying:

> The importance of the transition game, in modern ice hockey, has been greater and greater, as the defensive skills become more developed. There is a clear trend which shows that goals will be scored as a result of surprising your opponent and attacking [counterattacking] when they are still in their offensive positions. This is transition hockey (p. 3).

Most of the ideas proposed on this subject are based more on common sense, experience and observation than on scientific data. Time and time again, coaches refer to certain teams as being strong in their "transition" game. Many coaches believe that superior transition ability is what makes the difference between two otherwise evenly matched teams. Some coaches go as far as to make this their central focus during practices and games (Jacques Martin, personal communication, June 16, 1990). According to another coach, "Good offensive teams become great offensive teams with a strong transition game (Siciliano, 1989, p. 1)." Clearly, there seems to be no doubt about the importance of this phase and its relative impact on the outcome of a game.

In terms of some general action principles for players to consider during this phase, we propose the following guidelines:

1. Throughout the course of the game, anticipate turnovers or transitions by preparing mentally for the required adjustment.

2. Read and react to the transitional play situation with maximum speed. The quicker the transition, the better the opportunity for an excellent scoring opportunity. On a quick change to offense, a team can take advantage of an opponent's mistake; a slow reaction will not allow you to capitalize on the error. On a quick change to defense, a team can recover positionally so as not to be outnumbered, all other factors being equal; a slow reaction will give the opposition a chance to score.

3. Before turning to offense, certain players away from the puck should tactfully screen or complete their checks to delay the backchecking efforts of the opponents.

4. The first pass is also critical; it should be a forward pass. If diagonal, the pass must be made to an accelerating forward; otherwise, you lose the precious time required to produce the potent counterattack.

5. Execute offensive or defensive principles depending on the direction of the transition with total intensity and as a 5-man unit. We often find a few members on the team not reacting to the transition because they feel that the other players are performing the required adjustments or tasks. Always play the game with the "what if" question in mind, from both an offensive and a defensive perspective. When in any doubt about the role you should play for the immediate moment, give priority to your defensive responsibilities, except for certain game situations (e.g. your team is down by two goals with only three minutes left in the game) which require a "high gamble" type of action.

6. Finally and most importantly, when a team changes to offense, forwards should rapidly move in circular and curvilinear patterns with interchange to develop speed and acceleration. Defensemen should also quickly join the attack to create a numerical advantage and/or possible second wave of attack. Remember that every second counts, and speed of execution during the transition is imperative for a successful counterattack.

Ludek Bukac (1983), a Czechoslovakian hockey expert, emphasized the importance of cyclic coordinated patterns of movement by stating that "[this] pattern of movement by all the players has a bearing, not only on their mobility, but also on the duration and length of movement in action as well as the ability to instantaneously react offensively or defensively (p. 108)." While commenting on this latest trend in movement — which he also referred to as "whole-ice play" — Bukac went so far as to say that in any situation and at any moment, it is possible to attack and defend at the same time. European coaches, especially the Soviets, have played a major role in initiating these new movement patterns on the whole 5-man unit, which have helped players adapt more easily and efficiently to transitional play. As Lener (1990) recently stated: "Quality teams are able to apply whole-ice play, unifying the defense with the offense (p. 1)."

9.4 Offense and Defense — A Duality

In the preface to this book, we suggested that the game of hockey can be compared in some ways to the game of chess. Our main tenet was that, like chess, hockey is a game of strategy. We would now like to expand on that analogy.

If you are somewhat familiar with the game of chess, you will readily acknowledge and appreciate that each move has an offensive and defensive dimension. For instance, if you are under serious attack, you will respond by moving a piece to protect, or at least reduce the threat against, your king, but at the same time calculating the offensive potential of your move. Similarly, if you are thinking of checking your opponent's king with a series of attacks, you will also weigh the relative risks of these moves in terms of vulnerability to your own defensive position or alignment of your chessmen. Pelchat et al. (1980) captured this point extremely well:

> The game of ice hockey has gradually come to be made up of highly diversified but integrated tactical systems, to the point where the organization of the attack originates in the organization of the defense, and conversely, the potential for the organization of the defense is part of the progress of the attack. In other words, the game of ice hockey is one integrated unit like the game

of chess: offensive movements are protected defensively, and defensive movements are potentially attacks (p. 13, our translation).

In hockey, this offensive-defensive relationship or duality also holds true, at least in a general sense. On the whole, we can legitimately say that many offensive movements are protected defensively and that, similarly, many defensive actions are also potentially the start of an attack. However, the game of hockey is not exactly like chess, and the differences must be pointed out in relation to this topic.

The game of hockey requires players to make many action-decisions. Even though a large majority of these decisions are voluntary, requiring that players acutely read and react to the playing situation, many of these decisions are reflexive or instinctive, due to the fast nature of the game. It is therefore inconceivable to expect players always to weigh the offensive-defensive value of each movement or action. In addition, because players on the ice routinely concentrate on accomplishing one specific task, such as protecting the puck, screening a player or shooting the puck under pressure, it is also unrealistic to expect players always to take into account this offensive-defensive interplay in the execution of their movements. The fact remains, however, that in many situations, action-decisions by the players are or should be based upon the relative merit of both the offensive and defensive components of the movement.

To complete our discussion of this subject, one other pertinent question must be raised. What factors influence players to select a more offensive or defensive-minded approach, whether on offense or defense? This question patently implies that the duality concept functions on a continuum, from a highly defensive to a highly offensive approach or orientation, rather than on an all-or-nothing basis. Again, in attempting to answer this question, many factors influence the approach a particular player − and by extension, a team − may adopt in regard to this offensive-defensive duality. Moreover, this is not a constant over the course of a season or game. *En passant*, we should mention that this subject is very closely linked to the topic of strategy because, directly or indirectly, we are referring to a game plan or approach in relation to the opposition. Before we leave this subject, let's look at the major factors that affect a player's mind-set, and consequently his actions, vis-à-vis this offensive-defensive duality. These are:

1. Individual tendencies
2. Composition of team
3. Coach's emphasis
4. Adjustment to opposition
5. Specific playing situation
6. Area or zone of play
7. Time remaining in game
8. Period (1st, 2nd, 3rd and overtime)
9. Stake in the outcome of the game
10. Other contextual factors

9.5 The Phases of an Attack

The various phases in an attack have been described by a number of North American coaches (Meagher, 1973; Watt, 1973; Smith, 1976; Schofield, 1979; Shero and Beaulieu, 1979; Vairo, 1980; Chambers, 1981; Smith, 1984; Gingras, 1986). European offensive systems have also undoubtedly had a profound influence on the way hockey coaches currently conceive the development and progression of an attack (Aldcorn, 1973; Bukac, 1977; Lindberg, 1977; Johansson and Lindstrom, 1980; Horsky, 1983; Evensson, 1984; Kostka et al., 1984; Larsson, 1986). Going over this material has inspired us, and helped us to formulate our own thoughts and insights on the attacking phases during the course of a game. These are:

1. Breakouts
2. Attacking in the neutral zone
3. Attacking in the offensive zone
4. Attacking the net

Now that we have set the stage, let's turn our attention to the development and progression of an attack.

9.5 The Phases of an Attack

10

Progression of an Attack

10.1 Introduction

Now that we've identified the various principles and concepts that foster movement and puck control for both individual and group tactical actions, we can turn our attention to developing and building a concerted attack in the direction of the opponents' net. Attacking, including the preparation of the attack, means progressing or advancing towards the opponents' end. *Progression of attack* is therefore our third fundamental principle of offense.

An effective attack must logically progress towards the opponents' net and culminate in an excellent shooting opportunity. The progression of an attack is characterized mainly by synchronized movements of the players, puck control and the ability to "strike" at the opportune moment, when the opposition is most vulnerable or off-guard. This requires a high degree of skill and coordination from both puck carier and players away from the puck. Partially based on Kostka et al. (1984), the success of a progressive attack depends more specifically upon:

1. The ability to maintain control of the puck in various 1 on 1 situations
2. Continuous movement by the players, especially the non-puck carriers, to maximize the support role by availability and/or other forms of support

3. Frequency, timing and accuracy of passing
4. Creating a favorable grouping around the puck carrier to overload (outman) the area
5. Mastery of all offensive combinations or group tactical actions
6. Perfect execution of the basic attack and counterattack formations and flow patterns
7. Players' ability to vary the pace and tempo (accelerate and decelerate)
8. The ability to attack or strike from various vantage points
9. Creative decision-making (reading and reacting) to come up with instant solutions for various defensive tactics
10. Exerting pressure on the defense through speed, quick passes and overloading

Most of these points can be dictated by the team in possession of the puck. However, we must recognize that the outcome of an attack also depends on the behavior of the opposition — a significant factor to consider. This illustrates the importance of reading, adjusting and reacting in a collective way to the opposition's defensive play and alignment. This is an extremely critical function of the entire coaching staff, not only in the advanced scouting of the opposition and in pre-game preparation of the players, but also in the adjustment of the game plan during a contest. Despite the importance of adjusting to the opposition's defensive play, a team must still master certain principles and concepts associated with a sustained and progressive attack.

Some of these principles and concepts have already been mentioned under the heading of movement and puck control; our emphasis at this point is on the effective development and progression of an attack. Once again, we must always keep a global and integrated view. We cannot dissociate the principles and concepts that fall under movement and puck control from those that fall under the progression of an attack.

We will first introduce these principles and concepts and then see how they apply to the different phases of the game. Many of these principles and concepts apply no matter where the attack originates and develops.

10.2   The Principle of Counterattacks

Counterattacks inherently represent a quick *transition* from defense (or the "undetermined" possession phase) to offense with the purpose of catching the opposition at a numerical or positional disadvantage. This transition is in reaction to a turnover. The primary emphasis is on minimizing the length of this transitional phase followed by a quick pass and forward acceleration. The result will be a "surprise" attack. For example, if a defenseman stops a 3 on 2 attack just inside his blue line with a smart play, he can "turn up" and quickly pass the puck to a forward (see Figure 10.1). Depending on the playing situation, of course, this quick forward pass will most likely create a numerical advantage. The defenseman could have chosen to pass laterally; this would not have produced a quick transition. In other words, you don't want to give the opposition time to recover their ideal defensive alignment. The key ingredients of a counterattack are surprise and quickness. Kostka et al. (1984) expressed their views on this subject:

> The degree of surprise and quickness of the entire action — the speed of all actions must be decisive in order to be successful since the opposition will be able to return into their own defensive zone within 7-10 seconds (p. 52).

There is one other issue related to the effective execution of a counterattack. It stems from the offensive-defensive duality theory described earlier in which we noted that players must anticipate and capitalize on turnovers. Meunier (1980) emphasized this point by stressing the importance of an aggressive backchecking system to prepare the eventual counterattack. With backchecking speed, the players are in the ideal mode to launch a rapid counterattack. In a discourse on Soviet hockey tactics, Ruel (1980) also supported this idea, stating that all [most] defensive actions must be turned into counterattacks. After regaining possession of the puck, a quick pass must be made *immediately*. This is based on the hypothesis that a puck can move faster than a player. Hence, the quickest way of launching a counterattack is by a quick pass, either diagonally or longitudinally.

Whether by a quick pass, rapid skating or both, the foundation of any effective counterattack is to maximize speed in the transition.

FIGURE 10.1   Counterattack from an intercepted pass

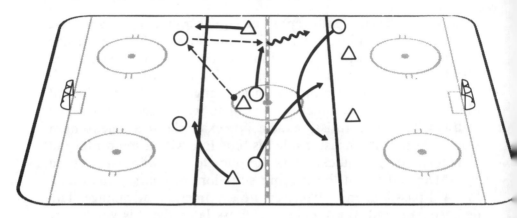

In many playing situations, the counterattack represents the first priority rather than regrouping or getting organized. This is an extremely critical and quite often difficult decision to be made by the puck carrier who has just regained possession of the puck. Somewhere in between lies the decision to establish good puck control. Sometimes you have no decision to make because the pressure is so intense that your first action/reaction is more defensive than offensive. This of course depends on the specific playing situation as well as the playing context, such as the amount of time remaining in the game or whether you are leading or trailing on the score board.

There is also a higher risk associated with opting for a counterattack rather than the more controlled regrouping or puck control option. If the initial action (usually a pass) of the counterattack fails, you may find yourself vulnerable to the opposition's own counterattack. The decision rests on the shoulders of the puck carrier; he must read and react, choosing what's best for the team.

In summary, effective counterattacks are created by:

1. Rapid transition from defense to offense
2. Quick pass(es)
3. Speed and acceleration of players

The principle of counterattacking is imperative to any potent offense. It is a very important factor in the execution of many fast

breakouts; and, as we shall discover later, counterattacks can originate from virtually anywhere on the ice — defensive, neutral or
offensive zone. The Soviets have incorporated this idea into their
attacks, as we have seen in many international competitions.
Aldcorn (1973), describing certain Soviet attacking tendencies,
made the following comment:

> You will recall that one of the basic tenets of Soviet hockey is the
> concept of counterattacks. This simply means that upon gaining
> control of the puck in their own end [...] the immediate reaction of
> the puck carrier and his teammates is to counterattack or create a
> play which is designed to move the play up ice as quickly as possible
> in order to get the [opponents] at a disadvantage (p. 9).

10.3 The Principle of Regrouping

The object of regrouping is to reorganize the movements of the
players to produce a more threatening attack. Frequently, an attack
is met with a solid defensive alignment, and rather than clearing
the puck off the boards or "dumping" with the risk of losing
possession, the more rational decision is to retreat and regroup. The
principle of regrouping is based on sound judgement, the specific
playing context and overall team strategy dictated by the coaching
staff. Regrouping can occur in the defensive or neutral zone, the latter
being more frequent.

For example, let us consider an attack taking place in the high
neutral zone. If your team is behind in the score and time is a factor, your best option would most likely be to "throw" the puck in
and try to regain possession. The puck carrier may even insist on
trying to beat the defense. Given the situation, it may be worth the
risk. At times, the defensive alignment is such that you have little
choice but to "dump and chase," and regrouping would not change
their "standing up at the blue line" type of defense. But let's face up
to reality! There are many worthy occasions in which a team should
regroup.

The principle of regrouping consists of knowing when to back-
track for better development and progression of the attack. This
principle can be applied in the normal organization of an attack *or*

in the case of reorganizing an attack (as described above) due to the difficulties of penetrating the opponents' blue line with good puck control.

Inspired by Boulonne et al. (1976) and Vairo (1980), the principle of regrouping is derived from the interaction of the following concepts:

1. Back-passing and/or carrying the puck back
2. Spreading the defense with one higher than the other
3. Forwards interchanging, accelerating and developing good width (lanes) and depth (zones)
4. Isolation with eventual support
5. Improvising to "take" whatever the defense is giving

Let's explore each of these concepts to more fully appreciate the mechanics behind the principle of regrouping. Refer to Figure 10.2.

1. *Back-passing* simply creates more time and space, both for the defense receiving the puck and for the non-puck carriers. The puck has moved from an area of intense action to a place where there is more room to maintain good puck control. This is logically the only place to reorganize the next attack.
2. *Spreading the defense* as shown provides support both offensively and defensively in case of a mishap. More space is also created for the accelerating forwards.
3. *Interchanging with balance (width and depth)* produces an attack which is very difficult to cover. The degree of balance desired is of course dependent on the defensive alignment; however, as a general rule it is advantageous to "spread out" in the middle of the neutral zone. Flow and counterflow movements are also important to add spice to the attack. Remember, we are always attempting to confuse and surprise the opposition.
4. *Isolating* an attacker (or attackers) is usually performed by means of a lateral pass with the purpose of gaining either territorial or numerical advantage (overload). The classic example comes from the sport of football, where a receiver breaks for the end zone while the rest of the receivers execute a "short" pattern. In hockey, a long or wide pass produces the same effect. It allows the attacker(s) more time and space to

FIGURE 10.2   Regrouping

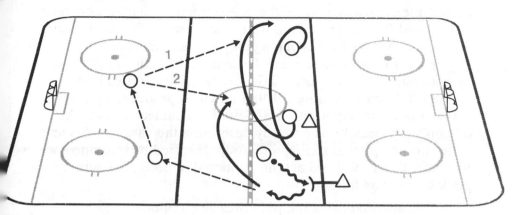

execute an individual or group tactical action on defenders who are trying to recover or adjust from the newly established point of attack. In certain play situations, isolating a player and/or the area of attack also implies support to maximize the action. This is clearly the case in a power play situation, when the "point" man forces the defender to move in a certain direction to free a forward ready for a one-time shot. The whole tactical action is aimed at isolating the shooter.

5. *Improvising* is a necessary ingredient in hockey due to the ever-changing nature of the game. As we have seen, the modern hockey player must continually read and react to adjust to the specific playing situation. While respecting the fundamental principles and principles of movement, players must still be given enough room for creativity and improvisation. This is what makes the game of hockey so exciting.

To improvise is to produce an action without prior thought or preparation. Many successful group tactical actions are a result of creative, spur-of-the-moment decisions. Improvisation also means adjusting to the defensive formation, and exploiting defensive weaknesses by finding attack solutions to situations and relationships among teammates. No two plays in hockey are ever exactly alike. The power of your intellect, imagination and creativity must be brought to bear on your individual and group tactical actions.

The success of a regroup depends on the interaction between defensemen and forwards — the defensemen as quarterbacks read the play while the forwards move to locate space for the eventual active pass. Although a regrouping play is often initiated by a simple back pass from a forward to a defenseman, the actions that follow, by both puck and non-puck carriers, determine the effectiveness of the attack. Wayne Fleming (1989), in a video produced by Hockey Canada in cooperation with the Canadian Amateur Hockey Association, emphasizes this point by describing the various roles and actions of the players during a regroup. Inspired by this video, we have identified roles and actions (options) of both puck and non-puck carriers as follows:

1. Defenseman with the puck has five options:

    1) Quick up, that is, a quick lead pass to a forward
    2) Quick turn-up toward the middle or outside lane followed by a pass
    3) Drag to the middle to create more passing options
    4) Pass laterally to his partner to shift the origin of the attack
    5) Carry the puck

2. Defenseman without the puck has four support options:

    1) Staggered or diagonal position to receive a pass
    2) Skate behind to create a drop pass option
    3) Support above to accept a forward pass
    4) Support by picking or screening a checker

3. Forwards should think about the following actions:

    1) Interchanging
    2) Locating space more than once
    3) Control skating to establish perfect timing
    4) Establishing good receiving angle
    5) Accelerating into pass
    6) Screening away from the puck
    7) Low forward supporting the defense and/or creating second wave
    8) Middle forward available for quick up
    9) High forward (decoyer) stretching the defense

The defenseman with the puck must read the oncoming pressure and select the best option. Non-puck carriers must also read the play and choose the most appropriate support role. Communication, reading and reacting and quick judgement are the key ingredients in producing a successful regroup. Reading the play means not only looking at what the opposition is doing, but also observing the movement of your teammates. This latter point is especially important to non-puck carriers attempting to choose the optimal support role. In Chapter 12, we will describe some specific regrouping plays.

10.4 Camouflaged Attacks

Closely linked to the ability to improvise is the concept of camouflaged attacks, also referred to as indirect attacks. As mentioned earlier, many successful attacks contain the element of surprise. Hockey players are not chameleons capable of disguise by changing colors, but they can conceal themselves in certain tactical actions. A camouflaged attack is often accompanied by an unorthodox movement of a particular player. One example would be in a power play situation, when a defenseman slowly moves down into the slot while defenders are looking elsewhere (see Figure 10.3), or when two speedy forwards cross diagonally in front of a defenseman to execute the shuttle play (see Figure 10.4). In both instances, the attack is camouflaged. In the first instance, the attack is completely hidden from all defenders, while in the second the attack is anticipated *but* not entirely revealed. In a split second there can be a different puck carrier moving in the opposite direction. The defenseman is momentarily frozen because the players are concealing or camouflaging the eventual direction of the attack.

10.5 The Marriage of Overload and Balance

During the course of an attack, there is a time and place for overloading but also for balance produced by spreading out or dispersing. Area overload mainly provides close support to the puck carrier, while dispersion stretches out the entire attack and the defense. Both overload and dispersion have their place and time, depending on the situation and the phase of the attack. As a general rule, it is wise to have both width and depth somewhere in the development of an attack, especially in the neutral (including the extended zone) and offensive zones. Establishing width and depth has also been referred to as a *balanced* attack (see Figures 10.5 to 10.7).

Overload and balance are not necessarily opposing principles. They can coexist at the same moment in time. In the course of an attack, balance can be created by a certain number of forwards while area overload (such as a 2 on 1) can be accomplished by others. Furthermore, balance does not necessarily imply that all three lanes and areas of a zone must always be occupied. This is especially true when you are working in a more restricted area of the rink, such as the offensive zone (see Figure 10.8). The object of balance is to force the defense to spread out in their coverage while overload creates a group tactical advantage in a particular area.

Kingston (1981) explained the complementary nature of these principles:

> These principles [balance and spreading out] may seem to be contrary to that of area overload or numerical superiority, but it must be borne in mind that two or three or sometimes four players can create numerical superiority while the remaining number of players create balance and spreading out. In fact both sets of principles and techniques should operate simultaneously in order to make offensive team play more effective (p. 13).

FIGURE 10.3   Camouflaged attack (power play situation)

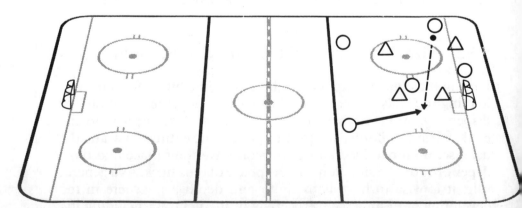

FIGURE 10.4   Camouflaged attack (shuttle play)

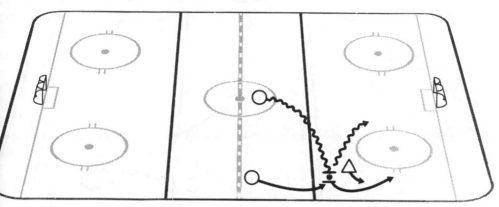

FIGURE 10.5   Developing depth by back passing

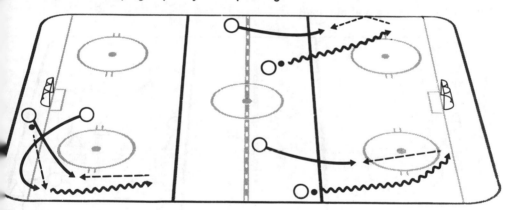

FIGURE 10.6   Developing width by lateral passing

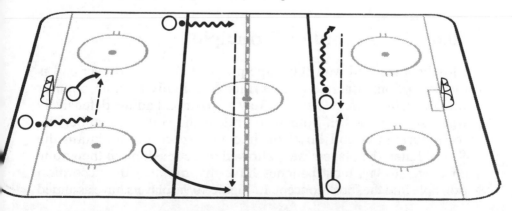

FIGURE 10.7   Developing width and depth by diagonal passing

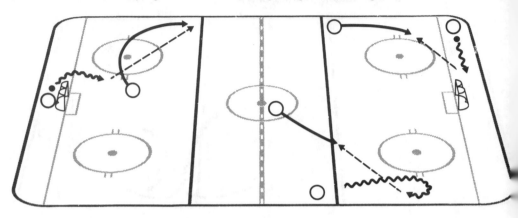

FIGURE 10.8   Balance and overload

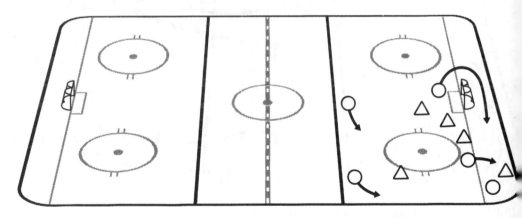

10.6   The Accordion Principle

Closely associated with the principles of balance and overload is the accordion principle. This principle initially became popular when coaches were describing how to align and adjust defensively when shorthanded in your own end of the rink. Remember the "box" formation and how you had to respect and maintain the "box"? Later, the players were allowed more freedom in their zone coverage. Today, most coaches have incorporated the accordion principle into the "box" concept. In Figure 10.9a, players have assumed a more expanded "box" formation with the puck close to the side. In Figure 10.9b, the puck is deep (low); hence the "box" formed by the players is tighter or smaller. Drake (1985), describing the many ways the box can be modified, stated: "This requires continuous disciplined adjustment − stretching and shrinking − good stick and foot positioning to minimize the high percentage chances to score"(p. 95).

On *offense*, the same accordion principle can be applied. Players can swarm (overload) an area and a split-second later disperse to create more balance (width and depth) in the attack formation. This principle is particularly effective during a loose puck situation (the "undetermined possession" phase). King (1983) discussed the positional responsibilities of forwards in the offensive zone:

> One of the most difficult things in offensive team play is what I call the "accordion principle." This means that sometimes you may have three players in one area to gain control of a loose puck, but once you do, then you spread out again (p. 67).

> On a loose puck they [the Europeans] overload − they have three guys in one small area − then when they get it [the puck], before you realize it they have expanded again. THEY STRETCH THE DEFENSE AND CAUSE A LOT OF THINGS TO HAPPEN. This principle doesn't seem to exist enough in our game (p. 68).

Here's an example to illustrate the application of the accordion principle on offense. In Figure 10.10a there is a 1 on 1 battle for a loose puck by the side of the boards in the neutral zone. The non-puck carriers read this situation and swarm in for close support in a circular pattern to maintain movement (overload phase). Having recovered the puck (see Figure 10.10b), the players now disperse to provide various forms of support (expanded phase).

In summary, the accordion principle incorporates the concepts of balance and overload. The principle can be applied on offense and defense and in all the different phases of an attack under normal, power play or penalty killing situations. And, as we mentioned above, this principle also has particular relevance when a team is switching from the "undetermined possession" to the attacking phase.

FIGURE 10.9a   Expanded "box" formation

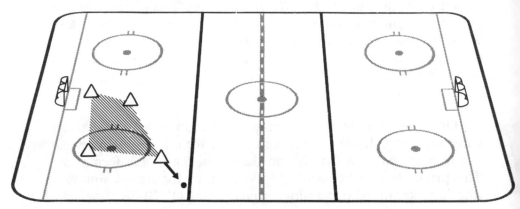

FIGURE 10.9b   Collapsed "box" formation

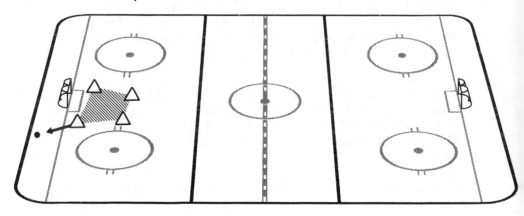

FIGURE 10.10a   Overload phase (fighting for possession)

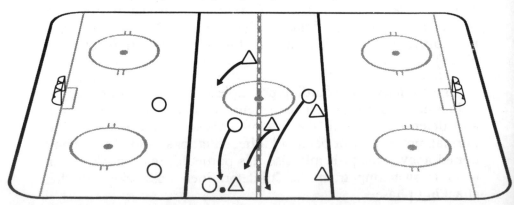

FIGURE 10.10b   Expanded phase (after regaining possession)

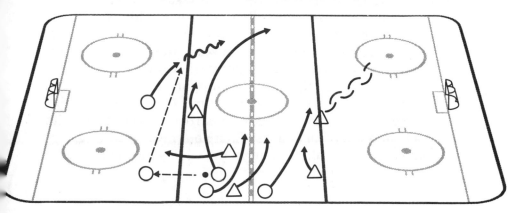

10.7 The Principle of Pressure

Applying pressure on the defenders will force them to retreat, weaken their defensive alignment, catch them off-guard or place them in a vulnerable position. Pressure also includes movement of non-puck carriers (see Figures 10.11 and 10.12). The principle of pressure is created by:

1. *Speed and acceleration* of all players combined with quick puck movement to establish a high tempo game. For the puck carrier in the offensive zone, this is accomplished either by "driving" to the net or by an outside drive to force the defenseman to commit himself. In the defensive zone on a breakout play, a puck carrier will also create more pressure by moving with speed. Flow and counter flow also produce favorable conditons on breakouts. For the non-puck carriers, this means assuming the various support roles. Movement by all five men, as described in an earlier chapter, creates an attack which is always more difficult for the opposition to cover.

2. *Numerical advantage* or outnumbering (overloading) the opposition where the puck is located. Overloading an area not only favors puck control but also produces an attack which is more difficult to guard against.

3. *Concentration of attack* to isolate or pressure a defender, especially as you near the offensive zone. This will create pressure on the defender(s) who have to contend with the attack, forcing the defender to make a wrong decision in his zone or man coverage. At the point where the attacker(s) isolates or challenges the defender, support should be provided as a means of creating extra pressure. The idea of isolating an attacker which we discussed earlier is also linked with concentration of an attack. When an army is attacking, they will select the weakest point in the enemy line and attack it with all their might.

FIGURE 10.11   Principle of pressure

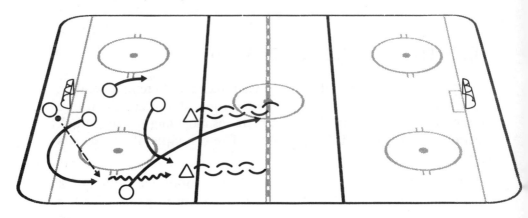

FIGURE 10.12   Applying pressure

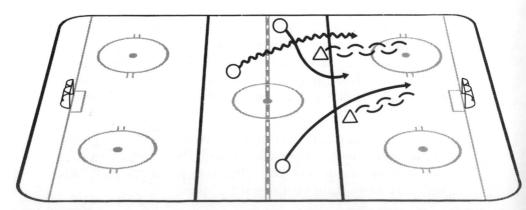

10.8   The Principle of Waves of Attack

Multi-waves of attack are created by the movement of players flushing through a certain area or zone of the ice. The concept of attacking waves in the *offensive* zone has received a great deal of attention in hockey manuals and at coaching seminars (King, 1981, 1984; Kingston, 1981; Evensson, 1983). However, waves of attack can also be applied in breakouts and while attacking through the neutral zone, as we shall see later.

Waves of attack occur along the length of the ice, that is, longitudinally. They are created by the puck carrier and non-puck carriers (the supporting cast) as they move through a particular zone one after another in a relatively short period of time. The object is to provide a sustained attack, give the puck carrier maximum support and put pressure on the net to create a good scoring opportunity.

Attacking in waves is almost a natural phenomenon when penetrating the offensive zone. The puck carrier leads the attack to avoid the off-side, the other forwards enter the zone and the defensemen move up quickly to complete the support from behind. There are a host of group tactical actions and team plays characterized by waves of attack. Let us examine one in detail as a team enters the offensive zone (see Figure 10.13). The waves can be classified as follows:

First wave :   puck carrier enters the zone with another forward driving to the net

Second wave :   forward (trailer) moves into high slot area

Third wave :   defensemen support the attack by closely following the play to inside the blue line

When discussing the principle of waves, we should also introduce what is commonly referred to as the concept of delays. As the term implies, the attack is purposely delayed by the puck carrier executing a tight turn near the boards (usually) to buy time for the second wave of attackers. Occasionally, the puck carrier is forced to think of delaying the attack due to the reaction of the opponent.

FIGURE 10.13   Waves of attack

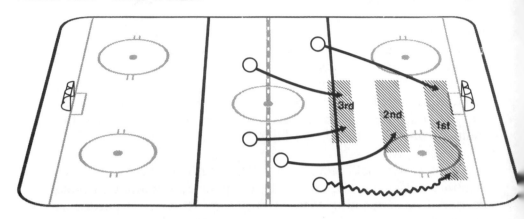

These delays can be classified as *high*, *middle* or *low* depending on where the puck carrier executes the turn (see Figure 10.14). The quality of execution of these turns is vital to the play. The puck carrier must first drive to the outside, forcing the defender to retreat; second, he must execute the turn quickly to prepare for the pass intended for the second wave of attackers; and finally, protect the puck from the defenseman pressuring him along the boards. In short, the success of the delay depends on the fine technical and tactical skills of the puck carrier.

Closely integrated with the concept of waves are two other principles or concepts. A number of Canadian writers (King, 1981; Kingston, 1981; Siciliano, 1985; Intermediate Level Coaches Manual, 1989) have commonly referred to these as *triangluation* and the *1-2-3 principle of attack*. Let us examine the meaning of each.

1. **Triangulation** is created by the first and second waves of an attack. More specifically, it is accomplished by the puck carrier and two other players creating the width and depth (see Figure 10.15). Because triangulation is characterized by width and depth, it has the effect of stretching the defense both longitudinally and laterally. This gives the puck carrier (and succeeding puck carriers), more time and space and produces an ideal three-man attack formation against most defensive alignments. The concept of a triangle or triangulation is also common in other team sports. It represents one of the best configurations three players can create in most attacking situations.

FIGURE 10.14   Delays : high, middle and low

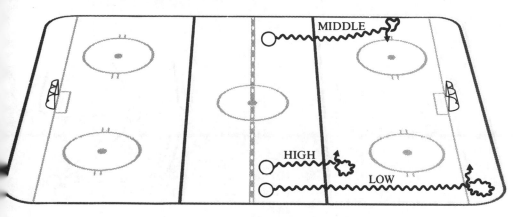

FIGURE 10.15   Triangulation

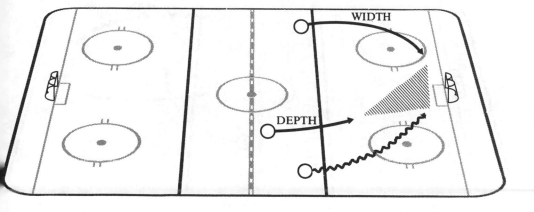

In a five-man attack, multiple triangles can also be created to enhance puck control, interchange and support. Figure 10.16 shows this formation along with interchange when the puck switches corners.

2. **The 1-2-3 principle of attack** is also created by the first and second waves of an attack and also incorporates the idea of triangulation. The difference is that players are identified by a number representing a distinct role (see Figure 10.17). These player roles are:

FIGURE 10.16   Multiple triangles

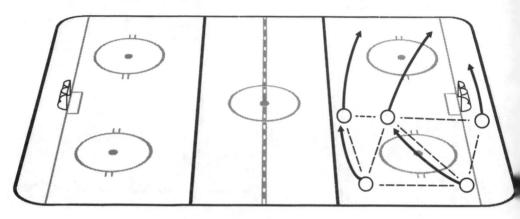

FIGURE 10.17   1-2-3 principle of attack

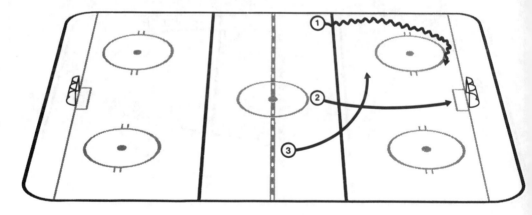

1. The *puck carrier* creates outside pressure by driving to the net (first wave).
2. The *second attacker* creates pressure to the net and produces width in the attack (first wave).
3. The *third attacker* assumes the trailer position producing depth in the attack (second wave).

The main objective of the puck carrier and the second attacker in the 1-2-3 principle of attack is to penetrate the offensive zone as deeply as possible. This will force the defenders deep on the first wave of attack and open up the slot area for the trailer representing the second wave. Some hockey coaches have referred to this as the principle of penetration.

It is important to emphasize that the 1-2-3 principle of attack is not always the preferred tactical play when entering the offensive zone. Although this particular play can be very effective, other group tactical plays, as described in Chapter 8, might be much more appropriate, depending on the defensive alignment.

The principle of attacking waves is most prevalent in the offensive zone; however, waves of attack, as mentioned earlier, can also be created in the defensive and neutral zones, even though flow and counterflow movements are more common in these zones. Flow patterns are more generally associated with maintaining puck control and regrouping, whereas waves of attack are more for progression, penetration and pressure. This partially explains why flow and counterflow patterns occur more frequently in the neutral zone, including the extended zone.

Figures 10.18 to 10.20 illustrate the application of the principle of waves in the defensive and neutral zones. During breakouts, waves are quite often associated with overloading and close support; in neutral ice play, waves are more closely related to interchanging and delays for timely penetration of the offensive zone.

FIGURE 10.18   Waves of attack

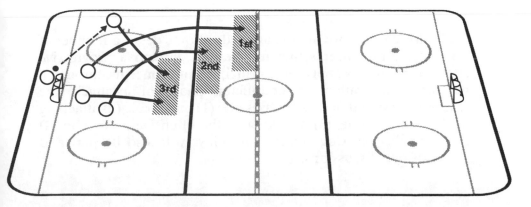

FIGURE 10.19 Waves of attack

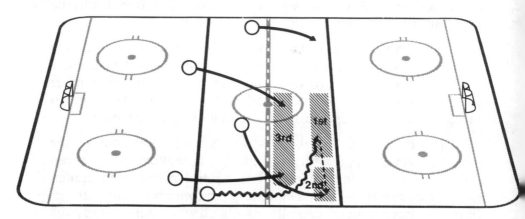

FIGURE 10.20 Waves of attack (first wave : players 4, 5 and 6 ; second wave : player 3)

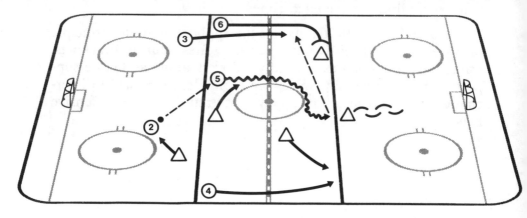

In this chapter, we have examined in some detail a number of principles and concepts that initiate and develop a progressive attack. We will now apply these principles and concepts, through a number of illustrations, to the different phases of an attack. The reader will recall that these phases are: (1) breakouts, (2) attacking in the neutral zone, (3) attacking in the offensive zone, and (4) attacking the net. Counterattacking plays will also be part and parcel of our discussions.

11

Breakouts

11.1 An Overview

The ability to effectively move the puck out of your own end is both an important defensive measure and the start of an attack. For these two basic reasons, it is imperative for every coach to establish some reliable breakout plays early in the season. Some coaches go so far as to say that the success of a team rests directly upon its ability to break out after regaining possession of the puck. Many teams who regain control of the puck in their own end fail to break out and consequently must return to defense, thus giving the opposition the advantage to re-attack in the most critical or vulnerable area of the rink. No turn-over is more dangerous than one which occurs in your defensive end. The common saying that "the best defense is a sound offense" is particularly meaningful in the context of breakouts — regaining and moving the puck out of your end successfully.

Some important observational studies and subsequent analysis (Bukac and Safarik, 1971; Dyotte and Ruel, 1976; Kostka, 1976; Littsola, 1976; Neale, 1976; Thifault et al., 1978; Pelchat et al., 1980;

International Ice Hockey Federation, 1981; Horsky, 1983) have revealed a number of interesting facts about breakouts. Specifically, the study by Pelchat et al. (1980) that we have chosen to describe looked at the frequency and relative value of various breakouts when the point of departure was primarily from behind the goal line. As we shall see later, it is important to establish and practice breakout plays based upon the location from which the puck is brought back. For this particular study, however, the discussion focuses on breakout plays that originate from behind the goal line. These descriptive statistics were noted at the 1971 World Championships.

The findings suggest that the most frequent (almost 30 %) and most effective way (almost 90 %) of breaking out was when one player carried the puck, especially through the middle lane. Peculiar as this may seem at first glance for a *team* sport such as hockey, there are two logical reasons for this. One, if no passes are made, the element of error is minimized; second, since many players tend to move or are limited to moving in the "quiet zones" to control the puck, this often leaves more open space in the middle lane. This of course depends on the specific playing situation, the type of forechecking used by the opposition and the ability of the puck carrier. It is interesting to note, however, that this option ranked highest in terms of both frequency and rate of success (see Figure 11.1).

A close second with a frequency of almost 30 % and an efficiency of 80 % is when a defenseman behind or in front of the goal line passes to a winger near the boards by the hash marks. The success of this particular play depends to a large extent on the direction or circular movement of the receiver. If the receiver obtains the pass while he is moving towards the middle lane, there is a greater likelihood that he will successfully come out of the defensive zone (see Figure 11.2). Again, this depends on a host of factors, but in the main, it is advisable for the receiver to get the pass at that specific moment in his skating pattern. A variation or subsequent step in this play is to make a second pass towards the middle lane, up towards the blue line (see Figure 11.3). This also increases the degree of success of the breakout play. The pass to the receiver by the boards is often referred to as an "outlet" pass, and rightly so, because it is quite often the only option a defenseman has in attempting to move the puck out of the zone.

FIGURE 11.1 Breakout option

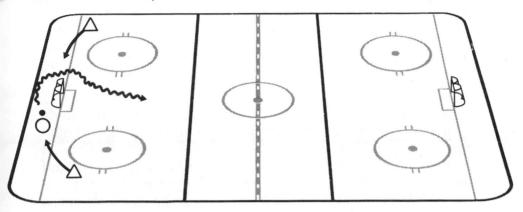

FIGURE 11.2 Breakout option

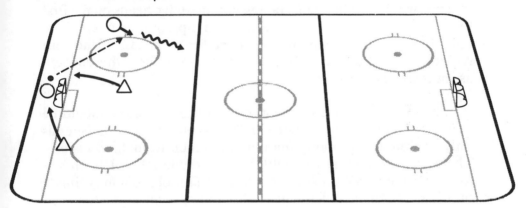

FIGURE 11.3 Breakout option

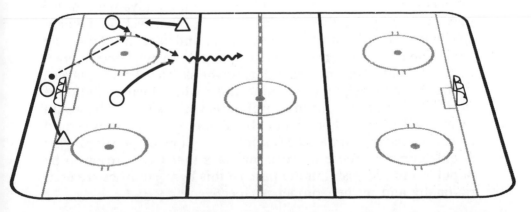

The third, fourth and fifth most popular breakouts in the study were each used approximately 10 % of the time, each having a success rate of roughly 70 %. These breakouts were: defense to defense and to a winger by the boards; defense to center in the middle lane; and defense to high forward off the boards (see Figures 11.4 to 11.6).

But what does this study — or for that matter any study — reveal? How should we interpret such findings? How should coaches use these statistics? Descriptive statistics pinpoint important tendencies, trends, probabilities and likely occurrences; they *do not* reliably predict occurrences, not to mention the outcome of a single event. The flip of a coin is the classic example. Even though we can reasonably expect a 50 : 50 ratio between heads and tails over a large number of trials, there is no guarantee that this will in fact happen. Having obtained five heads on the first five trials does not mean that the next five flips, or even one, will be tails. The probability remains the same for every toss of the coin regardless of the previous results. Statisticians refer to this concept as mutually exclusive events.

Statistics or the interpretation of statistics in hockey should be perceived in the same manner. Coaches should look at statistics as only one indicator among many upon which to make decisions. There are just too many variables in hockey to rely solely on statistics, whether in terms of briefing a team on the opposition or simply on where, when and what type of shot to use in various situations. However, statistics can and should play a function in coaching decisions. For example, in the above study on the types of breakout plays commonly deployed, it would be extremely advantageous for players to recognize these tendencies both offensively and defensively; this would increase their reading and reacting skills. The coach should also be encouraged to review these breakouts in practice first. In addition and depending on the skill level of the players, it would also be helpful to examine under what playing conditions (forechecking pattern for instance) these various breakouts would be most effective. Although other breakouts and variations should be considered or emphasized (for instance, during a power-play), it is only common sense to work on plays that have proven to be popular and successful in the past. In this light, statistics are used rationally and in their proper perspective.

FIGURE 11.4   Breakout option

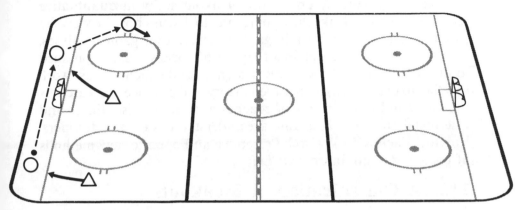

FIGURE 11.5   Breakout option

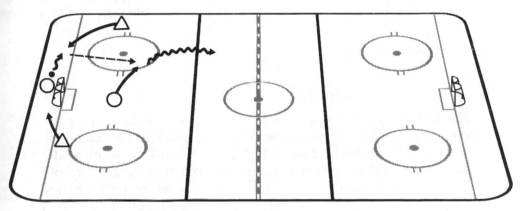

FIGURE 11.6   Breakout option

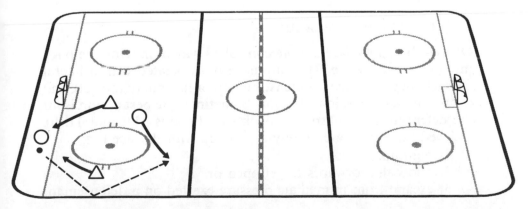

Our slight digression from the main subject of breakouts was intentional. Having described the breakout study in quantitative terms, we wanted to take the opportunity to discuss how we view the proper use of research findings. We believe that game analyses, observations and research in all aspects of hockey must be pursued to further advance our game. Researchers and coaches must work together to bridge the gap between theory and practice. Researchers must respond to the needs of coaches as well as disseminate and interpret their results in a language understood by the practitioners. Finally, coaches must also be receptive and open to new methods of coaching (Chouinard and Lefroy, 1987).

11.2 A Classification of Breakouts

Breakouts are classified in a number of ways. Using *time of execution* as the primary factor to describe them, we can classify breakouts as:

1. Fast
2. Delayed
3. Patterned

11.2.1 Fast breakouts

Fast breakouts are accomplished by means of a long pass (or two very quick passes) combined with skating speed and acceleration. A team should think about using the fast breakout when under heavy forechecking or when attempting to counterattack, or both (see Figures 11.7 and 11.8). A "fast" breakout, as the term implies, basically means that the team is opting for the quickest way to get the puck out of their end while still attempting to keep control of the puck.

11.2.2 Delayed breakouts

Delayed breakouts are a more controlled way of moving the puck into the neutral zone. They are usually associated with a lateral pass first (e.g., defense to defense behind or in front of the net), and later a forward pass, long or short. Sometimes the best option is for the defenseman to carry the puck (see Figures 11.9 and 11.10). Delayed breakouts are closely associated with the need to:
1) regroup
2) allow the forwards to get open or
3) escape from immediate pressure exerted on a defenseman.

FIGURE 11.7   Fast breakout

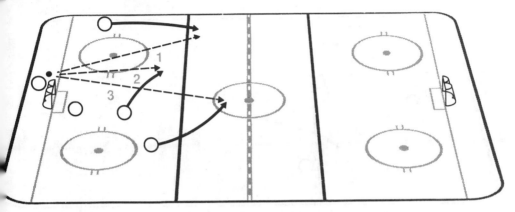

FIGURE 11.8   Fast breakout from defensive alignment

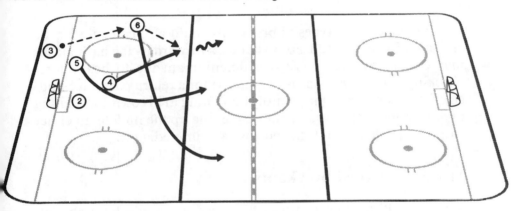

FIGURE 11.9   Delayed breakout

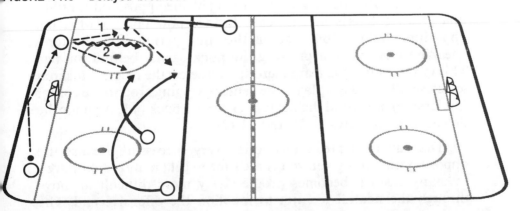

FIGURE 11.10   Delayed breakout

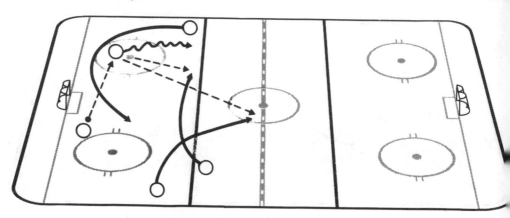

Of course, other types of breakouts could also come under the classification of delayed. For instance, a forward by the hash marks may choose to back pass to a defenseman due to heavy forechecking and move towards the middle for a return pass (give-and-go). Or a puck carrier may simply be skating in his own end waiting to draw opposing forwards before passing up the middle. In either case, the puck was not moved forward immediately.

11.2.3   Patterned breakouts

A patterned breakout is most often used when you have enough time to set up a specific play known by all the attacking players, most commonly when the forechecking by the opposition is rather unaggressive. This is often the case during a power play or when the opposition holds a big lead in the final period with the forechecking forwards not pressing the puck carrier behind the net. This lets the attacking team regroup and select the type of breakout to be used. The classic play is the center swinging around the corner (preferable) or behind the net to pick up the puck or leave it for the defenseman (Figures 11.11 and 11.12).

The patterned breakout is often very successful because the opposing team has given you some time to get organized; however, in many cases it becomes progressively more difficult to move through the neutral ice, not to mention the offensive end. The defense may have allowed you to break out of your end, but allowing you to penetrate into the optimal shooting area is "a horse of a different color."

The various breakouts all have their time and place during the course of a game, and each has its own advantages and drawbacks. Sometimes you have control over which breakout to use, but in many cases, the situation dictates your options. Fast breakouts emphasize the quickness of moving the puck out of the defensive zone while sacrificing – relatively speaking – certain principles of attack such as puck control. Patterned breakouts emphasize puck control rather than speed, thus allowing the opposition – relatively speaking again – more time to adjust defensively. Delayed breakouts lie somewhere in between the two.

While fast breakouts and counterattacks often complement each other, there is a slight difference. A counterattack, as you will recall from the previous chapter, relates to the rapid transition from defense to offense. Fast breakouts, on the other hand, emphasize the quickness of exiting the zone. A fast breakout, for example, could be used after having regained possession for some time. In this case, the fast breakout is not a counterattack.

Several other types of breakouts also merit special mention:

FIGURE 11.11 Patterned breakout

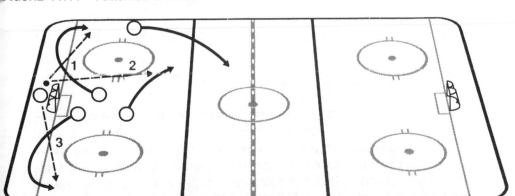

FIGURE 11.12   Patterned breakout

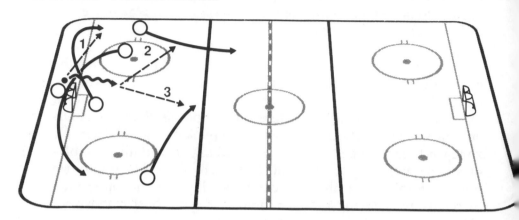

A. The reverse

The reverse breakout can be one of the most effective ways of sur-
prising the opposition when forecheckers have already committed
themselves. It reverses the flow of the attack which gives the puck
carrier more time and space to break out of his own end (Figures
11.13 and 11.14).

B. The natural or situational breakout

Since breakouts can commence from practically anywhere in the
defensive zone, we can also describe them in terms of where the
team regains possession of the puck, the potential start of a breakout play. We refer to these as natural or situational breakouts.
Breakout possibilities vary according to the location of the puck.
The possible scenarios are almost infinite, but we have selected two
in Figures 11.15 and 11.16.

C. From face-off situations

By extension, we can also analyze breakouts from face-off situations. Since these breakouts begin from a static alignment, it is
possible to develop set plays around face-offs, describing the role of
every player in the event of winning the draw. As a matter of fact,
this is a very good place for coaches to begin working on breakout
plays, as in football (see Figures 11.17 to 11.20).

FIGURE 11.13   Reverse

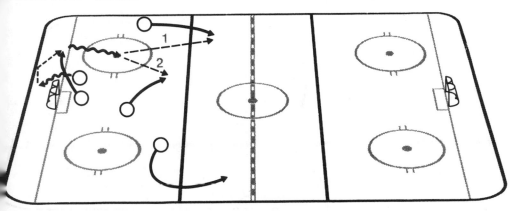

FIGURE 11.14   Reverse

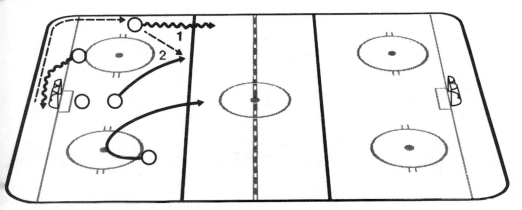

FIGURE 11.15   Situational breakout (quick turn-up)

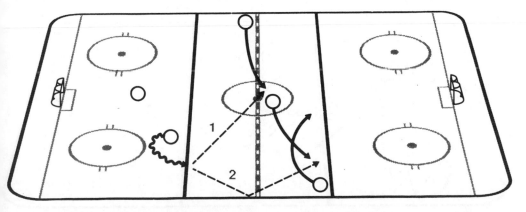

FIGURE 11.16   Situational breakout (regroup)

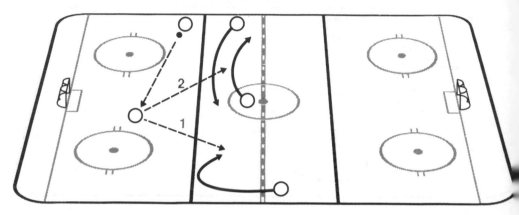

FIGURE 11.17   Breakout from face-off

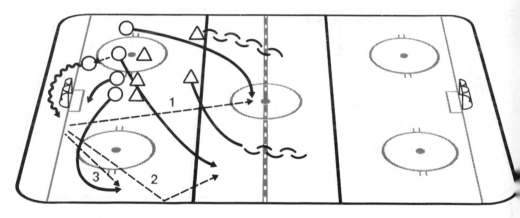

FIGURE 11.18   Breakout from face-off

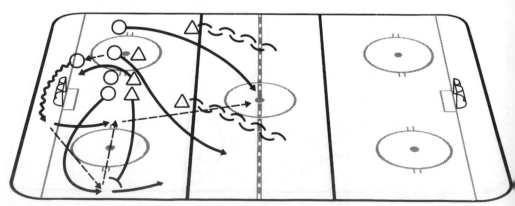

FIGURE 11.19   Breakout from face-off

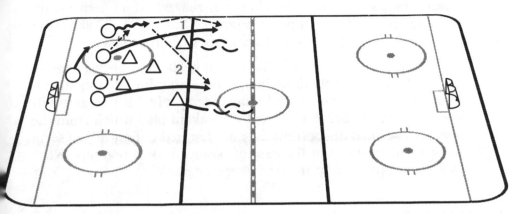

FIGURE 11.20   Breakout from face-off (reverse)

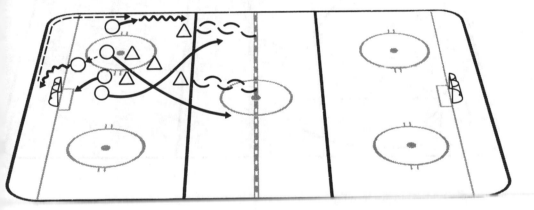

D.   *Flow breakout*

A flow breakout is basically characterized by the coordination of a number of players turning or skating in the same direction. This type of motion, as we have seen earlier, produces a numerical advantage, usually in the area of the puck. European hockey teams are known for this style of breakout as well as other offensive plays. Regrouping, flow (primary and secondary) and interchanging positions are all closely related to this type of breakout. Most of the breakout plays described above contain flow; some even contain secondary flow. Flow breakouts are usually more effective than linear breakouts. They are characterized by more movement, pressure, overload and support. Figures 11.21 and 11.22 show the difference between flow and linear types of breakouts.

At this point, we would like to emphasize the need in many breakout plays to apply the principle of regrouping, starting again. Think how many times it would have been profitable to regroup in your own end rather than accept a breakout play which from the very start seemed uncoordinated and destined to failure. We seem to be more receptive in the case of power plays to regroup. Why? Why not apply this principle in regular play?

FIGURE 11.21   Flow breakout

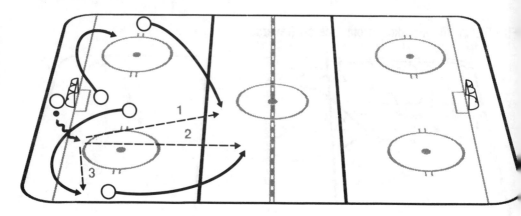

FIGURE 11.22   Linear breakout

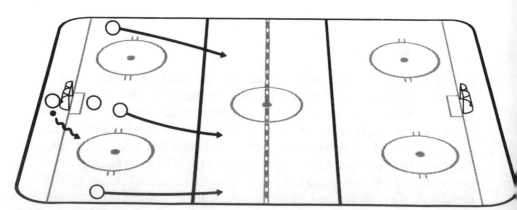

Regardless of the type of play utilized to move the puck out of your own end, some action principles should be followed to increase the success of the breakout play. In brief, these are:

1. All players should be in motion, even if this requires the receiver to remain in a relatively confined area (e.g. outlet pass to receiver close to the hash marks). Flow should also be incorporated in the movement of the players.

2. At least two players should be truly available to receive a pass (this creates options).

3. Crossing, circular and curvilinear patterns should prevail over linear (longitudinal) skating.

4. One player should, depending on the playing context, provide *close* support to the puck carrier.

5. One player could, on occasion, provide support by screening for the puck carrier or the players away from the puck.

6. Two options or passes should be established; one long for the fast break, the other short for a more controlled or delayed breakout.

7. One player (usually a defenseman) should assume a more defensive role — a defensive approach or mind-set in the eventuality of a turn-over. This may seem to contradict the principle that all five men should join the attack; however, until there is "clear" possession of the puck outside the blue line, this precautionary measure should be taken.

8. And finally, depending on the situation, a player could assume the role of clearing to create more space for the puck carrier or decoying to spread the defense.

Although many breakouts may appear to involve only one or two players in the execution of the play, it is nevertheless crucial that all players assume an appropriate role — as described in the above principles — to enhance the likelihood of success. The perfect pass to an open winger (a group tactical action) is what seems most evident and important; however, the players *away* from the puck also play a significant role, not only in terms of the breakout but also in regard to later plays. This latter point epitomizes the notion of team play.

11.3   Other Breakout Plays

We complete our analysis by illustrating some other breakout plays, including some effective counterattack, regrouping and goalie-initiated plays. Once again, which breakout play should be used to come out of your own end depends strictly on the specific playing context (see Figures 11.23 to 11.28).

FIGURE 11.23   Delayed breakout with flow (player 3 passes to an open space for player 2)

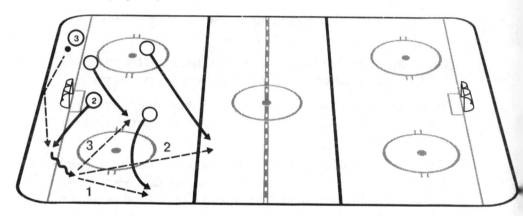

FIGURE 11.24   Fast breakout (goaltender initiates attack with quick forward pass)

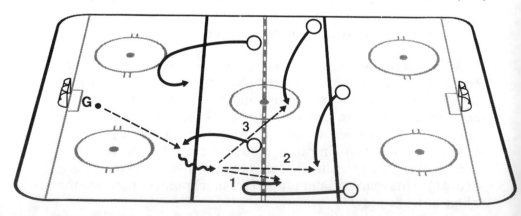

IGURE 11.25   Flow breakout (goaltender initiates attack with pass around the boards)

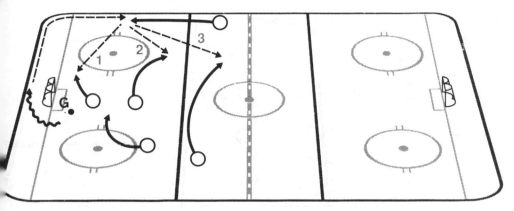

IGURE 11.26   Fast breakout (counterattack)

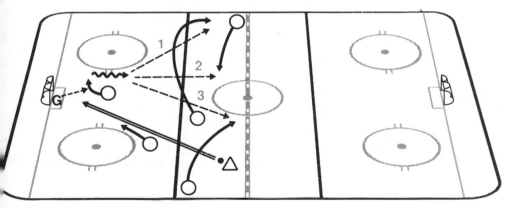

FIGURE 11.27   Regrouping

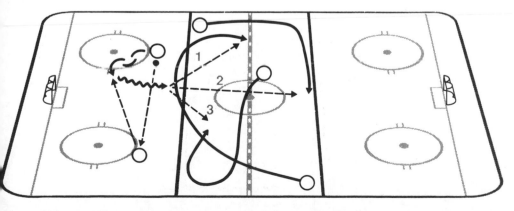

FIGURE 11.28   Fast breakout

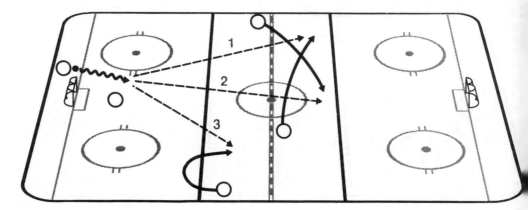

12

Neutral Zone Offense

12.1 Introduction

The literature specific to neutral zone offense is relatively sparse. With very few exceptions (Smith, 1976; Làrsson, 1981, 1985; Evensson, 1983; Kostka et al., 1984), most writers on offensive hockey have given more attention to breakouts and offensive zone play. This emphasis has also been noted in the amount of time coaches spend during practices on neutral zone offense. However, with the new wave of hockey coaching, which places more emphasis on movement and puck control, our approach to neutral zone offense seems likely to change.

The time between coming out of our own end and putting the puck in the net is very important. Neutral zone offense is particularly significant when continuing the attack following a breakout or preparing the counterattack after regaining possession in the neutral or extended zone. Breakout plays initiate the attack, but neutral ice play determines the potency of the eventual attack on the opponent's net.

While the "dump and chase" tactic may occasionally be a fair to good option in certain neutral zone plays, there are definitely more viable and effective alternatives for penetrating the offensive zone. Again, Soviet hockey has had a strong impact on this particular aspect of the game. The Soviets and other European countries have patently demonstrated the importance of regrouping and counter-attacking at the proper time in this area of the ice. Maintaining puck control and the progression or development of an attack should dictate the system of play, especially in the neutral and extended zone, where the greatest amount of space is available for movement by all five players. As in basketball and soccer, puck possession is a precious commodity. In most playing situations, neutral ice play should be used to continue building the attack or to prepare a counterattack in order to strike the opponent's goal most effectively.

Before classifying and describing some specific neutral zone plays, we would like to suggest some action principles as general guidelines to follow in neutral zone offense. Depending on the type of neutral zone play, some of these principles are more appropriate than others. They are:

1. Try to move through the zone quickly.
2. Maximize movement in all directions.
3. Interchange with flow and counterflow.
4. Maintain depth and width (decoys).
5. Create open ice for one another by using screens.
6. Use the concept of waves of attack.
7. Execute quickly (transition) after regaining puck.
8. Regroup with speed and gradual acceleration.
9. Make "active" passes.
10. Be creative and improvise.

Although we have emphasized creativity and improvisation as important factors in group tactical plays throughout the book, there is no question that these elements have special significance in the neutral zone. As mentioned earlier, the neutral zone with the extended zone offers the greatest amount of space for both puck and non-puck carriers to maneuver. The puck carrier must make an "active" pass to an open man. This space or area of the ice facilitates movement patterns such as flow, interchange, crisscrosses and waves of attack. It is also where players need to outsmart the opposition if they are to successfully penetrate the offensive zone. In their every-day practice coaches should encourage players to be creative in this zone, especially in the middle and top of the neutral zone, where deception has the highest payoff. King (1981), in a discussion of neutral zone offense, reiterated this point:

> It is in this zone that we must generate more deception in our attack by encouraging our player to "read" coverage — the other team's backchecking efforts — and moving away from it. This sounds like football and this is possibly a teaching cue that can be used. Consider the neutral zone to be a football field; the puck carrier, the quarterback; and the players without the puck as the pass receivers. The pass receivers have the responsibility of avoiding coverage and finding open areas to create a play or option for the "quarterback" (p. 146).

The application of the principles above creates a five-man attack with movement. This motion attack by all five, especially the forwards, produces certain technico-tactical advantages, as we saw in Chapters 4 and 5. Adapted from King (1981, 1983), these advantages are:

1. An attack with speed and acceleration
2. An increased passing range for the receiver
3. A better passing angle for the passer
4. An increased number of options for the passer
5. Greater difficulty for the opponent, especially the defensemen, in checking players who are moving laterally and crisscrossing
6. Enhancement of overall puck control with the option to regroup and counterattack
7. More difficult attack for the opposing defensemen to cover

12.2 Neutral Zone Plays

Based upon our observations of the game, neutral zone play can be analyzed from the following perspectives:

1. Following a breakout
2. After regaining possession
3. Regrouping
4. Face-off situations
5. Dumping to recover the puck (shoot-in pass)

12.2.1 Following a breakout

After a successful breakout, players must now continue to move through the neutral zone before penetrating the offensive zone. A variety of plays and options are possible, but many of these depend on the type of breakout used and the opposition's defensive alignment.

If the breakout was a fast, counterattack type of action, then you should maintain this tempo through the neutral zone. In this case, your primary objective is to minimize the time spent in the neutral zone by accentuating speed, and longitudinal and diagonal passes (see Figures 12.1 to 12.3). This will help you maintain the numerical and/or territorial advantage you created as a result of the quick breakout. On the other hand, if the breakout was quite controlled, then lateral movement, interchanging, flow and counterflow, and waves of attack may be more effective tactically (see Figures 12.4 and 12.5).

12.2.2 After regaining possession

In even play, there should never be any question in a player's mind that the first option after regaining possession in the neutral zone is to counterattack. This is especially true when a defenseman recovers the puck around the extended or the bottom of the neutral zone. Figure 12.6 shows a defenseman recovering a loose puck, executing a quick "turn-up" and passing options to the forwards. Notice how the forwards are maintaining movement and balance (width and depth) while interchanging. This form of diagonal skating creates visual screens, confuses the opposition and facilitates the long breakthrough pass between the opposing defensemen. Figure 12.7 also shows a rapid counterattack with a slight variation in the movement of the forwards.

Counterattacking in the neutral zone is the best means of creating a numerical and/or territorial advantage with an excellent opportunity of scoring. Rapid transition in the neutral zone can be a lethal weapon for any team. This requires both puck and non-puck carriers to react quickly, executing with precision and acceleration. However, if the nature of the play does not lend itself to counterattacking, then regrouping is certainly another viable alternative.

IGURE 12.1   Neutral zone play

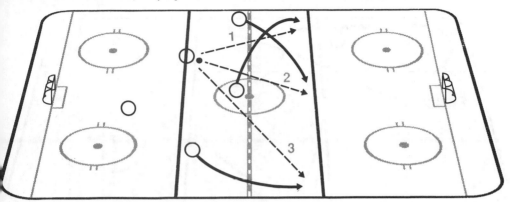

FIGURE 12.2   Neutral zone play

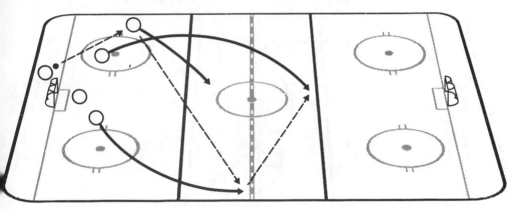

FIGURE 12.3   Neutral zone play

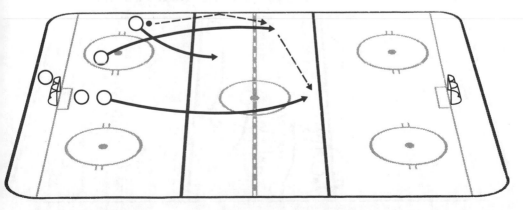

FIGURE 12.4   Neutral zone play

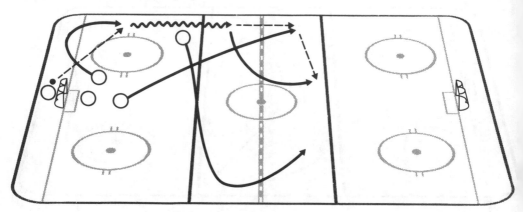

FIGURE 12.5   Neutral zone play (goaltender's pass initiates attack)

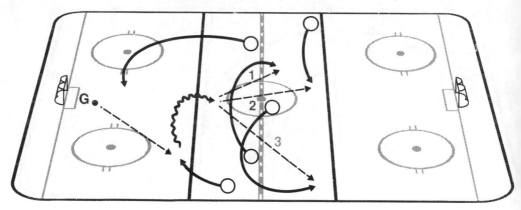

FIGURE 12.6   Neutral zone play (quick turn-up creates quick transition)

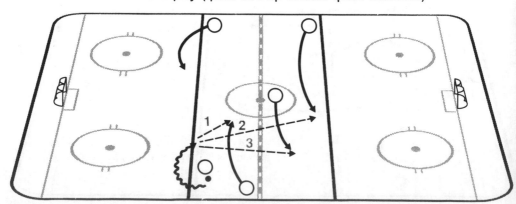

FIGURE 12.7 Neutral zone play (quick pass for rapid transition)

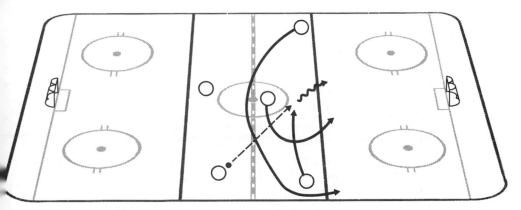

12.2.3 Regrouping

As we saw in Chapter 10, the main purpose of regrouping is to reorganize the attack, in other words to redesign the attack for a more effective penetration of the offensive zone. The decision to regroup is initiated by the puck carrier by means of a backward pass or back-tracking or both. Numerous combinations are possible after the original back-pass which triggers the regrouping play. Certain plays are more of the delay type, while others produce a faster transition "back to attacking." Note that we did not say "back to offense" because this would imply that you were initially on defense. The fact of the matter is that you were on offense but chose not to attack and penetrate the offensive zone. Instead, you opted to regroup to create a stronger attack.

A back pass to a defenseman creates more room in the neutral zone. You have in fact stretched the zone to help forwards locate open ice — to "go for the hole." With speed and interchanging of positions, the opposing defensemen become tentative and vulnerable. They tend to back off, making it easier for the forwards to "take the blue line."

Players away from the puck have the most difficult job. Following the back pass, the non-puck carriers must coordinate their actions almost perfectly to successfully implement the principle of regrouping and regenerate the attack, whether the puck goes from defenseman to defenseman or immediately back to a forward. Certain technical and tactical points can help forwards in their action regrouping mode.

1. Try to maintain balance while interchanging. Swing across at different depths and widths.
2. Time your move to be available for a pass. Don't turn up too soon. Read the developing play.
3. Time your acceleration, usually at the moment the defenseman passes the puck or slightly before.
4. Locate space and give target for passer while maintaining contact with the puck at least peripherally.
5. One forward can screen for another.
6. Because the defensemen are quarterbacks looking for the best (active) pass, be patient when they decide to hold the puck or go D to D. You may have to keep interchanging.

Figures 12.8 to 12.14 illustrate a number of regrouping plays in the neutral zone, each with various back to attacking speeds.

12.2.4   Face-off situations

Because face-off situations allow you time to set up, a number of patterned plays can be devised, depending of course on your having won the draw. As we describe various plays, we are reminded that face-off alignments can range from a totally offensive to a totally defensive orientation or purpose. In our description of plays, we have assumed that the players' orientation is offensive. This is not and should not always be the case. Bearing that point in mind, we would like to suggest some neutral zone plays originating from various face-off dots (see Figures 12.15 to 12.17).

12.2.5   Dumping to recover the puck (shoot-in pass)

In certain situations, especially when the opposing defensemen and a few defending forwards retreat to their blue line, the dump-and-chase tactic can be successful. The object should not be, however, to give up possession of the puck, but rather to penetrate the offensive zone with the likelihood of maintaining puck control. Unless this purpose is absolutely clear, you have simply given up the puck foolishly. There may be one exception to this general rule.

FIGURE 12.8   Regrouping using the extended zone

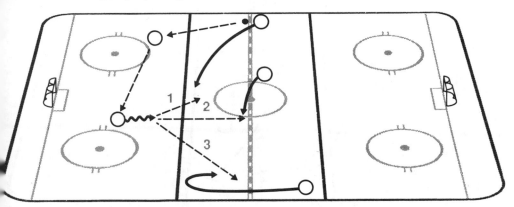

FIGURE 12.9   Regrouping using the extended zone

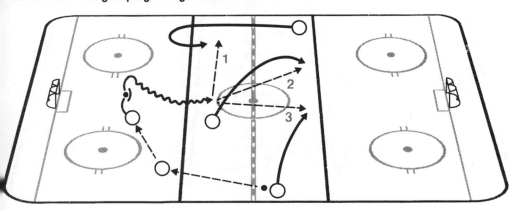

FIGURE 12.10   Regrouping

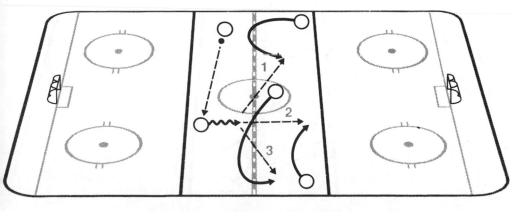

FIGURE 12.11 Regrouping

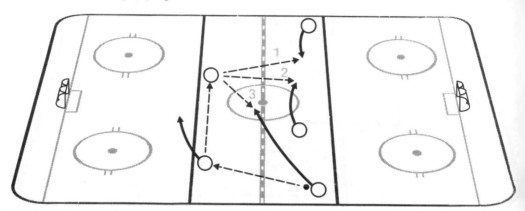

FIGURE 12.12 Regrouping

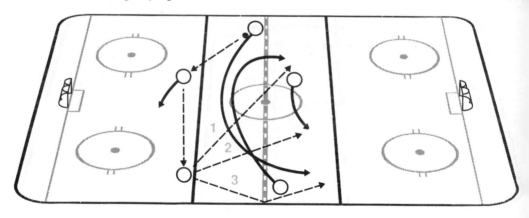

FIGURE 12.13 Regrouping

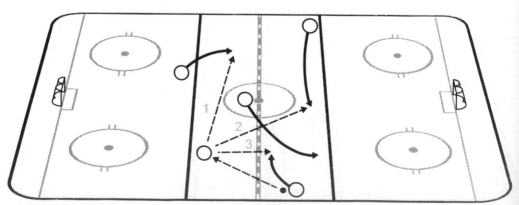

FIGURE 12.14 Regrouping using the extended zone

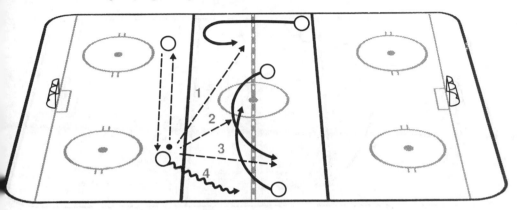

FIGURE 12.15 Face-off play in neutral zone

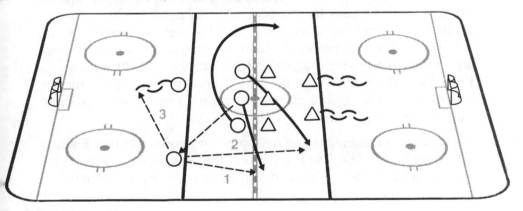

FIGURE 12.16 Face-off play in neutral zone

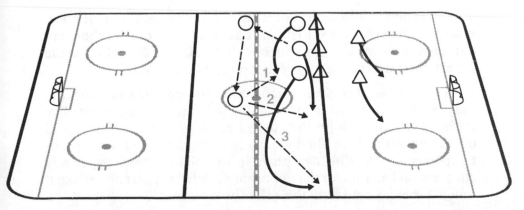

FIGURE 12.17　Face-off play in neutral zone

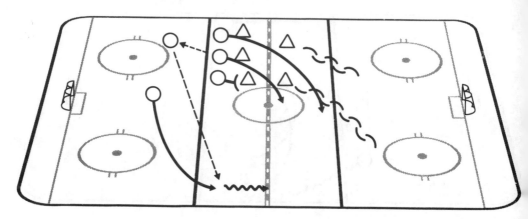

North American hockey teams are often willing to relinquish possession of the puck by dumping when in need of a line change. At first glance this may seem logical. However, we would like to raise the following point: could line changes be accomplished without having to give the puck away? Based on our observations, the habit of dumping with little or no chance of recovery is virtually unseen among European and Soviet teams. These teams consider puck control a priority.

Now let's examine the two most popular approaches (see Figures 12.18 and 12.19). The first is a pass off the far boards, the second a pass around the boards, commonly referred to as a "rimmer."

12.3　Other Neutral Zone Plays

To complete our discussion of neutral ice play, let's look at some other effective plays (see Figures 12.20 to 12.28). Some of these are variations on certain plays which we have already described, while others emphasize a new aspect of neutral zone play.

This chapter has given you a systematic overview of attacking plays in the neutral zone by grouping the various plays under five different headings. With the current emphasis on movement and quick transition, these plays are particularly important for the contemporary coach. Effective plays in the neutral zone, especially counterattacks, will tear the opposition's defense apart and make it much easier to penetrate the offensive zone.

FIGURE 12.18 Dump and chase (shoot-in pass)

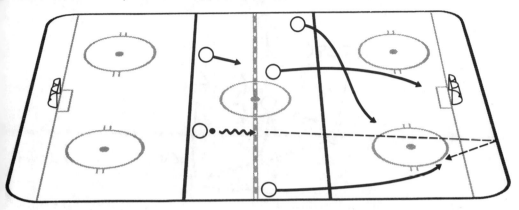

FIGURE 12.19 Dump and chase (rimmer)

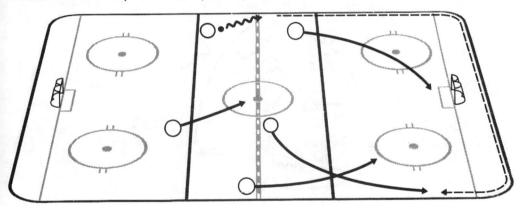

FIGURE 12.20 Regrouping with quick puck movement ("one-touch" passes)

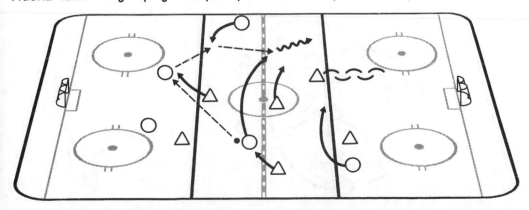

FIGURE 12.21 Wingers go across

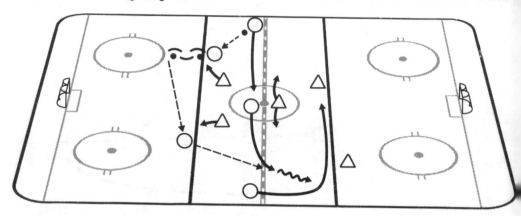

FIGURE 12.22 Winger supports (player 4 remains in right lane for support)

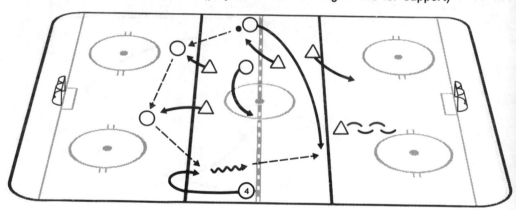

FIGURE 12.23 Regrouping (give-and-go)

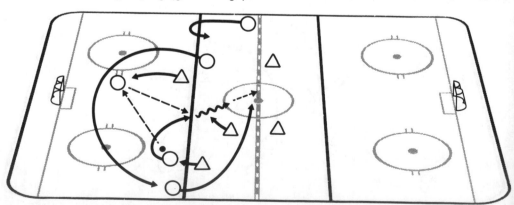

FIGURE 12.24 Back pass to change point of attack

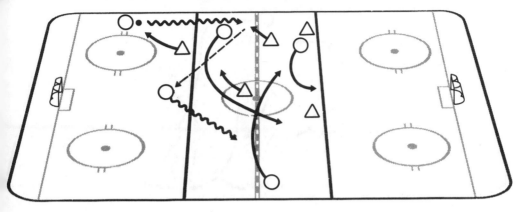

FIGURE 12.25 Neutral zone play (give-and-follow creates area overload)

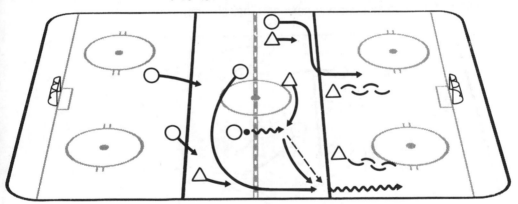

FIGURE 12.26 Neutral zone play (a variation of Figure 12.25)

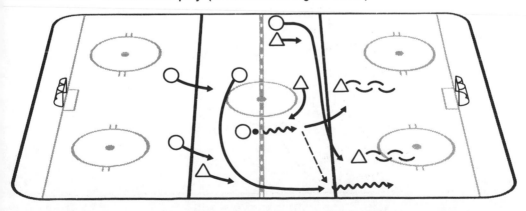

FIGURE 12.27   Change of lanes (quick lateral pass shifts point of attack)

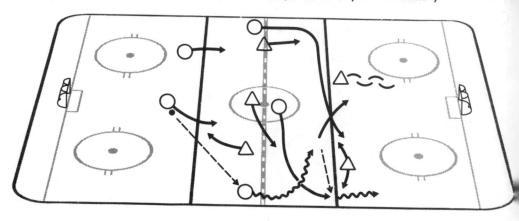

FIGURE 12.28   Two-man weave (pass and interchange)

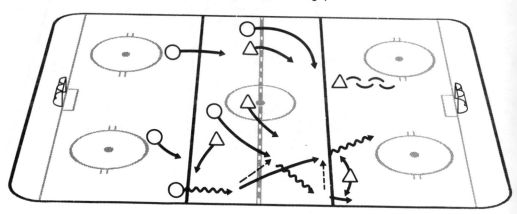

13

Attacking in the Offensive Zone

13.1 Introduction

Attacking in the offensive zone is one of the most exciting facets of the game, especially when the attack culminates in an excellent scoring opportunity. Obtaining the goal you so meticulously prepared is a high emotional reward, both for the players dirrectly involved in the attack and for the rest of the team vicariously experiencing the joy. Scoring the winning goal in overtime to win it all for Canada is nothing short of ecstasy!

A thorough review of the literature pertaining to offense in the opponents' end and careful observation and analysis of team play, especially in international competition, have helped us synthesize the nature of various attacking tactics in the offensive zone (Boulonne et al., 1976; Kostka, 1976; Littsola, 1976; King, 1981, 1983; Kingston, 1979; Larsson, 1981, 1985; International Ice Hockey Federation, 1981; Kostka et al., 1984). We have divided the analysis of attacks in the offensive zone into two main parts:

1. Penetrating the zone
2. Attacking the net

13.2 Penetrating the Zone

Because of the off-side rule, players are not free to do as they wish as they approach the blue line. The puck carrier must first attempt to penetrate or "take the blue line" at the opportune moment, while the non-puck carriers slightly delay their entrance to remain "on-side." The players have to adjust to the opponents' defensive alignment and to the blue line to avoid the off-side. This frequently poses a difficult task for the attacking players given that the opposing defensemen usually try to take advantage of the off-side rule by "standing up" at the blue line. Entering or penetrating the offensive zone is a critical task, a major step towards attacking the net.

As a general rule, you should "take the blue line" whenever possible. The puck carrier should take advantage of whatever space the defenders are giving. The non-puck carriers should analyze the situation and support accordingly. Again, this support may take the form of picks, clearing the area, availability or close support. This will usually create more time and space for both puck and non-puck carriers. As you enter the blue line, an attack will usually have some width but little depth. After penetrating the offensive zone, depth in the attack can and should be developed with the newly available forward space. This, as we have seen, is extremely important in producing a strong and versatile attack, a more balanced and threatening attack.

Several potentially effective plays can be used to penetrate the offensive zone. The success of these group tactical plays depends on the application of the various principles and concepts related to the progression of an attack, as described in Chapter 10. With these principles and concepts in mind, we will now discuss some of the most effective plays for various playing situations.

There are a number of ways to illustrate and describe plays used to penetrate the offensive zone. Based upon the amount of space available between the opponents situated around the blue line and the attacking players, namely the puck carrier, we will consider *three* possible scenarios and describe various plays for each. These scenarios are: (1) *ample space*, (2) *limited space*, or (3) *no space* inside the blue line for attackers to execute a play.

Let us now consider the most appropriate group tactical plays used to enter the offensive zone based on these different scenarios or playing situations created by the opposing defenders. Some of these penetration plays can apply to more than one scenario described above. Our purpose, however, is to illustrate the plays and options that would be most effective in a particular playing situation.

The main object of these plays is to penetrate the blue line. Our figures show both the entry into the zone and the various finishing options to the net. It is difficult to analyze penetration plays without examining the resulting potential attack on net.

13.2.1 Ample space situation

If ample space is available inside the blue line for the attacking forwards, they should penetrate the offensive zone as quickly as possible and generally apply the 1-2-3 principle of attack (triangulation). In the classic 3 on 2 situation, this will let the players reach the goal rapidly and avoid the encumbrance of one or more backcheckers. A number of plays and options are possible, all of which rest on the principle of triangulation (see Figures 13.1-13.5). In these plays, the puck carrier must drive to the outside and be a threat to score, one non-puck carrier must apply pressure to the net, and the other must trail for support. Time is of the essence in these playing situations. A forward pass to the leading forward is imperative in accomplishing this objective. The players must complete the attack quickly to capitalize on their numerical advantage.

FIGURE 13.1   Penetration play (puck carrier forces opponent 3 to commit himself)

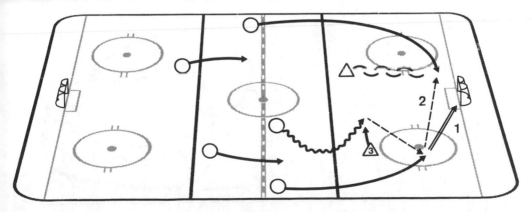

FIGURE 13.2 Penetration play (driving to the net)

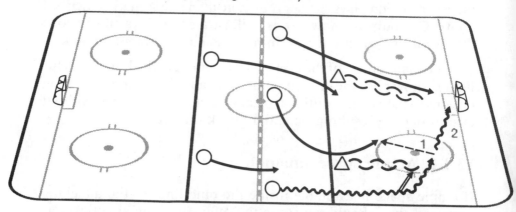

FIGURE 13.3 Penetration play (note interchange between players 5 and 6)

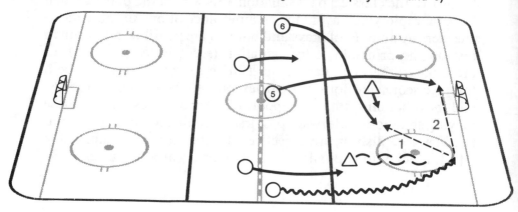

FIGURE 13.4 Penetration with near and far post pass-out

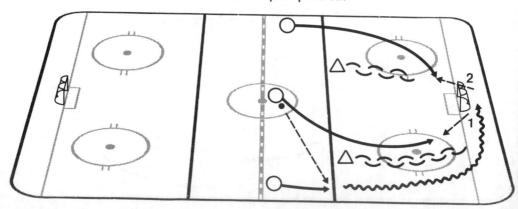

IGURE 13.5   Penetration with interchange

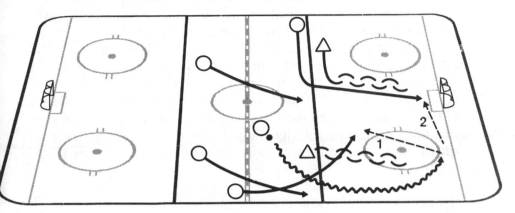

In a 3 on 2 with the puck carrier slightly leading the play in the middle lane, a different approach should be taken. In this case, the puck carrier should slow down slightly after crossing the blue line and both wingers should drive to the net. The puck carrier's objective is to draw one of the defensemen to him, thus opening a winger for a pass. The available options are interesting, as illustrated in Figure 13.6.

FIGURE 13.6   Middle lane penetration

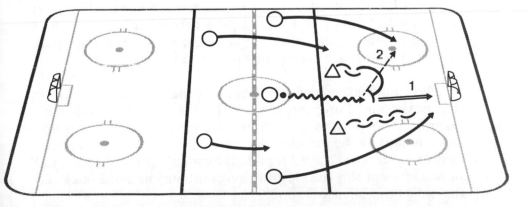

After successfully entering the zone, the puck carrier can elect to delay the attack and wait for additional support (third wave). This option should only be considered if there is little or no chance of obtaining a high percentage shot on net with the initial cast of attackers forming the first and second wave. Delaying gives the defense time to recover. Once again, it becomes a "read and react" decision on the part of the puck carrier. Delaying could allow a player to become open for a pass-and-shot, or produce an entirely missed scoring opportunity. Sometimes delaying becomes your only option, however, as we will discover in the next scenario.

13.2.2 Limited space situation

In many playing situations, especially with mobile and challenging stand-up defensemen, the puck carrier finds little room to negotiate a group play inside the blue line. He must therefore improvise, which in this case means delaying by locating space. Space gives the player time to maintain control of the puck, but more importantly, time to allow his teammates to enter the zone as well and offer support. There are usually two areas inside the blue line where some space can be found to accomplish this objective: (1) along the boards and (2) along the blue line. Let's look at these two delay situations and the possible plays.

The puck carrier who delays along the boards has many options, and the resulting plays can be extremely powerful. Puck protection, waves of attack and creating width and depth are vital elements in producing these plays. Figures 13.7 and 13.8 illustrate a middle delay play created by the puck carrier. Some coaches refer to this as the "J" play because the puck carrier's movement traces the shape of that letter. Other ways of using the longitudinal space along the boards are shown in Figures 13.9 to 13.14.

Plays that make use of the space along the blue line are popular with Soviet and European players. This is consistent with their general style of play, which features interchanges, crisscrosses and close support. In the past decade, more and more North American teams have adopted a similar pattern of play. Figures 13.15 to 13.22 show a series of plays inside and along the blue line as the puck carrier enters the offensive zone.

FIGURE 13.7 Penetration, delay and waves of attack

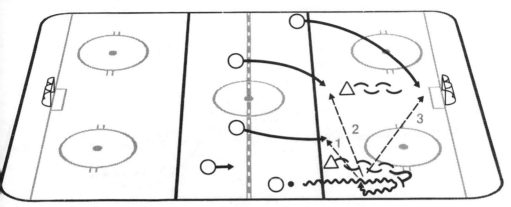

FIGURE 13.8 Penetration, delay, cycling and waves of attack

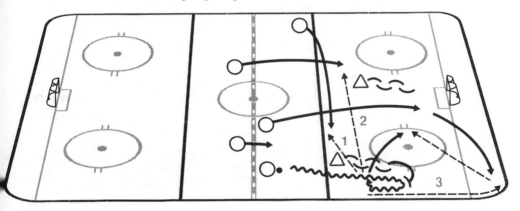

FIGURE 13.9 Penetration, delay and waves of attack

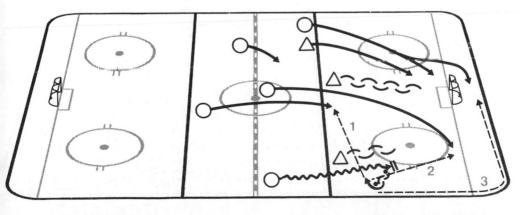

FIGURE 13.10 Penetration with back pass

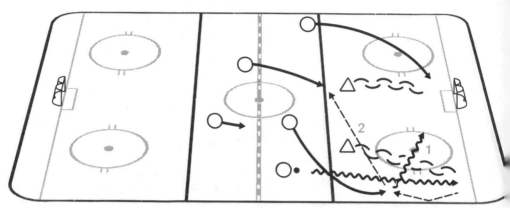

FIGURE 13.11 Penetration with lead pass to accelerating forward

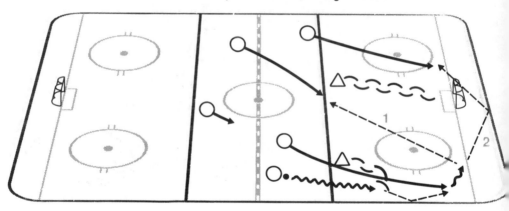

FIGURE 13.12 Penetration with high delay

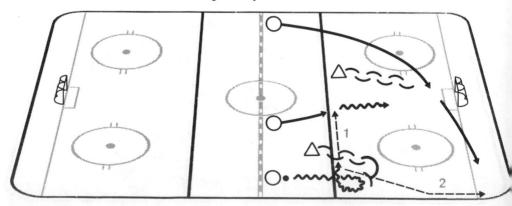

FIGURE 13.13   Penetration with low delay

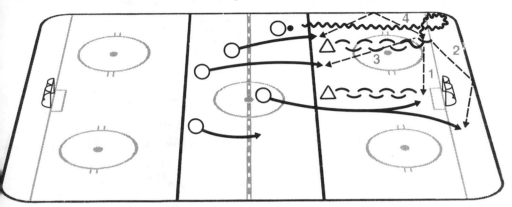

FIGURE 13.14   Penetration with moving screen

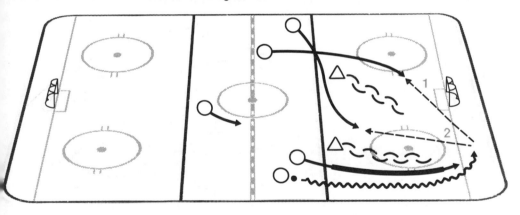

FIGURE 13.15   Penetration using shuttle play with drop pass

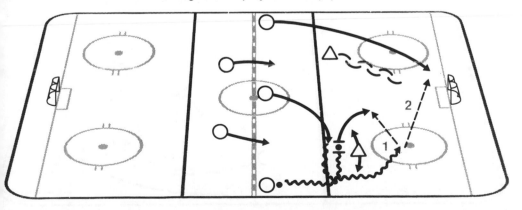

FIGURE 13.16   Penetration using shuttle play (note the fake drop pass)

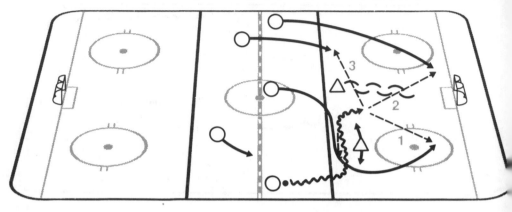

FIGURE 13.17   Penetration with crisscross play and drop pass

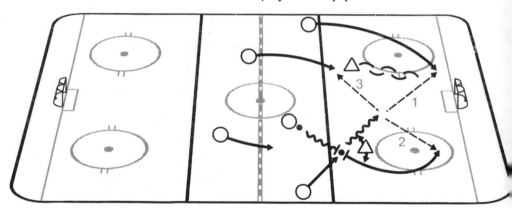

FIGURE 13.18   Penetration with crisscross play (note the fake drop pass)

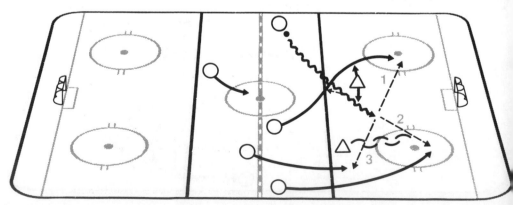

FIGURE 13.19   Penetration and delay along the blue line

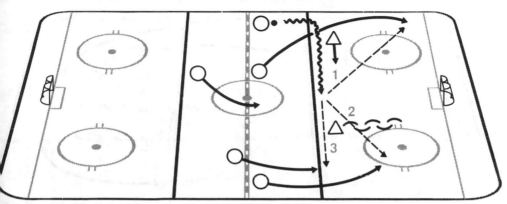

FIGURE 13.20   Penetration using a pick play

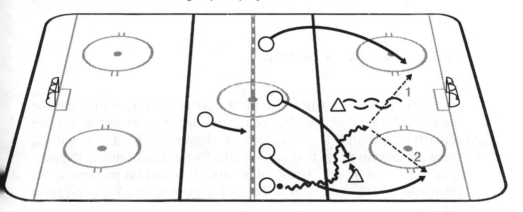

FIGURE 13.21   Slick maneuvering "à la Wayne Gretzky"

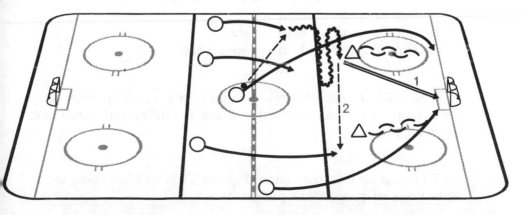

FIGURE 13.22   Slick maneuvering "à la Wayne Gretzky"

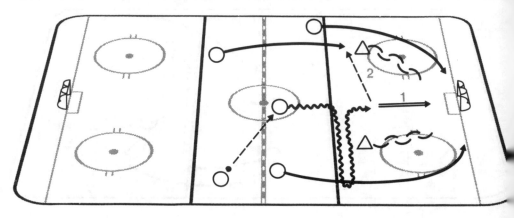

13.2.3 No space situation

There are occasions when the puck carrier is unable to "take the blue line," in other words, locate an opening to penetrate the offensive zone due to the defensive alignment. In this situation, there are certain plays that can be effective in maintaining the progression of the attack. These plays are all based on passing to an open space with the intent of regaining possession. We can group these as follows:

1. Passing to an open space
2. Soft dump to an open space
3. Rimming the puck to an open space

Figures 13.23 to 13.26 illustrate a series of plays and options using the concept of passing to an open space, including soft dump and rimming plays.

To complete our discussion, Figures 13.27 to 13.30 show some other types of penetration plays.

GURE 13.23   Penetration with "no space" situation (pass to an open area)

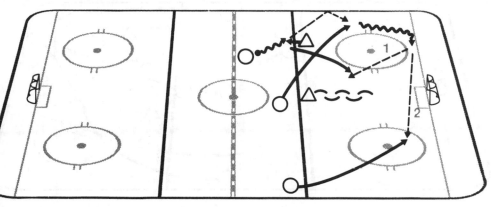

GURE 13.24   Penetration with "no space" situation (pass to an open area)

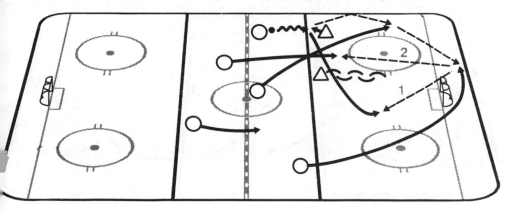

GURE 13.25   Penetration with "no space" situation (rimmer)

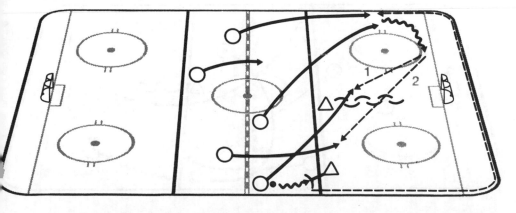

FIGURE 13.26 Penetration with "no space" situation (shoot-in pass)

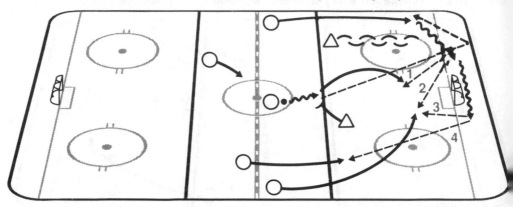

FIGURE 13.27 Back pass to establish second wave of attack (note pick set for player 3)

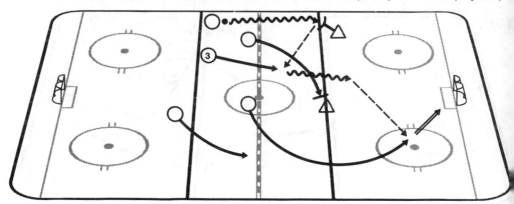

FIGURE 13.28 Camouflaged attack (note pick set for player 6)

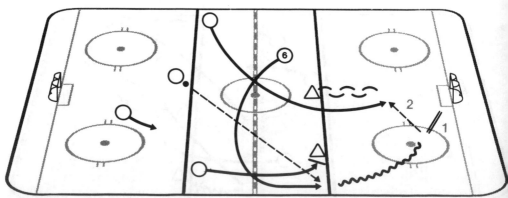

IGURE 13.29   Penetration with crisscross

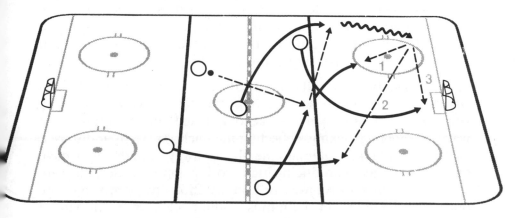

GURE 13.30   Penetration with multiple back passes (waves of attack)

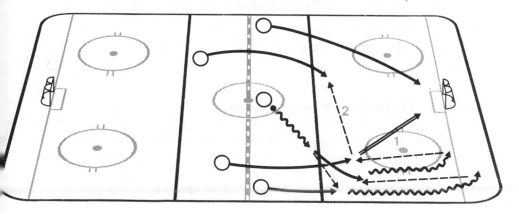

13.3   Attacking the Net

Attacking the net or goal is the culmination of an effective attack. In this final phase of attack, players must eventually penetrate the slot area and create plays which result in a high percentage shot on net. An attack — regardless of whether it originates from the defensive, neutral or even the offensive zone — is not complete unless it results in a good scoring opportunity. Directing the attack towards the net is a prerequisite to optimal shooting.

Optimal shooting is our fourth and final fundamental principle of offense. This principle states that players must attempt to create the best scoring opportunity as they complete their attack on net. After all, the ultimate purpose of an attack is to release a high percentage shot on net and score a goal.

In this section, we will examine different group tactical actions which produce sound scoring opportunities in various playing situations. Scoring can be accomplished in a number of ways — shooting, deking, deflecting the puck. As we shall discover, both the eventual shooter and the players away from the puck have vital roles to play in producing high scoring opportunities. The rare exception is in a breakaway or penalty shot situation, where the outcome rests solely in the hands of the puck carrier. Individual technical skills related to the art and science of scoring will be examined in the following section.

The finishing phase of an attack on net to create an optimal shooting situation can be analyzed from three perspectives:

1. Following a penetration
2. From natural situations
3. From face-off situations

13.3.1 Following a penetration

We have already discussed finishing plays following immediate penetration. Because the type of penetration plays into the offensive zone also influences the final phase of attacking on net, the illustrations in Figures 13.1 to 13.30 show both phases.

13.3.2 From natural situations

Many goals in hockey are scored as a result of pressuring the opponents in their own end, causing them to make a bad pass or lose possession. If the opposition makes a bad pass during an attempted breakout, the principle of counterattacking should be applied. If such a play occurs, we cannot overemphasize the importance of all five players reacting quickly to the transition. Not all intercepted passes in the offensive zone are of the breakout type, however; many passes by the opposition are to establish or maintain better puck control. In that event, counterattacking is less likely in the event of a turnover. In other playing situations, you simply win the 1 on 1 or 2 on 2 battles in the corner or along the boards. Many initial attacks do not culminate with a shot on net, with the result that you are now attempting to redesign a play to attack the net. You did not lose possession of the puck; you either opted to postpone or were forced to delay the action of going to the net.

For whatever reason, you are now faced with the task of creating an effective attack on net, starting from the offensive zone. Given the number of players in this confined space, the task is far from easy. As a general rule, you should emphasize movement, even by the defensemen, numerical advantage close to the puck, short, quick passes, converging on net in units of two or three, screens/ picks and quick release of shots. Figures 13.31 to 13.46 depict a series of plays from various positions in the offensive zone.

Pick and screen plays are a very important means of creating scoring opportunities. As in basketball, picks let a player get free from his check to release a shot on net. In hockey, the player planting the pick or screen must be careful not to get caught for interference by the referee. The screen or pick must be executed subtly to avoid attracting the referee's attention, and unexpectedly to be effective against the player who will be screened. Power and physical strength also play an important role for players attempting to penetrate the slot area, especially when coming off the wall (board side) or from behind the goal line.

FIGURE 13.31   Attacking the net (note pick play by player 4)

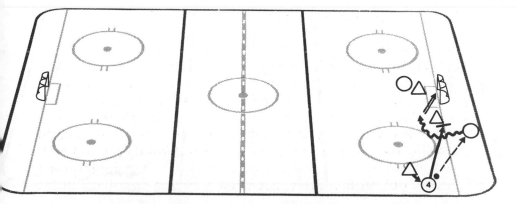

FIGURE 13.32　Walkout

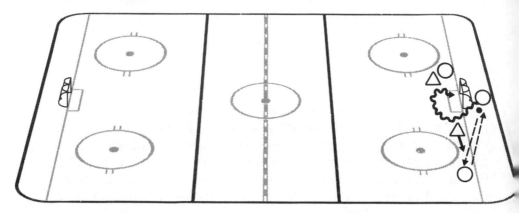

FIGURE 13.33　Walkout with pick play

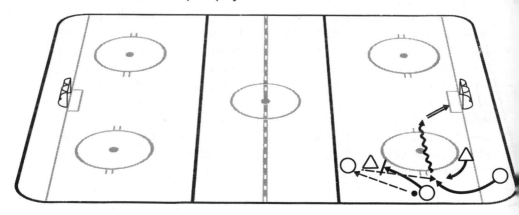

FIGURE 13.34　Attacking the net (note pick play by player 2)

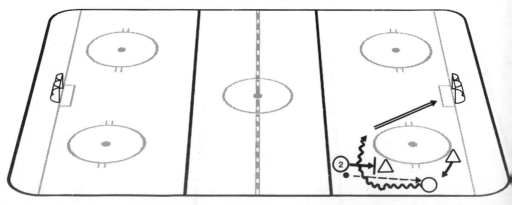

GURE 13.35   Clockwise cycling

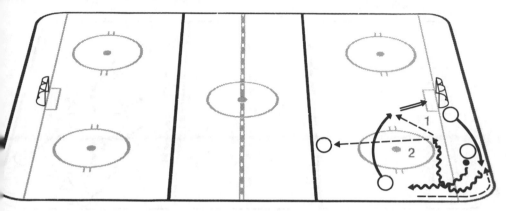

GURE 13.36   Counterclockwise cycling

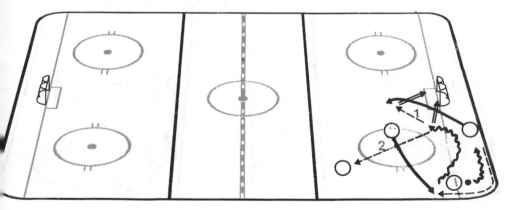

GURE 13.37   Cycling around the net and walkout

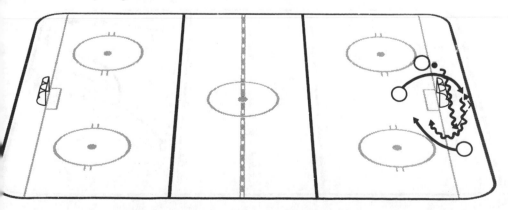

FIGURE 13.38   Attacking the net starting from the blue line (note side door option created by player 6)

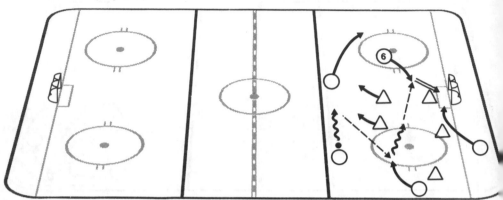

FIGURE 13.39   Attacking the net starting from the blue line (horseshoe play)

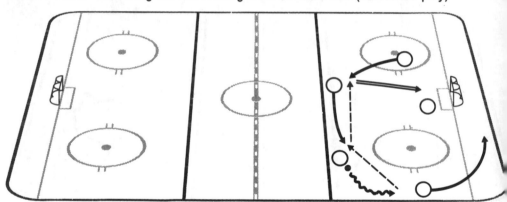

FIGURE 13.40   Attacking the net starting from the blue line

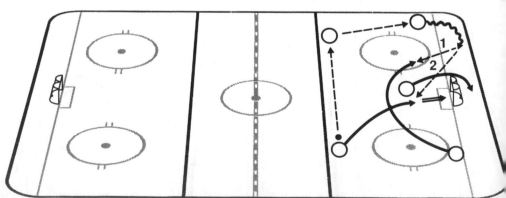

FIGURE 13.41   Shuttle play along the boards with drop pass

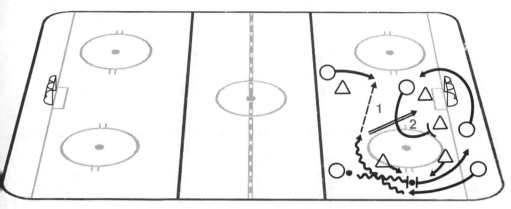

FIGURE 13.42   Shuttle play behind the net with drop pass

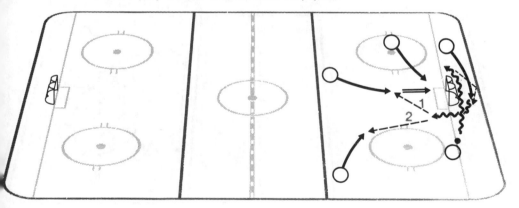

FIGURE 13.43   Give-and-go with pick play

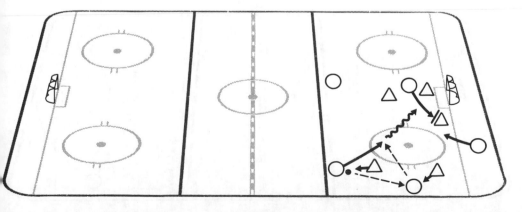

FIGURE 13.44 Give-and-go with pick play

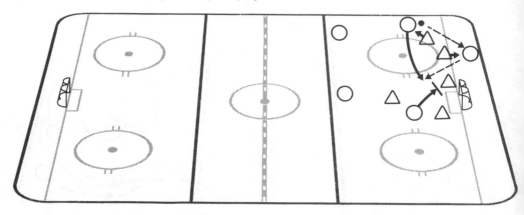

FIGURE 13.45 Defense to defense with pick play

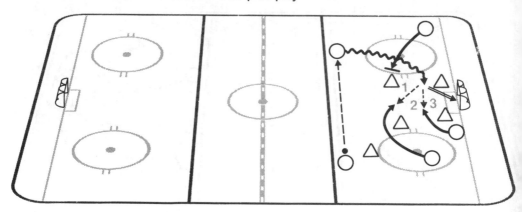

FIGURE 13.46 Defense to defense with bank pass

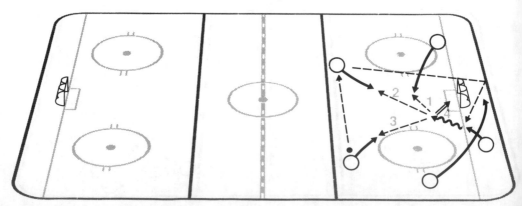

13.3.3 From face-off situations

A face-off in hockey is a unique occasion where a set play can be
developed and executed as planned, providing of course that you
win the draw. Granted, the face-off player must be successful, but
players away from the puck must also perform their respective
duties, screening players to give the shooter more time and space.
This will result in an excellent opportunity to score.

Generally, in keeping with the spirit of today's hockey, a
forward should take the draw (and not always a centerman), the
wingers should provide the picks and screens and the defensemen
should take the shot (see Figures 13.47 to 13.50).

FIGURE 13.47   Set play from face-off

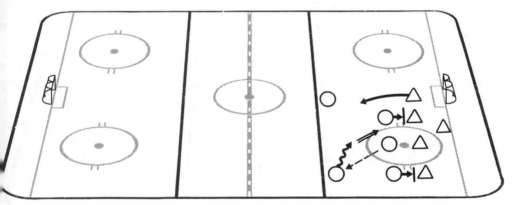

FIGURE 13.48   Set play from face-off with only a few seconds remaining in the game
(goaler has been replaced by an extra forward)

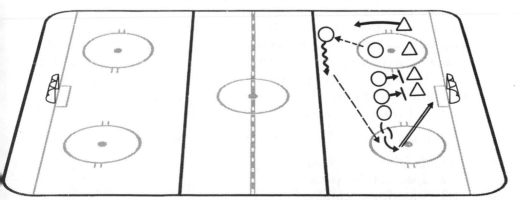

FIGURE 13.49   Set play from face-off (power play situation)

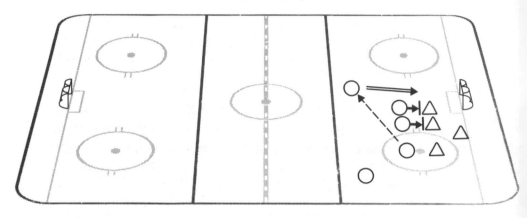

FIGURE 13.50   Set play from face-off

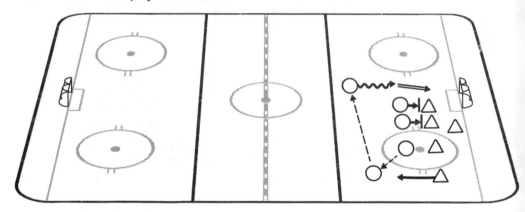

13.4 Technical Skills of Optimal Shooting

Scoring goals in hockey is both a science and an art. The art is the sixth sense of knowing when and where to shoot, a special gift that natural scorers seem to have. The science lies in the ability of the player to apply the technical and tactical skills which will augment his chances of scoring. Here we are referring to the skills specific to the act of shooting. Deking a goalie will be examined later.

The technical skills that affect optimal shooting are:

1. Quickness of release
2. Speed of the puck
3. Shooting accuracy

13.4.1 Quickness of release

Players who possess a quick release regularly catch the goalie off-guard. The quickness of release allows very little time for the goalie to prepare himself. Surprise! The shot has left the stick and is well on its way to finding the back of the net. There are two classic scenarios. The first is the one-time shot, where the goalie literally never even has a chance to face the shooter and prepare himself for the shot (see Figure 13.51). This is frequently the case when the puck comes from behind the net with the shooter in the slot. The goalie must look behind and then all of a sudden face the shooter already in action. The second scenario is when the goalie is clearly focusing on the puck carrier but is tricked by the unexpected shot. The shooter in essence didn't "telegraph" the shot. The shot was in a sense hidden or camouflaged among his other actions of skating and stickhandling. As Spassky said:

> When learning to shoot at the goal, see to it that your shots are accurate, unexpected and powerful (p. 70).

> Then he [hockey player] must try to learn shooting after short preparation − immediately after stopping, during dribbling, by-passing, tackling, while skating or from an inconvenient position (p. 71).

> The secret of a shot today is much more complicated. You must learn to make a concealed shot. In other words, [you must] conceal your preparation for the shot and attack the goal unexpectedly (p. 74).

One of the most effective ways of concealing the release of your shot is to shoot in stride. This basically means that you release the puck without changing the rhythm of your skating.

Darryl Sittler, one of the best centers and natural scorers in the NHL, and Brian McFarlane (1979) had this to say regarding shooting:

> I can't stress enough the importance of getting the shot away quickly. So often the goalie is not set for a quick shot. As soon as he does get set, your scoring chance diminishes. He'll move out at you, ready to block your shot with pad, stick, or glove. And that open corner of the net, which looked so huge and inviting a split second earlier, now appears to be smaller than a mouse hole (p. 62).

FIGURE 13.51   One-time shot (power play situation)

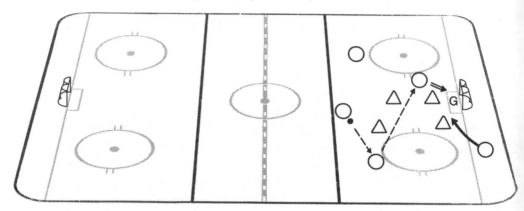

The type of shot naturally has a great deal to do with creating the element of surprise. The snap and the wrist are the best two shots to release the puck unexpectedly since they require very little backswing compared to the slap or sweep shot. As the late Valery Kharlomov once said:

> I think that the wrist shot gives the most results. It is particularly crafty because it is made without preliminary preparations, i.e., off-hand, and the goalie very often has no time to react. You can make the wrist shot at any moment even when surrounded on all sides by rivals (p. 76).

"Soft hands" help a player stickhandle, deke, pass and receive the puck, but "fast hands" let the player release the puck in the twinkling of an eye. This very special talent makes the shooter a feared attacker.

13.4.2 Speed of the puck

Goaltenders are often beaten by the mere velocity of the puck simply because of the human limits to reaction time. A good analogy is the penalty shot in soccer, where the odds of the shooter scoring are overwhelmingly high. The best soccer goaltenders are unable to reach for the ball heading for the corner. The same is true in hockey. A well placed shot released from a certain distance with a certain velocity is impossible to stop. Anticipation or "guesstimating" by the goalie is of course important, but the fact remains that puck speed is a determining factor, especially when coupled with a quick release.

There is no denying that shooting the puck with speed is related to upper body strength, particularly the arms and forearms for the wrist and snap shots. But technique is also very important, especially fluidity of motion. Many excellent shooters with fast shots do not have massive upper bodies but their shooting movement, like the swing of a golfer, is coordinated and smooth. The result is power. Guy Lafleur's slap shot is a good example. Compared to other players, Guy does not have a muscle-bound type of body, yet he can propel the puck with might. His quickness of release is also something to behold, not to mention the deadly accuracy of his shots.

13.4.3 Shooting accuracy

A shot executed with a quick release and good speed is worthless unless directed at the net. The puck must obviously be on target to have any chance of scoring. But great scorers do more than just shoot the puck in the direction of the goal. Great shooters pick their spots. They aim at the holes the goalie leaves open while standing in the crease. Normally, these openings are the top right and left corners, bottom right and left corners, and occasionally between the legs, depending on the goalie's style. Tarasov et al. (1973) addressed this subject:

> Some years ago a statistical analysis was made of all the goals scored during several NHL seasons. We Soviets have also made a similar analysis at home, besides keeping statistics of all our international games...

> According to the above mentioned statistical analysis most of the goals scored came from players who were right in front of the net and five to ten feet away from the goalie (note: goalie, not goal). By far the greater part of the goals were low, that is below the knee level, and went in at ankle level. Finally, many more goals went in on the goalie's stick side than on his glove side (p. 49).

Horsky (1983) stated that "the shooting effectiveness ratio of low to high is 10 to 1." His studies also revealed that low shots often rebound in front of the net, giving the attacking team a second chance to shoot.

Ideally, you should look towards the net and pick a spot before you shoot. This is quite often difficult in heavy traffic. If the shooter is in the slot area, his primary objective should be to release the puck rather than jeopardize his potential shot on net by taking the time to look. Under such conditions, the general rule is to shoot low. With experience and the use of your peripheral vision, however, you can develop a sense of locating and hitting the net without necessarily having to look. Darryl Sittler and Brian McFarlane (1979) had this to say:

> When the puck hits your stick you'd better get rid of it... if you sneak a quick look at the goalie in his net to see if he's left you an open corner, it's often too late (p. 61).

> The time to size up a goalie is before you get the puck. Then, if you have no time to look up when the puck comes to you, at least you'll have a sense of where he is in the net (p. 62).

In summary, the speed of the puck is an important factor in scoring goals, and quickness of release will increase your goal production by frequently catching the goalie off-guard. However, shooting accuracy is absolutely indispensable to put the puck in the net.

13.5 Tactical Skills of Optimal Shooting

As we have seen, there is an intimate relationship between technical and tactical skills. Every technical skill can be used tactically in the course of a game. The same applies to the technical skills of shooting that we have just examined. Quickness of release is a technical skill, but it can also be regarded as tactical, if it catches the goalie off-guard and scores a goal. In the next section, we examine shooting within the larger playing context, discussing various tactical actions by the shooter, as well as the role of the non-puck carriers.

We will examine the following tactical skills relating to shooting:

1. Type of shot, location and variety
2. Moving into position
3. Screening the goalie, deflections and rebounds
4. The breakaway

13.5.1   Type of shot, location and variety

A number of studies have examined the relationship between the type of shot used, accuracy and the speed of the puck (Alexander et al., 1963; Cotton, 1966; Roy, 1974; Roy et al., 1974; Perron, 1980; Jokat et al., 1986). A slapshot sends the puck travelling faster than the wrist or sweep shot, and the backhand shot is the slowest. However, the wrist and sweep shots are the most accurate shots, whether the player is in motion or stationary. These are also important factors when deciding what type of shot to use in a given location on the ice. Equally important is the position of the goalie at the time the puck carrier is about to shoot (see Figure 13.52).

Common sense suggests that in the slot area the wrist, sweep and snap shots are preferable to the slap (see Figure 13.53). This is not only because there is little time to release a shot more in the slot, where normally there is heavy traffic, but also because the shooter is normally going for accuracy as well. Further away, however, the slap shot can be more effective. But remember that quickness of release can compensate for a slower type of shot. As usual, you need to keep in mind your total playing context − your positioning, the pressure exerted by the opposition and your own personal strengths as a shooter. For instance, if a defenseman has limited time to shoot the puck, his preferable option is the snap or wrist shot to reduce the time of execution. However, if time permits, the normally heavier slap shot might be more effective (see Figures 13.54 and 13.55).

FIGURE 13.52   Quick release from high slot

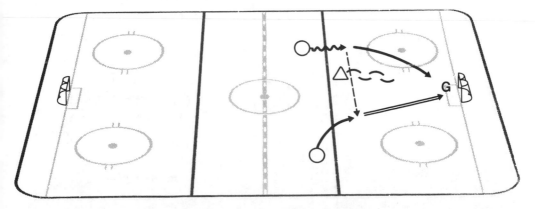

FIGURE 13.53   One-time shot in heavy traffic

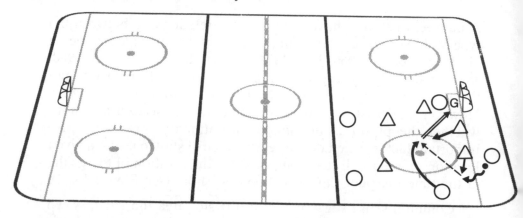

FIGURE 13.54   Creating time and space for slap shot (power play situation)

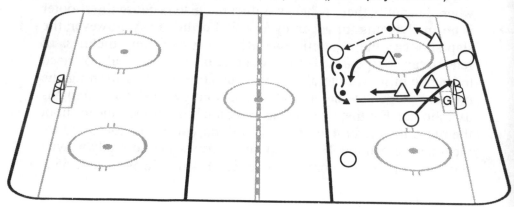

FIGURE 13.55   One-time slap shot with player 6 screening the goalie

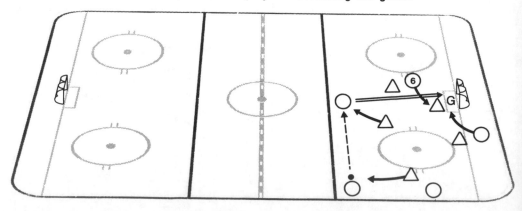

The use of various shots in hockey and the playing context bring up another important topic. As in basketball and soccer, the player who can shoot in various playing situations from different angles and who possesses a variety of shots at his disposal will be a more complete shooter (see Figures 13.56 to 13.58). A quote from the *Associate Coaches Manual* (1986) produced by the Amateur Hockey Association of the United States conveys that idea:

> Shooting situations within the game vary greatly. The skillful player must, therefore, have a variety of shots that match the opportunities that develop. The amount of time a player has, the location, and defensive player positioning require that different shots (or variations of the same shot) be used (p. 54).

Related to the topic of variety of shots is the "old" backhand shot. With the advent of the curved stick, the backhand (wrist, sweep or snap) went out the door, unfortunately. Players who shy away from using their backhand shot are committing a serious error. Just ask the goaltenders. Backhand shots surprise goalies because they are unaccustomed to them. Develop confidence in your backhand and the results will speak for themselves. Incidentally, the backhand flip is an essential shot to master if you are thinking of deking a goalie.

FIGURE 13.56 Shooting "against the grain" to displace goalie

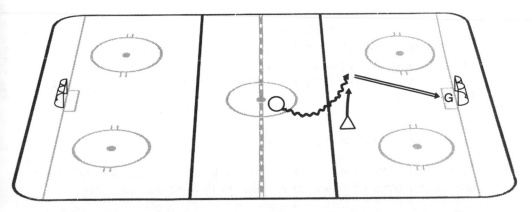

FIGURE 13.57   Backhand shot (left-handed shooter)

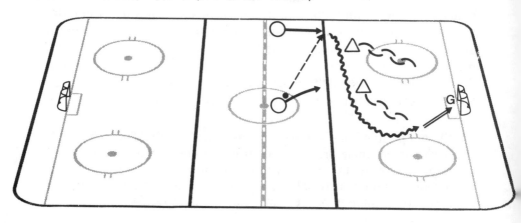

FIGURE 13.58   Wrap-around followed by flip shot

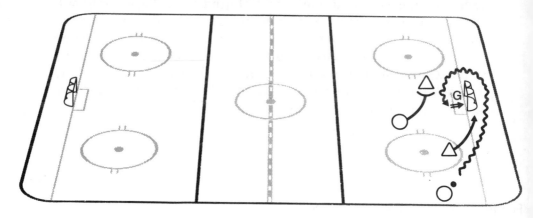

Players skating into the offensive zone must also learn how to use the opposing defenseman as a screen. If this maneuver is properly executed, the opponent totally obscures the vision of the goalie. This can be a particularly effective play in a 1 on 1 situation (see Figure 13.59).

13.5.2   Moving into position

There are two ways of analyzing this skill, as a puck carrier and as a non-puck carrier or potential shooter. Both have the same objective

— to create time and space in the slot area for shooting the puck. Group tactical plays can of course facilitate this task, as we noted earlier in this chapter. Here, we are concerned with individual actions or skills.

In the case of the puck carrier, the main skill required is the ability to attack the net. Stickhandling and puck protection skills are the key to penetrating the slot. But you have to attack the net with all your might — go for it, cut inside, crash the net! You have to negotiate your way among and between the defenders, maintain puck control and move into the slot area. The use of fakes (e.g., passing fake) can also be particularly effective for the puck carrier in this situation. Taking advantage of picks set by your teammates is equally important. Figures 13.60 to 13.62 show this type of play.

Based on one of his many studies, Tarasov et al. (1973) made the following comments about the importance of positioning for the shooter:

> The first conclusion arrived at was that only about one shot in 10 results in a goal. The reason for this is that players shoot from too close, from too far back, from too fine an angle, too high or too sluggishly. Many shoot without possessing proper puck control, while an equal number shoot without looking at the net or the goalie's position (p. 49).

FIGURE 13.59   Shooter using opponent as a screen

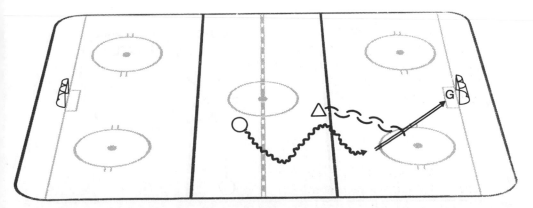

FIGURE 13.60   Accelerate, stop, start and shoot

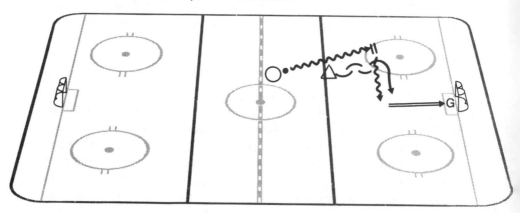

FIGURE 13.61   Accelerate, pivot, drive to the net and shoot

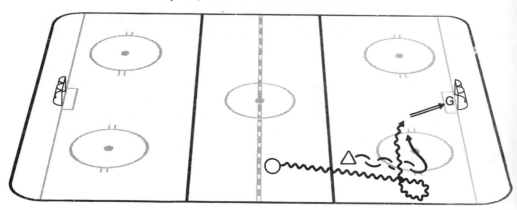

FIGURE 13.62   Driving to the net, puck protection and backhand flip shot (note pick set by player 5)

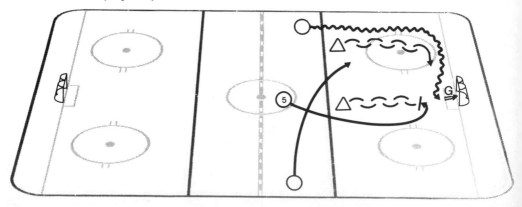

For the non-puck carrier, timing is everything! Being in the right place at the right time and moving into the slot area at the perfect moment is the way to get open for a shot. So many players just hang around in the slot waiting for a pass, knowing that the defenseman is right there ready to check them, or even intercept the pass. Players must read and react, watch the puck carrier and time their move into the slot. They must remain in constant motion, not only to make coverage difficult, but also to provide close support if required (e.g. cycling). Here again, the use of fakes, such as body fakes, can prove valuable to rid you of your checker.

13.5.3 Screening the goalie, deflections and rebounds

Players without the puck (one player is usually sufficient) should also think of screening the goalie when a shot is taken from the point (see Figure 13.63). The player in front of the net can also divert defenders, create a certain amount of commotion and distract the goaltender who is trying to keep his eye on the puck. Players in the slot should also be ready to deflect "tip in" shots coming from the point by facing the shooter and using his stick to redirect the path of the puck (see Figure 13.64). The screener should also be on the alert for any possible rebounds.

Timing, quickness and strength to jockey for position in front of the net are essential factors in obtaining deflections and rebounds. With limited space and aggressive checking by the opponents, you must be able to be strong on your skates, twist and turn and, at the same time, anticipate the shot from your teammate; and, when the rebound is there for you to take, you must shoot the puck with power and tenacity. The Advanced Level Coaches Manual (1989) emphasized this by stating:

> Sometimes the forward can anticipate where a rebound might go, but the two keys to corralling rebounds are to position aggressively in the scoring area (based on the trajectory of the original shot) and to concentrate on the puck with stick on the ice. The determination to drive the rebound home is the mark of good scorers and should be a main feature in all scoring [shooting] drills (p. 7.19).

FIGURE 13.63   Screening the goalie by player 4

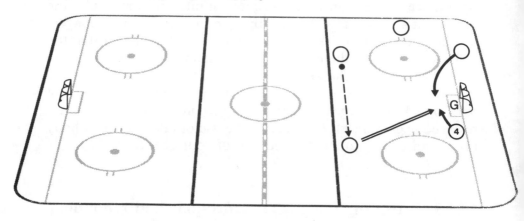

FIGURE 13.64   Deflection play ("shooting" for partner's stick)

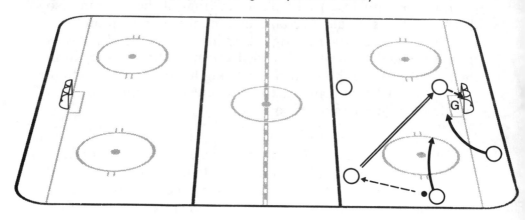

Speaking of rebounds, in many situations it is important for the shooter to follow his shot on net (see Figure 13.65). Catching rebounds can give you a second chance to shoot as well as allowing you to maintain control of the puck. When in close, rolling off your check is a good technique for obtaining a possible rebound (see Figure 13.66). The flip shot is particularly effective on a rebound close to the goal. Again, movement of shooter and non-puck carriers is very important to maximize your chances of picking up the loose puck. As a general rule, the puck carrier should be threatening to score, another player should go for the possible rebound and a third should provide support by screening the goalie, picking for the shooter or as a possible receiver for a one-time shot. After the shot, players should buzz to regain possession of the puck. Timing is everything — you must be in the right place *and* at the right time (see Figures 13.67 and 13.68).

FIGURE 13.65 "Crashing the net" for possible rebound

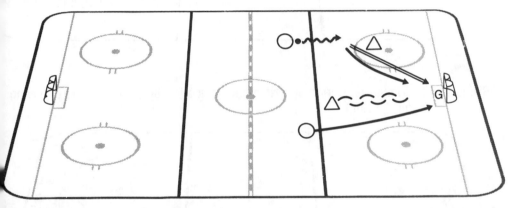

FIGURE 13.66 Rolling away from your check for possible rebound

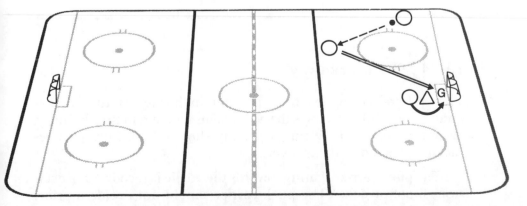

FIGURE 13.67   Right place at the right time (player 5 "control skates" for perfect timing)

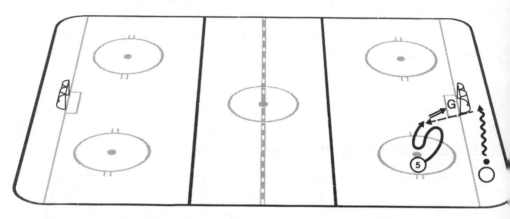

FIGURE 13.68   Timing is everything ! Note fake to the left by player 5 before moving to the right

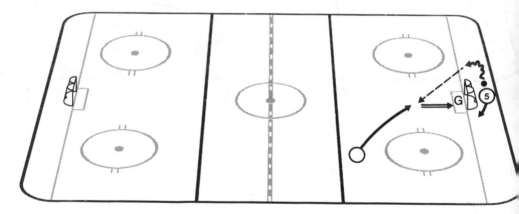

13.5.4 The breakaway

The epitome of an exciting moment in hockey is the "breakaway" — one player versus the goalie. This moment in time becomes even more dramatic during a penalty shot and absolutely nerve-racking in sudden death overtime.

The puck carrier skating towards the goalie is faced with a decision: shoot or deke? The puck carrier should not decide a priori what he will do, nor should he carry the puck in such a way as to tell the goalie his intentions. When a player decides to deke, the puck is in front; when he intends to shoot, it is on his side. Ideally, keep the puck between these two positions until you have made your decision. This is very important — just ask an experienced goalie.

It is also important to keep individual preferences in mind. Certain players possess deadly accurate shots, and their instincts and experience should naturally sway them to think of shooting as they approach the goal mouth. There is no problem with that kind of mind set; however, always leave your options open in case, for instance, the goalie has come way out with no possible angle to score.

Having confidence in your ability is particularly important on a breakaway. Statistically, goalies have the odds, but a cool and confident approach will help you make the right decision and skillful move to beat the goalie. Darryl Sittler and Brian McFarlane (1979) had this to say about the importance of self-confidence:

> If a player is going to score goals, he must have confidence in himself. He must believe he can score goals. A player's negative thoughts, his self doubts, are often a goalie's best friend. It's important to say to yourself, 'I know I can beat that goalie. I know I can deke him or hit the corner of the net with my shot.' You must acquire confidence (p. 55).

Having confidence is not only important in scoring goals; it is also fundamental to playing the game. Coaches must constantly attempt to instill confidence in their players.

We have come to the end of our journey. We hope this book will help players and coaches as they strive for excellence.

BIBLIOGRAPHY

ALDCORN, G. "Philosophy of the U.S.S.R. Play." *Proceedings, National Coaches Certification Program*. Level 5 Seminar. Ottawa: Canadian Amateur Hockey Association, 1973, 1-16.

ALEXANDER, J.F., HADDOW, J.B. and SCHULTZ, G.A. "Comparison of the Ice Hockey Wrist and Slap Shots for Speed and Accuracy." *Research Quarterly*, Vol. 34, No. 3, 1963, 259-266.

AMATEUR HOCKEY ASSOCIATION OF THE UNITED STATES. *Associate Coaches Manual*. Colorado Springs, 1985.

ANDREWS, D. "Team Play Problem Solving." *Proceedings, National Coaches Certification Program*. Level 5 Seminar. Ottawa: Canadian Amateur Hockey Association, 1983, 77-89.

BARNES, M.J. *Women's Basketball*. Boston: Allyn and Bacon, Inc., 1980.

BATTY, E. *Soccer Coaching the Modern Way*. London: Faber and Faber, 1969.

BOULONNE, G., CARON, J. and PELCHAT, C. *L'offensive rouge*. Montréal: Éditions du Jour, 1976.

BOULONNE, G., "Évolution de la tactique offensive du nord-américain." Montréal: *La revue de l'entraîneur*, 1986, April-June, 10-15.

BROKHIN, Y. *The Big Red Machine*. New York: Random House, 1978.

BUKAC, L. "A Comparison of Canadian and European Hockey." *Proceedings, National Coaches Certification Program*. Level 5 Seminar. Ottawa: Canadian Amateur Hockey Association, 1983, 105-112.

BUKAC, L., and SAFARIK, V. *Obrana V. Lednim Hokeji*. Prague: Olympia, 1971.

BUKAC, L. "Czechoslovakian Team Play." *Proceedings, National Coaches Certification Program*. Level 5 Seminar. Ottawa: Canadian Amateur Hockey Association, 1977, 217-268.

BUKAC, L. "Czechoslovakian Dryland Training." *Proceedings, National Coaches Certification Program*. Level 5 Seminar. Ottawa: Canadian Amateur Hockey Association, 1977, 158-169.

CANADIAN AMATEUR HOCKEY ASSOCIATION, *Advanced Level Coaches Manual*. National Coaching Certification Program. Ottawa, 1990.

CANADIAN AMATEUR HOCKEY ASSOCIATION, *Intermediate Level Coaches Manual*. National Coaching Certification Program. Ottawa, 1987.

CARON, J. *Le Grand Jeu*. Quebec: Presses de l'Université du Québec, 1985.

CARON, J. and PELCHAT, C. "Le hockey, sport collectif: modèle empirique ou théorique." *Mouvement*, Vol. 9, No. 1, 1974, 33-46.

CARON, J. and PELCHAT, C. *Apprentissage des sports collectifs*. Montréal: Les Presses de l'Université de Montréal, 1975.

CHAMBERS, D. *Complete Hockey Instruction*. Scarborough: LR and Associates Publishing Ltd., 1981.

CHAMBERS, D. "Skill Requirements for Defensemen." *Proceedings, National Coaches Certification Program*. Level 5 Seminar. Ottawa: Canadian Amateur Hockey Association, 1985, 33-40.

CHOUINARD, N. "Goal-Setting: A Motivational Approach." In T. Orlick, J.F. Partington and J.H. Salmela (Eds.), *Mental Training for Coaches and Athletes* (pp. 114-115). Ottawa: Sport in Perspectives and the Coaching Association of Canada, 1982.

CHOUINARD, N. and LEFROY, K. "Bridging the Gap Between Researcher and Coach". *Proceedings, International Association for Physical Education in Higher Education*, Trois-Rivières, Québec, 1987.

CHOUINARD, N. and MCKENZIE, A. "The Complete Coach." *A Paper Presented at the Fifteenth Annual Conference on the Teaching of Physical Education*. Victoria: University of Victoria, May 24-26, 1990.

COACHING ASSOCIATION OF CANADA. National Coaching Certification Program. *Coaching Theory, Level One*. Ottawa, 1989.

COSTELLO, M. "Reach the Peak." *Proceedings, National Coaches Certification Program*. Advanced II Seminar. Ottawa: Canadian Amateur Hockey Association, 1989.

COTTON, C. *Comparison of the Ice Hockey Wrist, Sweep and Slap Shots for Speed*. Unpublished master's thesis, University of Michigan, Ann Arbor, 1966.

DRAKE, C. "Penalty Killing Adjustment." *Proceedings, National Coaches Certification Program*. Level 5 Seminar. Ottawa: Canadian Amateur Hockey Association, 1985, 89-98.

DYOTTE, G. and RUEL, A. *Techniques du Hockey en U.R.S.S.* Montréal: Les éditions de l'homme, 1976.

EVENSSON, C. "Development of the 5-Man Attack." *Proceedings, National Coaches Certification Program*. Level 5 Seminar. Ottawa: Canadian Amateur Hockey Association, 1983, 39-54.

FISHER, C.W., BERLINER, D.C., FILBY, N.M., MARLIAVE, R., CAHEN, L.S. and DISHAW, M.M. "Teaching Behaviors, Academic Learning Time, and Student Achievement: An Overview." In C. Denham and A. Lieberman (Eds.), *Time to Learn* (pp. 7-32). Washington D.C.: National Institute of Education, 1980.

FLEMING, W. *Regroups* [Video]. Calgary: Hockey Canada in co-operation with the Canadian Amateur Hockey Association, 1989.

GAGNON, G. *Hockey: Système de jeu et tactiques*. Montréal: Les Presses de l'Université de Montréal, 1982.

GAGNON, G. *Hockey: Jeu d'équipe*. Montréal: Les Presses de l'Université de Montréal, 1989.

GIBSON, E.J. *Principles of Learning and Development*. New York: Meredith Corporation, 1969.

GINGRAS, Y. *Manuel Tactique*. Montréal: Les Éditions Topo Hockey Inc. et la Fédération québécoise de hockey sur glace, 1986.

GRATEREAU, R. *Initiation aux Sports Collectifs*. Paris: Collection Bourrelier, 1970.

GRETZKY, W. *Gretzky: An Autobiography*. Toronto: Harper Collins Publishers Ltd, 1990.

HORSKY, L. *Attack and Defence in Ice Hockey*. Colorado Springs: Amateur Hockey Association of the United States, 1983.

HUGHES, C.F. *Tactics and Teamwork*. Yorkshire: EP Group of Companies, 1973.

INTERNATIONAL ICE HOCKEY FEDERATION COACHES COMMITTEE. *Canada Cup Observation Project*. Ottawa: Canadian Amateur Hockey Association, 1981.

JEREMIAH, E. *Ice Hockey*. New York: The Ronald Press Company, 1942.

JOHANSSON, P. and LINDSTROM, C. "The 5-Man Attack." *Swedish Hockey Clinic*. Ottawa: Canadian Amateur Hockey Association, 1980.

JOKAT, B., CHOUINARD, N. and REARDON, F. "Relationship Between Upper Body Strength, Certain Anthropometric Measurements and Velocity of Various Shots in Ice Hockey." Paper presented at the *Ontario Exercise Physiology Conference*, Collingwood, Ontario, 1986.

KERR, R. *Psychomotor Learning*. New York: Saunders College Publishing, 1982.

KHARLOMOV, V. in SPASSKY, O. *Ice Hockey*. Moscow: Moscow Publishing House, 1981.

KINDING, B. "Transition Hockey — Defense to Offense." *Paper presented at the International Hockey Coaches Seminar*. Calgary, June 14-17, 1990.

KING, D. "Offensive Team Play." *Proceedings, National Coaches Certification Program*. Level 5 Seminar. Ottawa: Canadian Amateur Hockey Association, 1981, 135-161.

KING, D. "Positional Responsibilities of Forwards." *Proceedings, National Coaches Certification Program*. Level 5 Seminar. Ottawa: Canadian Amateur Hockey Association, 1983, 63-76.

KING, D. "Puck Control and Support." *Paper presented at the Coaches' Seminar, Program of Excellence*. Calgary: Canadian Amateur Hockey Association, 1984.

KING, D. "European Offensive Tendencies." *Proceedings, National Coaches Certification Program*. Level 5 Seminar. Ottawa: Canadian Amateur Hockey Association, 1985, 61-63.

KING, D. "Timing: The Key to Offensive Support." *Proceedings, National Coaches Certification Program*. Advanced II Seminar. Ottawa: Canadian Amateur Hockey Association, 1989, 168-183.

KING, D. *Puck Control and Deking* [Video]. Calgary: Hockey Canada in co-operation with the Canadian Amateur Hockey Association, 1989.

KING, D. "Reading and Reacting Offensively." *Paper presented at the International Hockey Coaches Seminar*. Calgary, June 14-17, 1990.

KINGSTON, G. "Practice of Individual Skill." *Proceedings of the International Coaches' Conference on the New Directions in Ice Hockey Training*. Prague: Czechoslovakian Ice Hockey Federation and Charles University, 1978, 126-138.

KINGSTON, G. "Developmental Concepts of Offensive Hockey." *Proceedings, National Coaches Certification Program*. Level 5 Seminar. Ottawa: Canadian Amateur Hockey Association, 1979, 153-173.

KINGSTON, G. "Age Group Practice in Ice Hockey: Developmental Tactical Concepts for Young Ice Hockey Players." *Paper presented at the Third International Conference on the Coaching Aspect of Ice Hockey*. Gothenburg, Sweden, April 23, 1981.

KOROLOV, J.V. "Game Analysis and Evaluation of Player's Performance." *Proceedings of the International Coaches' Conference on the New Directions in Ice Hockey Training*. Prague: Czechoslovakian Ice Hockey Federation and Charles University, 1978, 173-203.

KOSTKA, V. *Tactical Aspects in Hockey*, Québec: Olympia, 1976.

KOSTKA, V. "Systèmes Européens." *Délibérations, symposium international des entraîneurs*. Ottawa: Canadian Amateur Hockey Association, 1976, 173-196.

KOSTKA, V. *Czechoslovakian Youth Ice Hockey Training System*. Ottawa: Canadian Amateur Hockey Association, 1979.

KOSTKA, V., McDonald, D. and Wohl, P. *IIHF Coaches Manual* (Youth Hockey). Ottawa: Canadian Amateur Hockey Association, 1984.

LARSSON, K. "Swedish Team Play Systems." *Proceedings, National Coaches Certification Program*. Level 5 Seminar. Ottawa: Canadian Amateur Hockey Association, 1981, 186-227.

LARSSON, K. "Swedish Offensive Team Play." *Proceedings, National Coaches Certification Program*. Level 5 Seminar. Ottawa: Canadian Amateur Hockey Association, 1985, 65-79.

LENER, S. "Transition Defense to Offense." *Paper presented at the International Hockey Coaches Seminar*. Calgary, June 14-17, 1990.

LINDBERG, H. "Swedish Dryland Training." *Proceedings, National Coaches Certification Program*. Level 5 Seminar. Ottawa: Canadian Amateur Hockey Association, 1977, 170-216.

LITTSOLA, S. "La Finlande." *Délibérations, symposium international des entraîneurs*. Ottawa: Canadian Amateur Hockey Association, 1976, 97-108.

LODZIAK, C. *Understanding Soccer Tactics*. London: Faber and Faber, 1966.

MAHLO, F. *L'acte tactique en jeu*. Paris: Éditions Vigot Frères, 1974.

MARCOTTE, G. and CHAPLEAU, C. "Perfectionnez votre hockey en gymnase." Montréal: *Éducation Physique, Sport et Loisir*, November, 1959, 9-10.

MARTIN, J. *Personal Communication*, June 16, 1990.

MCDONALD, D. "Developing Canadian Hockey Players." *Proceedings, National Coaches Certification Program*. Level 5 Seminar. Ottawa: Canadian Amateur Hockey Association, 1985, 99-102.

MEAGHER, J. *La Stratégie au Hockey*. Montréal: Les Éditions de L'homme, 1973.

MEAGHER, J. "Variable Determinants of Performance — Intelligence and Strategy." Quebec: *Mouvement Hockey 2*. April, 1975.

METZLER, M. "The Measurement of Academic Learning Time in Physical Education." *Dissertation Abstracts International*, 40, 5365-A, 1979.

MEUNIER, N. "Les grandes lignes de mon approche tactique individuelle et collective." In G. Marcotte and C. Thiffault (Eds.), *Tactique individuelle et collective au hockey sur glace*. Québec: Éditions du Pélican, 1980, 56-58.

MOROZOV, Y. *International Junior Hockey Coaches Seminar*. Ottawa: Canadian Amateur Hockey Association, 1975.

NAYLOR, P.J. and HOWE, B. "Coaching Effectiveness: Issues in the Teaching and Evaluation of Coaches." *Proceedings, Commonwealth and International Conference on Physical Education, Sport, Health, Dance, Recreation and Leisure*. Volume 2: Sport. Auckland, 1990, 22-28.

NEALE, H. "Equipe E.U." *Délibérations, symposium international des entraîneurs*. Ottawa: Canadian Amateur Hockey Association, 1976, 83-96.

NEILSON, R. and SMITH, R. "Concepts in Team Play." *Proceedings, National Coaches Certification Program*. Level 5 Seminar. Ottawa: Canadian Amateur Hockey Association, 1978, 186-211.

PATTERSON, C. and MILLER, J. *Initiation Program, Instructor's Manual*. Ottawa: Canadian Amateur Hockey Association, 1986.

PELCHAT, C., KOSTKA, V., BUKAC, L. and SAFARIK, V. "La recherche tactique scientifique dans l'évolution tactique du hockey sur glace Tchécoslovaque." In G. Marcotte and C. Thiffault (Eds.), *Tactique individuelle et collective au hockey sur glace*. Quebec: Éditions du Pélican, 1980, 13-33.

PERCIVAL, L. *The Hockey Handbook*. Toronto: Copp Clark Publishing, 1951.

PERRON, J. "Étude comparative des lancers, passes et mise en échec lors du championnat universitaire canadien 1978." In G. Marcotte and C. Thiffault (Eds.), *Tactique individuelle et collective au hockey sur glace*. Quebec: Éditions du Pelican, 1980, 95-97.

PERRON, J. "Offensive Play and Tactics." *Fourth Annual Elite Hockey Coaching Symposium*. Toronto: York University, June 13-15, 1986.

PERSSON, V. "Analysis of Soviet Hockey." *Proceedings, National Coaches Certification Program*. Level 5 Seminar. Ottawa: Canadian Amateur Hockey Association, 1981, 74-92.

RATE, R. "A Descriptive Analysis of Academic Learning Time and Coaching Behavior in Interscholastic Athletic Practices." *Dissertation Abstracts International, 41*, 2998-A, 1980.

RATUSHNY, E. *Personal Communication*, September 5, 1988.

ROY, B. "Les lancers au hockey: rétrospective et prospective biomécanique." *Mouvement*, Vol. 9, No. 1, 1974, 85-88.

ROY, B., DORÉ, R., PARMENTIER, P.H., DEROY, M. and CHAPLEAU, C. "Facteurs biomécaniques caractéristiques de différents types de lancers au hockey sur glace." *Mouvement*, Vol. 9, No. 2, 1974, 169-175.

RUEL, A. "La tactique collective au hockey sur glace et l'Union Soviétique." In G. Marcotte and C. Thiffault (Eds.), *Tactique individuelle et collective au hockey sur glace*. Québec: Éditions du Pélican, 1980, 34-37.

RUSHALL, B. "Do You Really Think You Are As Effective a Coach As You Can Be?" *Coaching Review*, Vol. 3, No. 16, 1980, 27-28.

SCHMID, I.R., MCKEON, J.L., and SCHMID, M.R. *Skills and Strategies of Successful Soccer*. Englewood Cliffs: Prentice-Hall Inc., 1968.

SCHMIDT, R.A. *Motor Control and Learning*, Champaign: Human Kinetics Publisher, 1982.

SCHOFIELD, J. "Developmental Concepts of Offensive Team Play." *Proceedings, National Coaches Certification Program*. Level 5 Seminar. Ottawa: Canadian Amateur Hockey Association, 1979, 174-197.

SHERO, F. and BEAULIEU, A. *Hockey for the Coach, the Player and the Fan*. New York: Simon and Shuster, 1979.

SICILIANO, D. "Teaching Offensive Concepts." *Proceedings, National Coaches Certification Program*. Level 5 Seminar. Ottawa: Canadian Amateur Hockey Association, 1985, 51-60.

SICILIANO, D. "Drills to Develop Offensive Transition." *Proceedings, National Coaches Certification Program*. Advanced II Seminar. Ottawa: Canadian Amateur Hockey Association, 1989, 215-230.

SITTLER, D. and MCFARLANE, B. *Sittler at Centre*. Don Mills: Collier Macmillan Canada Ltd., 1979.

SMITH, M. *Teaching Hockey Systems: Philosophies, Diagrams and Drills*. St. Paul: Hockey Books, 1982.

SMITH, M. *Hockey Play Book*. St. Paul: Hockey Books, 1984.

SMITH, R. *Hockey Systems*. Toronto: Hockey Technical Director's Office and Al Stewart Enterprises Ltd., 1976.

SPASSKY, O. *Ice Hockey*. Moscow: Moscow Publishing House, 1981.

TARASOV, A. *Road to Olympus*. Toronto: Griffin House, 1969.

TARASOV. A. *Globe and Mail*. November 13, 1986.

TARASOV. A. and PERSSON, V. *Tarasov's Hockey Technique*. Toronto: Holt, Rinehart and Winston of Canada, Limited, 1973.

THÉODORESCO, L. "Principes pour l'étude de la tactique commune aux jeux collectifs et leur corrélation avec la préparation tactique des équipes et des joueurs." *Compte rendu du colloque international sur les sports collectifs*. Vichy, Paris: Ministère de la jeunesse et des sports, 1965, 122-138.

THIFFAULT, C., BRUNELLE, J., BÉRUBÉ, G., and PIERON, M. "An Observation System of Individual Tactical Actions in Ice Hockey." *Proceedings of the International Coaches' Conference on the New Directions in Ice Hockey Training*. Prague: Czechoslovakian Ice Hockey Federation and Charles University, 1978, 153-168.

TRUDEL, P., *Validation d'une stratégie de formation pour des entraîneurs bénévoles au hockey mineur*. Unpublished doctoral dissertation, Laval University, Québec, 1987.

VAIRO, L. "Controlled Breakouts." In L. Vairo (Ed.), *Hockey Coaching*. New York: Charles Scribner's Sons, 1980, 182-190.

VAIRO, L. "Regrouping in the Centerzone." In L. Vairo (Ed.), *Hockey Coaching*. New York: Charles Scribner's Sons, 1980, p. 201.

WAITERS, T. *Coaching to Win*. Toronto: Totem Books, 1984.

WATT, T. *How to Play Hockey*. Toronto: Doubleday Canada Limited, 1973.

WHITING, H.T. *Acquiring Ball Skill*. Philadelphia: Lea and Febiger, 1969.

SUGGESTED READING

Physical Preparation

DINTIMAN, G.B. and WARD, R.D. *Sport Speed*. Champaign : Leisure Press, 1988.

KOSTKA, V. *Czechoslovakian Youth Ice Hockey Training System*. Ottawa : Canadian Amateur Hockey Association, 1979.

MACADAM, D. and REYNOLDS, G. *Hockey Fitness : Year Around Conditioning On and Off the Ice*. Champaign : Leisure Press, 1988.

MARCOTTE, G. and POIRIER,G. *La préparation physique du joueur de hockey*. Quebec City : Éditions du Pélican, 1978.

SMITH, R. and WHITE, L. *Off-Ice Training for Hockey*. Toronto : Hockey Technical Office, Sport Ontario, 1975.

TAYLOR, J. *Lloyd Percival's Total Conditioning for Hockey*. Toronto : Fitzhenry and Whiteside, 1978.

WENGER, H.A. *Fitness : The Key to Hockey Success*. Victoria : British Columbia Amateur Hockey Association, 1988.

Psychological Preparation

CARON, A.V. *Motivation Implications for Coaching and Teaching*. London : Sports Dynamics, 1984.

NIDEFFER, R. *The Inner Athlete : Mind plus Muscle for Winning*. New York : Thomas Y. Crowell, Publishers, 1976.

ORLICK, T. *Psyching for Sport : Mental Training for Athletes*. Champaign : Leisure Press, 1986.

ORLICK, T. *Coaches Training Manual to Psyching for Sport*. Champaign : Leisure Press, 1986.

TUTKO, T. and RICHARDS, J.W. *Psychology of Coaching*. Boston : Allyn and Bacon, Inc., 1971.

TUTKO, T. and TOSI, U. *Sports Psyching*. Los Angeles : J.P. Tarcher, Inc., 1976.

RUSHALL, B. *Psyching in Sports*. England : Pelham Books, 1980.

SINGER, R. *Sustaining Motivation in Sport*. Tallahassee : Sport Consultants International, 1984.

Technical Preparation

BELLEFLEUR, R.J. *Characteristics of Goaltending*. Moncton : Speedy Print Moncton, 1983.

HOCKEY CANADA and the CANADIAN AMATEUR HOCKEY ASSOCIATION. *Canadian Hockey 1*. Agincourt : Sportbook Limited, 1975.

HOCKEY CANADA and the CANADIAN AMATEUR HOCKEY ASSOCIATION. *Canadian Hockey 2*. Agincourt : Sportbook Limited, 1975.

HOCKEY CANADA and the CANADIAN AMATEUR HOCKEY ASSOCIATION. *Canadian Hockey 3*. Agincourt : Sportbook Limited, 1975.

LEMIRE, V. and BIRD, W.D. *Goaltenders Are Not Targets*. North Vancouver : WDS Systems Inc., 1982.

FÉDÉRATION QUÉBÉCOISE DE HOCKEY SUR GLACE, 1980. *Manuel technique*. Montréal.

FÉDÉRATION QUÉBÉCOISE DE HOCKEY SUR GLACE, 1981. *Manuel II technico-tactique*. Montréal.

MCKEE, D. *Teaching Hockey Skills*. Toronto : Hockey Ontario. 1982.

PATTERSON, C. and MILLER, J. *Initiation Program. Lesson Manual A. B. C. and D*. Ottawa : Canadian Amateur Hockey Association, 1986.

GLOSSARY

Alignment   The formation or arrangement of players on the ice, usually in reference to a specific zone and a particular playing situation. It acts as a general framework or structure — a starting point to facilitate the various patterns of movement and the necessary permutations to maintain a certain balance among the players.

Concepts   Ideas that are closely associated with the fundamental principles and principles of action.

Flow   The general pattern and direction of movement by the players on the ice.

Fundamental principles   The foundation upon which tactics and systems of play are developed (adapted from Caron and Pelchat, 1975; Kingston, 1981).

Group tactics   Collective actions used consciously by two or more players to gain advantage over one or more opponents, whether offensively or defensively.

Individual tactics   Individual actions used consciously by one player to gain advantage over one or more opponents, whether offensively or defensively (adapted from Théodoresco, 1965).

Principles of action   Guidelines for players' individual and collective actions. Some authors refer to these as rules of play; others, as principles of play.

Strategy   An overall plan or approach to a game in relation to the opposition and the strengths of your team. This plan rests upon the physical, tactical and psychological dimensions of the game. In practice, this plan is reflected through a particular system of play deployed against the opposition in an attempt to exploit their weaknesses and neutralize their strengths.

System of play   The overall organization of the offensive and defensive actions of the players, with clearly defined roles and responsibilities assigned to individuals and groups of players for all the various playing situations.

Tactics   Individual and/or collective actions of players on a team in order to gain advantage over one or more opponents, whether offensively or defensively.

Team play   All individual and collective actions by the players on a team, organized, coordinated and unified rationally with the objective of winning the game (adapted from Théodoresco, 1965).

Techniques   Fundamental skills required to play the game, such as skating, passing, receiving, shooting, checking and blocking shots.

ABOUT THE AUTHORS

Jean Perron is one of the few coaches ever to win a Stanley Cup in his rookie season; a feat he achieved with the Montreal Canadiens, the team he coached from 1985 to 1988. After being named assistant general manager for the Quebec Nordiques, he finished the season as head coach in 1988-89.

Mr. Perron is a well-known figure in coaching circles in North America and Europe. He has coached teams to medal status in Canada and Germany and has worked with National Championship, World Championship, and Olympic teams.

He joined the Montreal Canadiens as an assistant coach after the Sarajevo Olympics in 1984, and rose to head coach within a year. He coached the top NHL players who played the Soviets at Rendez-Vous 1987 in Quebec City; that same year, he was an assistant coach to the Canadian team that beat the USSR in the finals. He obtained his Master's Degree in Physical Education from Michigan State University in 1973, and now works as a sports commentator for CJRP radio in Quebec City.

Normand Chouinard, Professor of Physical Education at the University of Ottawa, has almost twenty years of teaching and coaching experience in ice hockey. He is an instructor in the National Coaching Certification Program and Best Ever Program and a Master Coach at the National Coaching Institute.

After playing junior and university hockey in Canada, he pursued his playing and coaching career in Europe. He then coached college and university hockey in the United States and Canada. He has also coached both men's and women's hockey teams at the minor level.

Norm completed his Doctoral Degree in Physical Education at Illinois State University in 1979 and has continued his research activities both in the area of ice hockey and coaching. He has also managed his own hockey schools, advised a number of professional athletes, and acted as a consultant for major junior teams. Norm is presently an assistant to the coaches of the Ottawa Senators.